SILENT WISH

David G Thomas

Copyright ©2023 David G Thomas

All rights reserved

No part of this book can be reproduced in any form or by written,
electronic or mechanical, including photocopying, recording, or by any
information retrieval system without permission in writing by the author.

Designed and Printed by Fineline Print and Web

ISBN No. 978-1-8382487-5-8

Acknowledgements

Chris and Daniel Harper along with the staff at Minisport of Padiham for their support from start to finish through out the ups and downs on my World Tour as they called it.

Jim Brindle at R.A.C.E. Chorley, UK for the many Brews and full use of his workshop we're with Tugs Sherington's support and ideas we built a world beater.

Barry Knox at SHE Maritime Services Ltd. Barking, Essex United Kingdom.
Connie McKinnon at Schenker Logistics. Halifax, Nova Scotia, Canada.
All Cargo Express Inc. Richmond, British Columbia, Canada.
Tatiana Chernysheva DBS Cruise Ferry Co Ltd. Japan and Korea.
Yuri Melnikov at Links, Ltd. Vladivostok, Russia.

Rick and Elaine Higgs from Pitt Meadows, B.C. Canada.
Who made me feel at home so many times over my many visits. Very special friends, thank you both.

Larry and Ann Sutton from Maple Ridge B.C. Canada.
Who welcomed me and kindly stored the Mini over many winter months. Wonderful and welcoming people.

Bill and Barbara De Crefft from Homer, Alaska.
Thank you for the Drams, Bag pipe playing and many hours of flight time over the Glaziers around Homer. AK.

Keith, Deb and Girls from Mainly Minis of Montreal, Canada. An Oasis on my journey.

Mike and Sharon Lavie from Charlottetown, Prince Edward Island, Canada. My hideaway on a small island.

Shinobu, Hiroko and Aoi Kitani at Garage Grace, Kamigou-cho, Yokohama, Japan.
My Japanese family in a wonderful country of kind and special people.

Jack, Robert, Dave, Edmund, Bill, Ernie and Ron. All retired guys who once worked for Canadian Atlanta Tele-com. These well advanced in age men would give up there time to help underprivileged family's At the Lions Max Simms Camp in Newfoundland. My time and memory's with you guys will live on in me forever.

Ross Pattison. Thank you for giving your time into reducing my endless spelling mistakes though out my written word.

To Scotland's best trad-group. Skerryvore. And their "On the Road" hit track, thank you.

Mike McCann "Mr President" of Run-a-Muck Tours and his no plans shit happens attitude to life just seems to work. A man I thinks the world of and wishes I'd bumped into him a life time ago. He truly is a one of in this life. In the following years I would go back many times to join him up on the Yukon River in Alaska or down in Montana to do stuff, the stuff true stories are made of.

Mr and Mrs Unknown. The greatest gift I was given was to meet so many people and spend a little time with them. There are too many to mention but they are there in my memories, thank you one and all.

Finally. Top of the questions I would get asked, are you travelling alone?
My answer would often be. I don't do baggage.
Now on reflection after 4 years and 60.000 miles I wasn't alone at all
as my faithful companion Austin Minivan was always by my side.

More photos and Video's can be found on my FB Page The Wrong Way Round.
So have a look and LIKE the page.

You might find I've taken off again into the unknown.

Unexpected Foreword

Dave. I have read your book, twice, and can only express my admiration for your journey that you undertook and the wonderfully written account of it.

I would advise you NOT to change anything as I feel it would be detrimental to the outstanding piece of work that it is. You have not meant it to be a travelogue or an adventure story, but a personal account of your epic journey across continents. It is told in the ancient and universal tradition of storytelling, usually an oral version of ones endeavours and escapades. Like those storytellers of old, you have narrated your tale just as they did.

This book should be regarded as a written oral account, told in your own words, in your own way. This means that the rules of grammar, punctuation, sentence construction and all the conventional writing rules do not apply to amend the text, to make it a "proper book," would detract from the personal and inspirational memoir that it currently is.

As with all good stories, people are enthralled by the narrative, not commas, full stops, spelling and all the other literary crap. They relish and enjoy a well told story, which you certainly have.

So Dave, from someone who is an avid reader of all types of books, this is a brilliant piece of storytelling and is a tribute to your spirit of adventure, your great resolve and gritty determination, and your bravery in undertaking a journey into the unknown.

All in all a piece of work to be proud of.

Bob Melia

Zak and Sam
May you go out and see the World

Dedicated to the Memory of
Your Mums Mum

SILENT WISH

By David G Thomas

CHAPTERS

1	How it all started	3
2	A Mini story	5
3	The Build	9
4	Crossing the Pond	13
5	Bring it on	17
6	Life on the Rock	27
7	Dust and Dirt	37
8	Get out of my town	47
9	Mile Zero	53
10	Making for the Arctic	85
11	The last Frontier	93
12	This is the end of the Road	103
13	New Friends	113
14	Dead in the Water	119
15	Yanking my Chain	127
16	Run in with the Law	131
17	Into the danger Zone	137
18	Not telling the Truth	149

Chapter 1

How it all started

Yes, how did it all start? That has puzzled me for some time, I now believe the seed was sown back in my childhood, and not as I had previously thought in the early part of 2008.

I can remember back to my childhood. Dad had been in the army with the Royal Engineers clearing mine fields with a bulldozer and building bridges across the Rhine in Germany for our troops to advance during WW2. After the war dad got a job, and was never far away from plant and machinery in one form or another and as I grew up as a young child dad became a diesel fitter for a heavy haulage transport company. His place of work was just across the road from home and I can recall him coming home most nights in his dirty boiler suit with clean hands and dirt still under his fingernails.

From my teens until this day I have never been able to pick up a book and stick with it for to long, I have tried and failed time and time again. However, I do remember the commercial transport magazines that would appear at home and how I would find myself flicking through the pages on many occasions just looking at the articles and colour photos. I can still recall one picture and an article that will forever stay in my mind. "Hardship in Alaska" This was a story about those pioneering drivers and their trucks. It was their account about the lack of roads and the difficulties when it came to snow ice along with freezing diesel, with temperatures way below freezing point, with twenty-four hours of sunlight in summer and the short days of winter. This was the beginning of the fight to find oil in the arctic.

What an exciting snapshot, so much happening but all this was the other side of the world and I was only thirteen at the time. It was just a dream; it was just a picture in a magazine. Little did I know that one day I would find myself driving in the tracks of those pioneers? Late in the summer of 2009 and fifty years later I would cross the Arctic Circle and shed a tear of thanks to my dad on what is now called the Dalton Highway, a dirt road that takes you to the Arctic Ocean.

Dreams are an image in one's mind, but my childhood dream would become very much a reality sooner than ever imagined. On the eleventh of February 2008 just coming up to 6.00 p.m. as I opened the post box at my gate and took out the one and only letter, my mobile phone rang. It was my daughter's voice telling me her mum had passed away after losing her fight for the last time with cancer. I stood at the gate crying my eyes out. Still standing at the post box I finished opening the one and only letter and started to read the first few lines. This was when I felt a second wave of helplessness come over me. I had lost another person I cared so deeply for, and at that moment I felt as if I was falling into a black hole and nothing could stop me. I needed answers to why this was happening.

My closest family was my mother, forty miles away. I set off on the drive to see her. While at the crematorium we talked for an hour, me asking her questions that had never been asked before, seeking answers and eventually coming away with a purpose to move forward. Life had flicked a switch inside me that would send me on a journey around the world.

Over the following months I found myself at an all-time low, stuck in this black hole trying to fight my way out. I would fight hard to pick myself up and face the future. During that time my daughter Louise bought me a CD called, "On the Road" by a group named Skerryvore. One of the tracks on the CD is called "On the Road" and it was this track alone that gave me a purpose and motivated me into action.

~~~~~~~~~~~~~~~~~~~~~~~~~~~~~

These are the words to the song

The summer's here and the time has come
to hit the road and stop being a bum.
Better pack those bags and pack them full
It's gonna be a long one.

It's sure to be tough when you're feeling rough
You can feel alone when you're far from home.
But no need to fear the boys are near
When it's gonna be a long one.

We're on the road again, there's no stopping us
Were on the road again.
We're on the road again there's no stopping us
Were on the road again.

We'll meet old friends make new ones too
You'll take a dram we'll take one too.
Stay up all night then start again
It's gonna be a long one.

We'll see more places than people can
Fantastic journeys foreign lands.
Hours of mountains years of sands
It's gonna be a long one.

And when we're on the road
there's no stopping us.
And when were on the road
there's no stopping us

In the early part of summer 2008 I decided that life was too short, and I must do something and do it now. It would have to be travel and to see the world, but that is very expensive so how could I get started?
At the time I owned a mini which was quite unique being one that was used by the British Motor Corporation for publicity then moved on to the Race and Rally Department of the company. The money from the sale gave me the opportunity to put my heart and head into focussing on plans and the challenges that would hopefully give me a different outlook on life along with much needed answers for my loss.

After much thought and soul searching, with the ever presence of cost never far away from my thoughts, I decided that I would try and drive round the world. Driving had always been in my blood as I had bought and passed my driving test in a minivan when I was 18 years old, and these little cars had been part of my life and still are to this day.

As a person I like simplicity, and this was to be the format if I was to accomplish my challenge. It would be a Minivan, not a Land Rover or a big Toyota. I was the one who would have to fix it, so in my mind there was never going to be any other vehicle that I would choose and be confident to take care of me. It would become my office, my bedroom, and my kitchen, in general my home and the mini was the vehicle that convinced me it could do whatever I asked of it.

For the first time in many months I started to feel good and a determination to carry on fuelled me even though I am not a planner, more of a doer, someone who could be described as the practical type. I was aware my plan would involve paperwork and I was always mindful of this, but looking back there was minimum research, costings, or time-consuming paperwork involved in fulfilling this adventure. Yes, I did look into how much it would cost to ship my vehicle across such huge oceans, but when the answers came back that it could be done for less than the cost of a flight and a couple of weeks holiday in the sun, I was fuelled into action even more.

Much work lay ahead, a lot to be achieved in the coming months, but this was welcome to me, as I was now starting to work on my plan, a positive distraction from the two significant events that had led to this point in my life which would take me into a future of unknown adventures.

Chapter 2

A Mini History

Home for me is the Isle of Mull on the west coast of Scotland, which I love. However, the draw back to living there was the fact that I would want to build my mini from a bare shell, with the plan that it would evolve as the months passed by. With that in mind I contacted a long-time mini friend, Jim Brindle and the proprietor of R.A.C.E. based In Chorley Lancashire. I told him of my plans to which he responded, "You can use my place and build it here."

By now my friends at Mini Sport in Padiham had found me a 1973 Austin Minivan in perfect condition, and to help me with my project they stepped in with a very special package on the parts that I would need to rebuild the van, I was determined to use all new parts on such a simple vehicle.

My interest with the mini came about because at sixteen years of age I found myself slap bang in the middle of a decade that is still iconic to this very day for so many. The 1960's a time when it would seem everything was full on and so much in the world has happening. The U.K. was the place to be. For many of my age, having left school and securing a job, I could now spend time socially with people who were once school friends, boys and girls who become mates. There was a freedom about that time, you could meet up at the pub, have a drink and even play darts till you got bored, and then you would take off and drive to another pub in your car. Its interesting looking back now and considering the drink drive law's we have in place. Yes, we would have a drink but never to the point of falling over. One of us would offer to drive and not drink and then see us all pile into one car and leave another behind to be collected the next day usually on the Sunday. For me today it seems you have to drink alcohol to enjoy yourself, but back then my friends and I just wanted to be together and have fun.

At sixteen I remember seeing Mini cars everywhere and over the next few years they developed into many forms and by my eighteenth birthday the Mini Cooper could be seen in both Austin and Morris models. Not long after my eighteenth birthday I passed my driving test and with the small amount of savings I had, I brought my first car. My mind was set on a Mini Cooper but the purse could only stretch to what turned out to be a Minivan. I consoled myself by thinking ah well, there's plenty of room in the back for friends and possible camping adventures. Well I was young, and the world was out there to be explored.

I was lucky to have a job and be earning money and over the next couple of years my interests went in a couple of directions. Owning the mini I started to travel to motor sport events, and shortly after I joined a Motor Club and became a Marshall at race circuits, travelling around the country. As well as seeing the mini at race circuits I became aware of them taking part in and winning rallies. Getting to events involved using maps to find my way, and that's when I became acquainted with O.S. Maps (Ordinance Survey maps), they fascinated me with so much detail.

By the time I was nineteen I was on my first adventure with the Minivan. I had found an old O.S. map covering a part of Scotland and a place called the Pass of Condie, hidden it the middle of nowhere, the name alone fascinated me, and I thought to myself, I must go and find this place. That summer I fitted a roof rack to the Minivan, placing on the rack some spare wheels and tyres along with fuel and water cans, all tied down with rope. These items would be my insurance for any misadventures. In the back I put an old mattress, food and a primus stove, a few clothes and of course soap and towel. To make things more interesting I set off at night planning to arrive in the morning. Much more of that trip I can't really remember. This was my first adventure but what it did was to set in place a bond within me of three things, travel, adventure and my love of that iconic car they call the Mini, something that I still have nearly sixty years on.

I remember in late 1968 doing a car rally in the Lake District and then in 1969 going to the Isle of Mull where the same club put on the first Tour of Mull. I liked the people and the place so much, I moved there at the beginning of the 1980's. The early days living on Mull weren't easy and I lived in a static caravan with no electricity and a case of bucket and chuck-it, for sanitation. Living in the caravan seemed to go on forever, but it never worried me as there was such a magic about the whole island. Over the coming years I set about trying to earn a living, so I took on repair jobs. The first job I did on the island was to fit new brake shoes to of all vehicles, a Minivan. It's only now when I sit down, reflect and put pen to paper that I pinch myself. Things were hard but they went well, and in time money started coming in. I was making small steps to earn. I was earning and building my small business venture during the summer and winter. I don't know where else in the world I could have achieved all I did back then, setting up a small garage and engineering business while living with so little.

Living on an island you have to be able turn your hand to anything and that's what I did many times, sometimes not always knowing what I was doing often working by my own rules, simply so I could began to learn, but I was always honest with my customers. I would turn my hand to fixing pots and pans for the local hotel in our small village along side assorted farm machinery from the local farmers. This kept me going day and night and it wasn't unusual to get a phone call after nine at night. By then my potential customer would have finished their long day, but the phone would ring, and I would hear "I've bust the tractor and I need it first thing in the morning." "OK" I'd say, "I'll is there at first light." What they hadn't told was that it had broken down early the day before! Another group of people that kept me busy were the fishermen and their boats, again wanting my services at some very strange hours. It's true to say I spent a lot of time outside, some of it at sea, and in every type of weather day or night.

I loved my life on the island and I felt I was part of the community, where in the world can you go and you don't have to lock your door? I was made to feel part of island life and it was good to be putting something back into the community, very satisfying. I have a lasting memory from those early years of my life on Mull. It came in the form of a compliment given to me by a Mullach, a native of the island. One winter in our village pub, when most of the tourists had left the island, not that we weren't pleased to see them but when winter came it was good to get the island back. A hand full of us was sitting in the bar. Tom sometimes called the PMG (Post Master General) who ran the small post office and shop suddenly turned to me on his bar stool while picking up his rather large dram and said, "I like you Dave."
"That's very kind of you" I said, "But may I ask why?"
"Simple" he replied, "You're not super glued to your seat in the community". Hearing those words made me feel very good. Putting back into the community was a positive experience.

My interest in rallying and minis continued, and in October each year the Tour of Mull would return to this small island. This meant friends from far and wide arriving the weekend before the event with most of my work for that coming week would be put on hold. I listen for the rattle of my cattle grid announcing the invasion of my workshop was now underway. These were the service vehicles and trailers loaded with rally cars bringing old friends and new folks who would become friends before they left the island. I loved having them and enjoyed hearing their stories and tales about what they had been up to and what their plans were. This was an annual joy for me for many years to come.

Getting off the island was pleasing at times and none more so than in the 1990's. This proved to be a good decade for me and my involvement with minis. December '93 would see me buying my first ever new car, a 1.3 Mini Cooper and then in January '94 I would find myself joining Paddy Hopkirk and the team for a one-off return to the Monte Carlo Rally, celebrating his win of the rally in a mini back in 1964. I joined the team with my new mini as chase support car. I returned again over the following years to the Monte Carlo and RAC Rally's along with many other events. During that period I joined and supported the Plant Twins Michael and Robert in their Mini sponsored by Corgi toys, it became known as the Corgi Mini. Russell Brookes was a well known Rally driver at the time and he found himself getting back into a Mini for a one off drive on the RAC Rally of Great Britain with backing from Mini sport.

Right from the start the classic mini was always going to be my preferred form of transport for this incredible drive around the world I had planned and I had made the decision to go with the van version of this iconic little car. The classic mini first came into production in 1959; much time has passed since then so finding a good one at an affordable price would not be easy. Months and months passed with me searching magazines and the internet, all to no avail.

One weekend I found myself at a classic Mini car show and by chance I came across Daniel Harper from Mini specialists, Minisport of Padiham. We talked for a while and I told him of my plans to take off and drive round the world. He listened and at the end of the conversation he said "I'm sure we have a van body that we restored some time ago and is in primer hiding in one of our warehouses. I will take a look and let you know in the coming days." True to his word and a few days later he rang me to confirm that he had found the van and on inspection it was dry and rust free albeit a little dusty.

Keen to keep moving on with my dream, the following day I left Mull via the ferry to mainland Oban heading for Minisport. Half a day's drive and I was in Padiham looking over the body shell of the van. Being able to purchase this mini and build my dreams into it, felt like a huge turning point in my life, and by the end of the day I would be driving away with a package and the support from Minisport, they were prepared to give me favourable prices for all the new parts I would need to get the van ready.

Months and months had passed before getting the bare shell and in that time I had processed hours of thoughts through my head on what preparations it would take to maximise my chances of the Mini lasting the distance, I felt sure if I built it properly then that was one less worry once on the road. These months of diversions in my head helped me so much to level out my thoughts especially at night time.

Chapter 3

The Build

The basis for my adventure would be a humble 1973 Minivan. I started with the basic shell Minisport had sourced. Rather than take it all the way back to my garage on Mull, I took it to Jim Brindle at R.A.C.E. Motor Sport in Chorley. He let me use his workshop to do all the preparation work there. I have known Jim for many years because of our love of rallying, and he and his team of friends known as the "Withnell Mafia" would turn up on Mull each October to take over my garage for the week, to compete on the Tour of Mull Rally.

The many months of head planning trying to think it through where I could gain space in the Minivan would now start to take shape, where to put the boxes and where to make modifications. A lot evolved as it went along but most of it came from my background of rallies. I had to have a vehicle that would last the distance; this would require plenty of thought and clever innovation to make it suitable for the rough terrain and the wide range of temperatures I would certainly encounter.

Jim's workshop was always a place of people coming and going. There were plenty of brews, chats and conversations, and with that came interest, support and help. Long time friend Tugs Sherrington came onboard and helped a lot with the work that was needed and this speeded up the build time. Tugs was like me in many ways both similar in ideas and capability to do the job and do it properly, he must take huge credit for his work as I could leave him alone and he just got on with what was needed. Fortunately, I didn't have to waste time fitting new panels to the shell as the body was sound the only bit of rust was on the heel board. All we did was take the angle grinder and cut that out to make it good again. Most people would have left it, but I knew that in two or three years the rust would come back. However, modifications to the shell were vital to ensure it could withstand the rigours of the trip and that I had enough storage space. It never failed to excite me when I could extract those extra few inches hidden within such a small vehicle. A modified roll cage was fitted not for speed but to stiffen up the shell with gusseting added between the shell and the cage. The rear damper mounts were beefed up too. The subframes were a combination of a new modified rear, and a good second hand front one, which were both seam welded and stiffened. Elsewhere tubes were welded to the sills to ensure easy jacking. It was standard work that would normally be done to a rally Mini. One of these extra parts was the winch, which I could bolt onto either the front or rear of the Van.

The simple reason for bolting it on the back was that if I went off road, it's best to come out the way you went in. When the winch was bolted onto the front it would also give me extra space inside the vehicle. I can remove it which means I have all options covered which would be necessary as there would only be me on my own. Many of the further bodyshell adaptions evolved around the need for space. Space would be the biggest problem.
I would need to take lots of spares with me, and I needed space for my kitchen, my office and my bedroom.

To increase the space, I cut the boot floor to create a means of storage, also cutting the load bay overhang. The latter allowed space for a 50-ltr long distance fuel tank, which I had fabricated. The filler neck is original although the aperture in the body was moved further forward to suit.
To further boost space two spare wheels would be bolted to the roof using the fittings from the boot floor of any mini. That's a trick they used on the old BMC long distance Rally cars. Under the bonnet, mesh was added to protect the extra cooling fan, and along with the bulkhead that too was heavily modified to incorporate a large box for two very expensive Gel batteries. One of my main worries was the snow and the cold, so I spent my money buying two batteries, and a 12 volt diesel truck night heater so if I did get stuck I could survive and live for four or five days, with the knowledge the batteries would hold out and I could stay warm.

I always planned everything for the worst-case scenario and the need for survival and this made me think deep and long into whatever I was inputting into this one chance to make my dream come true. I was unable to create quite enough space in the van in some areas, so hence the tent innovation and construction at the rear was needed. The tent idea again from those endless nights of head planning and it would come in the form of a rod system extending from each side of the roof. I had two new rear doors when it got the Minivan shell, I didn't use the doors because by then all my designs for the roof rack, storage box and tent had all come together in my thought process, the two doors opened upwards and they would impede the tent so I sourced a one-piece fibreglass door that opened upwards and was flat.

Underneath, the modifications were quite restricted with most parts still in their original positions. The exhaust was placed at stock height but with added skid plates, a flexible joint and a side exit back box where the original fuel tank used to be. Rather than run under the floor the fuel and brake pipes were mounted inside. All the lines are Aeroquip equipment so I would not have to worry about them. If I had to drop a rear subframe for any reason I would have to disconnect the brake lines so I added an extra two foot of flexible line in so I could then drop the frame without losing fluid or pressure. To finish off, everything underneath was protected with aluminium guards. Suspension wise most parts came straight off the shelf, including the adjustable ride height and Spax dampers. The only major change was the hydrolastic competition bump stops front and rear. I bolted to the underside of the floor at the rear to both sides, a short length of two-inch box section steel.

The purpose for this extra addition was, should my suspension collapse I could still drive as the bump stops could ride safely on the steel sections. The brakes are stock Cooper assemblies up front with spacer drums at the rear albeit with some clever alterations I could change things if my front or rear brakes failed I could still maintain some sort of braking system. Concealing the brakes are standard 12-inch steel rims with Yokohama a 539 tyres. Steel unlike alloys can be bashed back into shape if they get bent.

When it came to paint, I was inspired by two young girls in a pink tuk tuk. No joke, I had read about how they had driven a tuk tuk from Bangkok to Brighton which they had painted pink, not because they were girls but because if it got stolen thieves wouldn't be able to hide it to well. That was such a sensible idea, so I thought I would go for bright yellow but black fly and mosquitoes really like that colour so in the end I fell back to my rally days going for the works colours of red and white roof's from the long-distance BMC cars like the 1800's and Maxi's with their matt black bonnets. Things like the lights on the wing weren't just for looks I was thinking of the deer, moose and the bears I might come across at night time.

The driving seat was from a Volvo and was one of my few concessions to comfort. The vehicle would be left hand drive and that was always the intension as most of the counties I was going through had left hand drive so for toll booths, and stuff like that it became very useful. Japan is one of the odd ones, as they drive on the left the same as the UK. The mini has to be the easiest vehicle to convert, you only have to buy a left-hand drive steering rack, and all else will change over. Cunningly most of the electrical switches had been relocated to the left-hand door. I had a new loom made by a specialist who builds them mainly for rally cars. A lot of thought went into the wiring; most of the electrical items had been relocated with some new ones added such as the winch, spot lights and two Gell batteries that would run of a split charger. The system was backed up with relays and fuses for all the individual items.

The power unit was collected ready built for the task from Minisport. Daniel Harper came in on the specification of the engine because of his engineering experience. The engine was a basic 1275cc unit with new cylinder bore liners fitted. This modification would play a huge part in my survival in temperatures in excess of 120 degrees while on the road, stranded in a desert the other side of the world. Happy with the engine block and cylinder head, attention was focused on the gearbox and the ratios to give me two very low gears with a twin pinned differential for plodding through mud and dirt, thus giving less strain on Verto type clutch. Also fitted was a taller top gear for paved roads and this would help with fuel economy. Some time was spent on the cylinder head because of the fuels in different parts of the world. Once the engine had been fitted and was running the car was put on the rolling road. A couple of reasons for this were to set the carburettor up, and also the timing. We marked with a steel centre pop and hammer the distributor and the engine block, this meant I had a reference point and I could move the distributor if I got poor fuel.

The whole car was prepared in a mere five months through the help of friends and in October 2008 it went for its M.O.T. Everything was solid after all new parts had been fitted even down to neoprene bushes to replace rubber ones. The final job in the van build would be my purposes built add on tent that could extend to the rear. It turned out to be simple to build once I had thought it through. Another tube inside the roof tubes would extend out and two vertical legs could be fitted making up the support frame. A heavy duty, water resistant cover was made with a zip entry on one side and this extra space served many purposes such as a kitchen, a storeroom or somewhere to sleep if it was safe to do so. Oh yes, there were to be some unsafe animals about, as I would find out about in time.

My final joy was to head back to Mull for the winter months with the van, and this would be a shakedown and test for the challenges ahead. Spring and a new year would soon come and nerves were starting to kick in. Payment for shipment of the van had been done and my outbound flight was also booked. Before the off I loaded the spares package. This consisted of everything and anything you could think of, after all anything can break down. The only thing I didn't have was a spare engine block, that would come back to bite me, but this was March and I didn't know anything about what the future was to bring in my direction.

In the early spring of 2009 the van was now placed on a container ship in Liverpool, bound for Halifax in Nova Scotia a place way across the Atlantic Ocean and a journey that would take it a third of the way round the world. I hoped she would make it, as I would be flying out of England some seven days later, planning to be reunited with my mechanical travelling companion.

Chapter 4

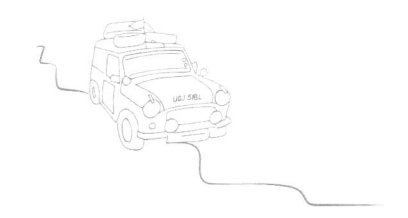

Crossing the Pond

Friday the 1st May 2009 would see me with an early start and my flight from Manchester airport to Heathrow were I would connect with my flight to Canada. Things didn't go too well when I checked in at Manchester. I have always made it a rule that when I travel by air I only take hand luggage and try to avoid any baggage in the hold. Unfortunately for me at the security check the baggage scanner operator saw something on screen and subsequently I was pulled to one side and asked to open my case. As soon as I lifted the lid, I saw the problem, a rather large one-inch combination spanner used for adjusting the ride height on the Minivan and I had forgotten to pack it in with my tool kit that was loaded in the van and was now on the high seas. I tried explaining why I needed this spanner and why it was a necessity but all to no avail and thus only when it was it removed was I allowed to pass though for my flight to Heathrow and my onward flight to Halifax, Nova Scotia.

After leaving Heathrow and once in the air, I settled down to an inflight movie, but after a couple hours we ran into some bad weather and instead of the flight getting smoother, the turbulence became a lot worse, with passengers being sick and children crying. Touch-down into Halifax was interesting, and a huge relief could be felt on hearing and feeling the wheels make contact with the run-way, so much so, the whole plane gave a round of applause for the pilot who landed us in a very wet and windy Halifax safely.

With no bags to collect and armed with my travel case, I cleared passport control and headed for the, Nothing to Declare Exit. Daydreaming and wondering about where I was going to stay, I suddenly found myself being ushered into a room by two smartly dressed border and customs men. "Welcome to Canada sir and what is the purpose of your visit?" they asked me.

Digression
The reason they had stopped me was I had bought a one way ticket so that sets the alarm bells ringing with the Border Agency. As a British citizen going to Canada I can stay legally 180 days and not 90 days as in most counties.
~~

"I'm driving around the world in my British Mini."
This then started a very relaxed and interesting conversation lasting for about twenty minutes, "So where is your vehicle just now then?" they asked. With tongue in cheek I replied, "Hopefully awaiting clearance in the port, then I will be onward to travel your vast country finishing in Vancouver before leaving and crossing the Pacific Ocean."
"Well enjoy your time here sir." I'm sure I will.
Just before leaving I reached into my hip bag and produced my Scottish passport It's not a real passport but one I purchased and brought with me and the intention of getting it stamped as many times as I could at border crossings and county post offices as my travels evolved. They kindly obliged and I thanked them. Turning and heading for the door they had the last word, which gave me a huge smile.
"Oh, one of your country men was in here at the weekend and we spoke with him. He was a kind and funny man; I think you guys call him the Big Yin."
"Ah yes" I said, "that will be Billy, Billy Connolly."
As I stepped outside and took a deep breath I felt warmth within, I had passed my first test and I knew what I was doing felt positive and right.

The weather had changed for the better and the sun was now shinning it was time for me to find a taxi and head for the city. The beauty of major airports is there are always plenty of taxis and within minutes my bag was whisked from me and into the boot or "trunk" by a large bubbly lady.
"Where to sir?" "Somewhere close to the port please as I have a vehicle coming in from the UK that I need to collect," and thus started a conversation that would be repeated many times before I got back home again.

The journey into town took about twenty minutes, during which time my driver made a few phone calls and figured out a good place for me to stay. It's at times like these that you put your trust in people, and for me it worked out well as I would discover over the coming days. My destination was to be Dartmouth on the north side of the Halifax. The area was very clean with single storey houses and lots of blossom trees, it was also very quiet. We pulled up at a bed and breakfast with the owners coming out to greet me. My hosts introduced themselves as Peter and Anne Freeman. After settling in they offered me food, but I was happy with just tea and a biscuits. I went through to the lounge with my tea, and while sitting in my chair I talked with Peter and recounted my experience at the airport with the nice customs people. I had been so busy telling him about the airport that I forgot to ask him what he did. Peter mentioned that he and Anne would be going out and they would leave me to settle in and I was to make myself at home.

When I had finished the tea and biscuits, I took my dishes to the kitchen and washed them along with a few other items that were in the sink, my mother would have been proud of me. I left them to drain and had a look round to find something to dry my hands on and that's when I noticed lots of stickers and magnets on the fridge door. One you couldn't miss was a card with a photo of Peter; with his name, which said Chaplin of Halifax Airport. With so many nice thoughts in my head about my journey so far, I headed to my room and the comfort of a soft bed. Tomorrow was Saturday so I wasn't expecting much to happen until the vessel carrying my vehicle docked?

I woke the next morning at about 7.30 a.m. and a note had been popped under the door to let me know breakfast would be ready at 8.30. I showered and dressed and went through to the breakfast room. Joining me at the table was John, a friend of Peter and Anne's who told me he would be staying for the weekend and would be interested to hear about my travel plans.

While serving breakfast Peter offered to drive me into Halifax on Monday as he was not working and he would try and help me to sort out getting the van clear of customs and the border agency. It was clear that Peter was keen to get involved and help he would become a source of constant support over the coming days. I thought to myself here I am a stranger in a stranger's house thousands of miles from home and now with the knowledge that somebody was taking care of me. I was amazed, who knew what other good things this country would gift me.

As it was Saturday and there wasn't much I could do, I decided to stay about the house and take it easy, thinking that on Sunday I will venture out and get some exercise. That evening I watched some ice hockey until I got bored, then headed to bed. Next morning was dry and sunny, and after a full breakfast I was off out for a walk, careful to remember the directions I had been given, not wanting to get lost in a strange country. I'd been walking at a leisurely pace for about an hour when I spotted a bridge towering over the houses ahead of me. Not one to turn down the chance to view large types of engineering I made a bee line for the structure, drawn almost like a magnet to it. Some fifteen minutes later I rounded the last row of houses, where it opened up to the noise of a large highway, with a view of the river and downtown Halifax. This was not to be missed, this was the MacDonald Bridge known locally as the Dartford crossing. Getting across the highway was not that easy and I had to remember that in this part of the world, like many others, they drive on the "wrong" side of the road.

Once clear of the traffic and standing at the start of the bridge crossing it was difficult to see the other side of the River due to the uphill curvature of the bridge. It looked daunting. The sheer size and shape had been designed to carry the colossal weights over such a large span of water. I recall stopping and just standing for some time looking and deciding whether to turn round and go back, and wait for Peter's offer for Monday, but niggling away in the back of my mind was, where are the docks and where would I find my vehicle? My mind was made up, so forward I went, taking to the left side of the crossing figuring that I could look out to the ocean that way and see any ships that came into view. The bridge is very wide carrying two-way traffic in three lanes, and now and again I would look right and catch a glimpse of some large building in the distance. Nearing the top of my climb across the bridge I thought I would stop, wait and watch for a while.

I could see ships passing by, most of them in the distance and too small for a container ship. By now I had made my mind up that once I reached the centre of the bridge I would stop and turn back. Nearing my chosen turning point, I decided to take some photos. My camera wasn't a good one, or an expensive model, but it did have a zoom lens, keeping a steady hand was not easy due to the wind, and zooming in on the buildings I had glimpsed earlier, I caught site of dock cranes, the type that could lift containers from large ships.

A feeling of anticipation and excitement came over me. Was my container ship there? I couldn't see it but I was hopeful that it would be there in the coming days.

It's strange how suddenly things can change in the blink of an eye as their just underneath me was a ship that I had dismissed as of no interest, but with a closer look it turned out to be a cargo ship.

I focused towards the stern of the ship hoping to catch a glimpse of its name. No such joy, a ship with no name! Damn, I thought with the realisation that the name was on the back and it would pass under me and I won't be able to get its name. Trying to calm myself I swung the camera forwards to the bow and zoomed in as the ship was about to disappear under the steel work beneath me. The words Atlantic Cartier popped into view and my anxiety at potentially missing the name turned into pure excitement, it was my ship and here I was in Canada nervously awaiting its arrival. Seven days previously I had packed the van off on the container ship. I had boarded a plane in the meantime and had arrived at my destination and was waiting with bated breath for the van's arrival. I had painstakingly prepared the van for this round the world tour, and for the first time when the vehicle was loaded onto the ship in Liverpool, the cars fate was out of my hands. I was anxious because I was in another part of the world I didn't know, which brought its own anxiety, and of course I was anxious that my precious vehicle would be OK. It was quite a heart pumping moment walking across the bridge and knowing that my car was down there below me and had crossed the Pond. I hurried back across the bridge to share the good news with Peter and Anne, eager now for Monday, and take Peter up on his offer to run me around Halifax.

Soon after breakfast on Monday, Peter and I and headed over the bridge and in the direction of the port to locate my vehicle. We drove along the dock road and spotted my tiny Mini tucked away amongst some large trucks. She felt so close but out of reach, and this was confirmed when I went to the dock gate to inquire about my car being released. "Sorry sir" was the reply "but the cargo has not cleared customs, try again tomorrow."
With the good news that we had located and actually seen the vehicle, it was time to head back across the bridge to Dartmouth for tea and biscuits. Next morning at breakfast Peter thought we should wait until after lunch before checking in with the customs office. We agreed that made sense so just after 2.00 p.m. I entered the customs office and inquired about the Mini.
"Ah it's yours is it sir? Well it certainly has created some interest."
I feared the worst on hearing those words, but my fear was unfounded. Getting the van through Canadian customs could have created all sorts of problems, but the Mini's inherent charm meant that I needn't have worried. Customs were more than helpful, doing all the paperwork for me that needed to be done. My worry was the possibility of a large payment or bond, a Carnet De Passage type of charge, but they waivered that with a cheery "Go on and enjoy Canada."
One of the customs guys even gave me a recommendation for his sister's campsite, should I travel to Newfoundland. I told him I would make time to go to the campsite, which I did some many, many weeks later.

I still smile when I think back about those first days in Canada, and about how the people and the country welcomed me. There is good and bad all over the world, but Canada, well it's special to me as it set me up with great thoughts of what may lay ahead.

Chapter 5

Bring it on

My last breakfast before taking to the road ahead turned out to be both fulfilling and educational, as a fellow traveller sitting with me ask what direction I was going in. Fearing he may be looking for a lift and as I only had one seat in the van, I casually replied I'm not sure I have not made any plans. You should go to Prince Edward Island." Why? I asked. "The bridge is 12 km long, and then you can return via the ferry."
Peter my host dug out a map to show me where Prince Edward Island was and with a quick glance I could see a route that would take me through Nova Scotia, New Brunswick and the bridge to Prince Edward Island then possible a ferry to Cape Breton and onward again by ferry to Newfoundland none locally as the Rock. By going this way I would be able to fulfil a promise that I had made to the kind customs man at the border agency and pay his sister a visit. For the first time I could feel a plan coming together that would focus me in a direction that could be exciting.

I'd held off buying maps or a Sat-Nav device as basically my head was my map on this drive round the world. While most people would decide to travel first through Europe and then head east, I would be travelling east to west, and as long as the sun was behind me in the morning and ahead of me in the evening I would be travelling in the right direction, it may have seemed a silly idea to many but it worked for me to go The Wrong Way Round.

Digression
Little did I know at this early point that word had got out of an English guy and his Austin Mini had landed in Canada and on there travels. All of this was unbeknown to me and it would not become clear to what extent until I made it to Montreal. Before I started this journey I can recall being approached and offered pen and paper along with a camera, seems they wanted me to report back regularly, I felt uneasy about the pressure it would put on me so I declined, in my mind this was a personal thing I was undertaking.~~

I spent my last morning after breakfast checking out equipment and bolting on the spotlights. That done I went out and bought my first lot of shopping for the coming days, all the things that you would tend to buy if you were living at home. However this was to change dramatically as I was to discover over the coming months.

Early afternoon I said my farewells to Peter and Anne. I settled into my comfy driving seat turning my back on Halifax and hitting the road. The highway was busy with lots of traffic and I was now encountering the big difference in vehicle size and traffic. The Mini felt lost amongst such huge vehicles added to this was a bigger worry the weather; a monsoon engulfed the driving conditions. I was being tested as the water poured into the foot well quicker than it would run out and that's when I remembered we had welded all the floor holes up. I was now a boat taking on water very quickly and my shoes and socks were splashing about in 2 inches of water, I had to do something and quickly. As quick as the weather had hit us it soon disappeared we were now bathed in sunshine, this gave me a chance to turn off the highway into the safety of a tourist information centre car park. I remember pulling up and sitting in my seat laughing and thinking was this to be the first of many surprises that would test me. If that's the only thing I have to worry over then bring it on.
In the pre van planning I had decided that a toolbox would need to be accessible at all times and not buried deep in my fully laden vehicle.

As it worked out, what was once the drivers' side made for an ideal location to fit the toolbox in. So, with the water still deciding to keep company with me I reached into the toolbox and found a hammer and a pointed chisel. Sensibly I had not fitted mats and I set about the floor and in next to no time punched three or four holes through the bodywork. The water was soon dispensed with, but my feet and jeans had absorbed water due to the tidal movement round the foot well and with that in mind I headed for the information building to make a recognisance, figuring that there could be toilets and wash rooms. Again, the Canadians had done themselves proud and as soon as I walked into the building, I was greeted by a lady who had seen me pull up. Excited at seeing my vehicle we talked, and I explained what had happened.

"Bring your clothes in and use the washroom, and we will dry your clothes for you" she offered.

Going back to the mini to collect dry feet and jeans, I saw that the van had by now drawn a small crowd, and an elderly lady with a small child, that I thought must be her granddaughter, stood there in silence. They both stood looking at the van and as I got closer the elderly lady said to me

"Is this your rig sir?"

"Yes, I've brought it from the UK and hope to drive round the world."

Still looking at the mini she rubbed her chin and said, "I know that vehicle I've seen them …." and before she could finish her words the little girl chirped up "It's a Mr Bean car." Those words from that innocent little girl would come in very handy on a continent that had long forgotten the Mini or perhaps many had never seen one this old.

After changing and thanking the helpful information staff for my dry clothes, I picked up a free map, something I would do on many occasions, as I made my way across the second biggest country in the world.

The day was moving on and I needed to start to find somewhere to set up my first night on the road. I drove for a while looking for a suitable safe place to stop. Darkness was moving in as I came across a couple of small wooden houses on the edge of a forest. Spotting a couple of people unloading their car I stopped to ask if there was a campsite anywhere close by. They told me I could find one about 6 km down the road if it was open, as it was still early in the season it may well still be closed. They then told me I would be safe stopping anywhere so I thanked them and I set off into the darkness of the forest. It was so quiet and spooky and for some reason wild animals came into my head. Excitedly, I turned on my two wing mounted spotlights for the first time and was really pleased that I had fitted them. My travels would take me through many forests, some of them bigger than my own county and with the fear of deer and elk along with bears confronting me while driving it would be a worry. I'd heard many stories about my biggest potential enemy, the moose. I remember them being described to me as being like a giraffe without the long neck, and antlers over two metres wide shaped like the jaws of a crocodile.

Digression

In the weeks to come I would witness such things in Newfoundland that would turn out to be a tragedy for one early morning traveller, when a moose came out from the undergrowth at speed and took the roof off the vehicle with its antlers.~~

After about half an hour of driving I gave up looking for the camp site. It was now 9.30 p.m. and the rain had returned, so I decided to turn off the road and onto what looked like a narrow forest road. Ideal I thought, as I drove along through the grass that had grown over the gravel. I kept going eager to find what I thought would be the best spot to camp. Even with the spotlights turned on the rain still made my vision difficult. The track I was following ended at a cliff face and nowhere to camp. Feeling pretty tired I decided to try and turn round and at least face the other way, as a precaution. Three-point turns in reverse are not unusual for me, having competed in driving and speed tests in the past. I could see that the track was none too wide and that it would take several turns to accomplish the turn round. I made the first couple of manoeuvres with no problems and I was now at the halfway point of completing the transition when fate kicked in. Selecting first gear the mini rolled back and I felt a thump as the rear wheels settled into a small ditch. I was now stuck, very stuck and no amount of traction from the front wheels would help. Darkness was all around the forest but reluctantly I climbed out of the van and into the rain. A quick look confirmed I was going nowhere without the use of my winch, and that was buried deep in the back somewhere. Climbing back into the van wet and tired I turned on my diesel night heater to get warm and try to dry out. Room in the van is limited and any chance of lying down to sleep at this point was not going to happen. Deciding there was nothing I could do till day light I settled down to spend my first night on the road sitting upright in the front seat listening to the sound of the rain and wind.

I woke the next morning to the sound of ticking. The noise was coming from the pump that keeps my night heater running. The rain had stopped, and I felt dry and warm. It was time to step outside and unload the many storage boxes and find that winch. Bolting on the winch was not difficult and I'd soon run the wire out to the base of a substantial tree. I pressed the go button and movement of the vehicle was soon underway and in no time, she was back on four wheels and I was underway, this time heading for Prince Edward Island and the 12 km Confederation Bridge.

Within a couple of hours, I had reached the entry for the crossing and was pleased to see there weren't any toll booths to greet me. I drove onward unable to see much due to the high concrete sides and the travelling became a little boring and the bridge disappointing. It was not what I had expected but turning back wasn't an option due to the configuration of the bridge, and before long I was out in a wide area with yes, you've guest it, toll booths. Clear of the bridge and on the island, I was keen to see if there were any similarities to life here that I could connect with from back home on the Isle of Mull. The lack of houses and traffic was evident at first and not long after I turned off the paved road.

Digression
Roads that are dead ends and seem to go know where I would drive on many occasions, having worked out that at the end of these roads something would be happening, and I was rarely disappointed.
I would go and prove this to myself many times, even to the point of driving distances of 500 to1000kms even to crossing the Arctic Circle, and on one such occasion just to prove that there was something there. Eventually having to turn round and return to my starting point. For me it was never a problem as every mile was interesting whatever direction I took. ~~

Turning onto a beaten track I followed the road for a while till it ended up at a small quayside with two old wooden sheds and a single fishing boat. I got out stretching my legs and took a look around. There was an air of quietness that I liked, and the place had the feeling of bye gone days. As I walked towards the small boat a head popped out of the deck hatch and a voice said "Hello" to which I replied,
"I've been down in those dark places a few times back home.
"Where are you from the man asked".
"Small Island off the west coast of Scotland" and over the next hour or so we talked about boats, their engines and what was caught and landed from the sea. He told me that crab and lobster was caught and I told him that was similar to back home. Ever mindful that I had not yet got into a routine for meals and sleeping I bid him farewell and went in search of an early night and the chance to put some basic routines into my days ahead.

Again, I found the road quiet with very little traffic still unsure where or where not it was both legal and safe to stop to set up my camp. Luck would have it and I came across an abandoned sand pit that seemed an ideal spot to stay for a few days. Just after lunch time I set about unloading the plastic boxes of different sizes onto the floor outside. Each box had been marked either with the contents or their purpose. The van now empty meant the inside was clear and I could test out my hammock bed. This was attached to the roll cage by chains to the hammock bed frame, and when not in use, it could be taken down and stored. The next ten minutes were interesting and very funny as I tried hard to climb onto the mattress. The hammock would not stay still, and I wasn't even lying down on it yet. I had let myself down, and this device was destined to be scrapped in the coming minutes and a new plan would have to be figured out for sleeping. I set about putting up the Van tent and this did go well and proved easy and quick to put up, turning out to be a great asset.

The plastic boxes could be stored or set up as a seat and table for cooking on, leaving plenty of room for me to sleep on the vans floor with an air bed that I had brought with me. However, this too turned out to be another waste of time, loosing air when I lay on it and that to be bound for the bin. Opening the box marked kitchen I took out the Colman stove that I was keen to use. It ran on petrol and not propane. Propane was never going to be an option for me because of safety and availability. Fuel I would always have. The stove had been recommended to me by Matty Green one of the young guys in the Withnell Mafia rally clan. The stove tuned out to be invaluable and would earn the nick name the Matty Stove. The time of the day seemed right to test it, and along with my food survival skills, and with a frying pan of eggs and spam the warm aroma of food soon circled my tent. The silence from outside was only broken by the sound of a vehicle approaching in my direction stopping just in front of the tent. I could see two guys in the vehicle and winding down the window the driver said "hello."
I responded with "Am I OK here?" "Sure, you're fine, you won't get bothered. How long you staying?" they asked.
"A couple of days" I said.
"We are just going fishing, so if you're still here we will drop some fish off for you." I thanked them and set about preparing my bed then turned to writing my daily log, something that became a habit for me at the end of each day.

I spent the next few days checking and playing about with my equipment, getting to know how and where everything fitted in for ease on my travels. The van was brand new and especially prepared for the days ahead. Silent Wish, as I had named her would take care of me and each day as I climbed into my seat, as a routine I would tap the steering wheel and say thanks to Silent Wish for taking care of me.

Getting low on food and in need of diesel for the night heater due to the evenings still being cold, I decided that I should move on and find a town to top up my supplies. After breakfast I packed up and got back on the road. I enjoy driving, and I like it even better the fewer vehicles there are. Driving this side of the world was turning out to be a real pleasure.

The evenings were cold, but once the sun came up, the day felt warm and spring like. Time seemed to slow down, and with it my driving as I reflected on this newfound comfort. Like most people it's the view and scenery that makes a journey interesting and aligned with that I seemed to be constantly looking for, the unexpected surprise, and to go to where others may not. I soon came to a T junction with a small red dirt track that ran straight across and on my right was a tiny petrol station. Pulling in a young lady greeted me and offered to fill the mini's petrol tank; leaving me to find the diesel can I use to top up the night heater. As I walked in to pay an elderly hillbilly looking gent in bib and braces overalls stepped out of the workshop and commented on the van. "That's an old Austin."

"Yes, it is" I said, and soon after I was inside the garage workshop looking at some well-preserved cars and a Mack recovery truck, the bull nose type that sat in pride of place in the garage entrance. It became obvious that the workshop did not take in work anymore; it was so tidy you could eat your food off the work benches and even the floor. I thanked the gentleman for his interest and the time we spent together and then headed to pay for my fuel, as I stepped into what was a small shop that had all the basics I needed to top up my food supplies.

Digression

Living on Mull teaches you to shop locally, buying fuel and provisions from the local small business. These stops made me feel close to home and reflect that you could in time loose these facilities if you don't support and use them. ~~

Turning back onto the road I decided to take the little red dirt track hoping that I was not trespassing and some fifteen minutes later I came to a dead end and the ocean. With not a soul about I turned the engine off and lay back in my seat feeling the sun through the screen I relaxed.

The air was still and motionless, with only the occasional sound of the rolling surf below the cliffs of red stone. It was so good I fell asleep for an hour before getting out and stretching my legs. Now armed with a towel and wash bag I made my way down to the red sandy beach. I could see for miles, the place was totally deserted. I lay down on the towel to take in the sun and silence, every now and then lifting my head to check on the privacy. It felt like the world was so different and as I lay back my thoughts turned to family and friends back home wishing they could have been here with me to experience these thoughts also.

Digression

One of the most asked questions I would be asked was "Are you travelling alone?" "Yes" I would say, "I don't do baggage."

I know it's a rather selfish way to deliver a reply and one that did not come easy to me, but it sat a lot easier with me than having to repeat the reasons why by reflecting on the past. This journey would have to be done alone as I was trying to rediscover myself while still reflecting on my loss's in 2008. ~~

Safe in the knowledge that I was alone on the beach I decided to take a full body wash and headed for the sea with just a towel and soap. The soap turned out to be hard work and, in the end, useless, as the soap wouldn't lather try as hard as I could it would not lather in the sea water. I improvised a wash with the seaweed lapping about me and managed a scrub down before drying off and returning to the van. Feeling refreshed I headed back to the paved highway. All sorts of vehicles would pass me, and passengers would wave to me, bikers would pull alongside and join me for a while, then take off with a salute and often I would be beckoned and signalled to stop. The drive eventually brought me to a small harbour, a little larger and with more activity than the last one.

Sitting with van on the quayside my thoughts turned to the lack of houses. I had not seen any since crossing the bridge and where did everybody live was becoming a mystery that was about to change in the coming hour. Happy just to sit and people watch from my vehicle, it wasn't long before two young boys on cycles turned up to view and spin round my vehicle. They waved a couple of times then took off. Not long after a pickup truck pulled up alongside me, the driver got out along with the two boys that had previously been on cycles. The driver greeted me, and I stepped out of the van and shook his hand. "I'm Dave from Scotland," I introduced myself.

"You're a long way from home, I'm Mike and these are my boys. They came back home and told me about this strange little parcel van, and I had to come and see. Where are you staying tonight?"

I didn't have any plans on that just yet I told him.

"Follow me, there's lots of space back at mine and you can camp there if you want."

I followed Mike's truck from the harbour back onto the highway and in a short distance we were in town, Georgetown, a small oldie world place with wooden buildings some of them empty and in need of repair. There weren't many shops and while driving down the main street you couldn't miss the large concrete boat sitting on a trailer on a small grass plot slap bang outside the town's council office. As I passed, I laughed thinking they must have had a high tide to get that there. Now we were out of town and it wasn't long before we arrived at Mike's. I was introduced to his wife Sharon who straight away put the kettle on and we settled down to talk about the new man and van in town. Mike told me I could stay as long as I wanted, and I could stay in the bunk house at the bottom of the garden if I wished.

He added that it had a great bed, a hot shower and stove and I could just bed myself down there. I was overwhelmed by the family's generosity and I offered to put myself to work while I was there. Don't worry about that for now just settle in and enjoy and be sure to come to the house for breakfast in the morning and have some pancakes with us.

That evening I went for a walk just round what was the back yard but in actual fact I soon became aware it was fields, more than one. Finding myself at the furthest point I came across an area full of VW Beetle cars, trucks, pickups and camper vans of all ages and colours, with trees and bushes growing through them. I'd never seen anything like it before I just kept walking and looking, occasionally stopping to lift a hood and find a missing engine, or the odd seat from much of the rusty mix that lay about. Somebody had a passion for these vehicles, and I felt they had cornered the market. It was truly an amazing sight.

Next morning, I was up early and looking out from the bunkroom I could see activity in the house. Grabbing some shorts and T shirt I fought my way down the track at speed wrestling with a pair of flip flops not wanting to be late for proper Canadian pancakes and maple syrup breakfast. Sharon and the kids were sitting down while Mike was busy at the stove. Pulling up a chair I joined then at the table, eagerly attacking a plate full of lovely warm pancakes. Mike joined us and asked me if I would like to go into town and take a look at a wooden building he had been working on for some time, seems he had been trying to replace the rotten timbers that supported the house in the basement. "Sure" I said "it sounds interesting to me."

We arrived at the site and Kenny a friend of Mike's was busy taking doors down that would be re hung once the house had been jacked up and the new timbers had been installed. I set about helping Kenny with removing the doors. Mike went out to get some food and at lunch time we stopped to eat, and talked mainly about me and what I did back home for work. The rest of the day passed quickly, and I did feel I had been of use. I was covered in dust and dirt having ventured into the basement to help with the daunting task of replacing timbers below ground level. With life teetering on the edge down there, I was enjoying it in a strange way.

Once again, I was invited to join the family to eat that evening and during the meal Mike asked me if I would like to do a job for the community. I agreed willingly adding it would not be a problem.
"I haven't told you what it is yet" he said.
"It doesn't matter" I replied, "I'm just glad to be here."
Mike told me about the large boat down in town the one I had seen yesterday. The town had wanted it moved for some time and welding work was badly needed on the trailer so it could be moved safely. Mike explained he had the steel work, in the form of large girders, that need cutting and welded into place and if he could source the welding equipment to do the job would I do the work? I willingly agreed provided I wasn't paid. Mike's retort was "We will see about that."
Next morning, I drove down to the town in the Minivan to take a look at what I had let myself in for. Mike tuned up with a loaded trailer that looked full of all I would need to do the job. I gave him a rough idea of what I thought would work okay and he said he would leave me to get started if I was happy to get going, and he would call back later in the day. I reckoned an hour had gone by when I spotted Mike's pickup coming down the street. He pulled up and told me he had to go and get some screws for Kenny to use on the doors. I smiled and thought to myself, has Kenny really started refitting the doors already? Mike took a quick look at what I was doing and seemed happy enough. It was some time before I saw him again. Over the rest of the week I kept going cutting and welding with the odd passer by stopping to chat. Friday morning at breakfast Mike asked me when I thought the work would be done. I was able tell him it would be completed by the end of the day.
"That's great Dave" he said "We are planning to make tracks to Marie's for the weekend. She's my sister and has a cottage, the plan is to join the rest of the family and you are welcome to come with us."

Friday's work to the boat trailer went swiftly and by 3.00 p.m. I'd tided up and packed the tools and equipment onto Mike's trailer. As expected, he arrived not long after and we returned to his place to get ready for the weekend. We would be saying over till Monday, so I put a few clothes in a bag and by 4.30 p.m. Mike, Sharon myself and there two boys had piled into Mike's truck and drove for about thirty minutes before arriving at Marie's. What a beautiful location it was, there were assorted trees set in about ten acres on the edge of a small bay. We drove up to the cottage and got out to meet the family members, young and old. Once introductions had been made Mike took me on a tour of the property and we finished up walking to the shore. Mike removed his shoes rolled up his jeans then walked a short way into the water. He bent down and picked up a shell, it was an oyster. He opened it up and passed it to me to eat, before long I had eaten four or five, it was enough. The seabed was full of them growing wild. Back at the cottage the ladies were all busy preparing food while the men drank beer and got their musical instruments out and warmed up. Early that evening we all gathered together in the main room with food and drink in no short supply settling down to an evening of varied instruments and music. It's at times like these I feel a little left out being unable to play any type of musical instrument.

Digression
I have always wanted to be able to play the banjo. My rallying friends and my family gave me a send-off party and presented me with a banjo before leaving on this adventure. I took it with me, and God love them I think they thought I would have loads of time to sit on a log in a forest and practice. ~~

The evening's enjoyment went on to the early hours of Saturday morning, so it was close to midday before most people were up and about. Barry, Marie's husband was up and working, banging nails into the roof of his new boat shed. Not wanting to feel left out both Mike and I climbed gingerly up the ladder and onto the partly finished roof offering help for the afternoon, be it at a slow pace, with long breaks for tea and coffee.
Something we didn't have was electricity. It's not a big problem you just adapt, and before long you forget about it. Lighting candles or taking a Tilley lamp for a walk in the darkness to find the outhouse was normal in this part of the world. This is all part of life still in some places and it makes for interesting times.
Saturday evening was much the same as the previous evening. This time we had a barbeque outside on a homemade spit that turned round slowly over a log fire. The large piece of meat on the spit turned out to be elk. The evening was warm so we took our seats outside and settled round to watch the sun and light fade to the sound of the fiddle and a guitar.

Mike had spoken to me earlier saying he would like to get back handy on Monday as he had lots to do work wise. I told him that was fine by me as I must make tracks and move on. After all it had been nearly ten days since meeting Mike and being made welcome by his lovely family. The following day I said my farewells and after one last call, this time to Mike's brother's garage for a quick check up and oil change on the van I headed for the ferry, but not before a bus stop call into Charlotte town the biggest town on the island.

Arriving at the small port called Woodlands I paid my $68 x $5 fuel tax then joined the queue of twenty cars and six big rigs, mainly freightliners and Kenworths hauling two or more trailers with fridges or logs a plenty. The passage takes about an hour and a half to reach the port of Caribou, Nova Scotia and I spent most of the crossing catching up on my daily log. I had found a tourist map of my next destination Cape Breton, so I searched for interesting places. A couple of names and places that jumped out at me were Meat Cove the other was Cape North both sounding very appealing and mysterious. They were at the top of the island and about a week away at the speed I was travelling.

Cape Breton is an island with a manmade causeway as access. The main road goes round a lot of the outer edge of the island above the steep cliffs. The road is known as the Celtic trail. Finding a place to stop and camp became very easy and I set the tent up for the first time in a while. The sun was setting in the west so I left the side curtain open on the van tent and got the Matty stove on the go to make some soup. Climbing into bed clutching my bowl of soup I reflected on the last ten days, and the place and the people that had surrounded me with so much affection and how it had been so hard to leave.

Digression
We all feel emotions in one form or another. I sought for an answer to the feelings that produced so much emotion and tears for me. I could only conclude that it had to be a mixture of meeting new people, new places and my recovery bubble that I was floating along in.~~

Over the next few days, I drove and travelled the Celtic trail passing many signs more akin to one's back home with name places like Craigmore, Inverness and Iona. The following days I would visit a small Celtic college where music and dancing were taught, spending a little time talking about life back home in Scotland. I was amazed to find that this part of the world felt more Scottish than home. The coming week and my activities would very much reinforce these thoughts.

Digression
I had lived on Mull in Scotland for longer than I had lived in my birthplace, which was the Wirral in England. Born English with a Welsh forename and surname trapping an English saint in-between, I worked at, and bonded with my community back home on Mull and that pleased me immensely. I find it both interesting and sometimes amusing the relationship between the Scots and the English. It's similar this side of the world with the Canadians and the

Americans, while metaphorically throwing hand grenades at each other now and then. The Canadians have more history than the yanks and that hurts them as their history only goes back a couple of hundred years. ~~

Saturday morning, I got up cooked breakfast and made a plan to try and find Meat Cove and possibly set up camp there for a couple of days. The weather was mainly warm and dry and the traffic was starting to increase with trucks and camper vans the size of a small house now starting to appear. Come lunch time I found myself rounding a corner on to a junction with an oblong shop with plenty of parking area. Pulling in I parked up to decide if I needed anything. While sitting there two guys each carrying a white plastic shopping bag in one hand and a case of beer in the other stepped out from the shop. I said hello to them and told them pointing to the beer that looked like a great idea. One of them made the observation I wasn't local, I told them I was from Scotland. We shook hands "My name's Jarred and this is my brother Dave"
"That's my name" I said. "Do you want some where to stay and have a beer?" If you do then follow us back to moms place.

Normally I would think hard before taking up an offer from two guys but the fact they had added their mother into the conversation made things rest easier with me. I took up their offer and followed them till we reached a dirt turning. After passing two sheds with an old red Massey Ferguson tractor outside we soon came upon a small single house in a clearing, which looked like work in progress. I was invited to Come in and meet mom, and still a little cautious I stepped inside to be greeted by a lovely little lady of good age. She reached out and told me her name was Theresa she wrapped her arms around me and said "Hello, my boys have a beer for you and if you don't mind drinking outside, we can eat on the porch."

Dave was already outside and had a barbeque on the go with buffalo steaks the size of a frying pan sizzling and smelling good. It seemed I was to eat and stay the night, it all now felt more comfortable with me. Food on the go and after a beer or two talks turned to Scotland with Jarred telling me that he had been to Oban and had sailed to the outer isles. He knew lots about Scotland and his brother Dave had also been to different parts of the world but with the army in the Special Forces. I told them I hoped to go to Cape North and Meat Cove while I was here. We agreed they would take me the following day and show you me some interesting places. Feeling sleepy I thanked everybody and took myself of to bed. The next morning, I awoke to the smell of bacon and headed to the kitchen. Jarred was cooking breakfast and mum was pottering about the place. I could feel the guys were keen to get going and show me around their community. After breakfast the brothers and I got into their truck and drove for about 12 km before taking a turning to the left and another dirt road which climbed for some distance. The scenery was stunning and as we reached the headland the road ran out and we could go no further. We climbed out of the pick-up and walked the last bit of track to the headland where we came across an old wooden building where a huge guy was busy cutting planks of wood with a chain saw. The boys obviously knew him and I learned his name was Allan. On seeing us he stopped the saw and we talked for what must have been an hour. While there we were asked if we fancied a cup of tea, and with that all four of us got into the pickup and headed back down the road to a small café where Allan's wife worked. We order tea and coffee and while we were waiting, I looked at the photographs on the wall. They were all in black and white and were pictures of local people who had left this part of the world and travelled far to fight in a war on the other side of the world many years ago.

Digression
One thing I did begin to notice while travelling was flags and lots of them. Something you don't see too often back in the UK, maybe on special occasions but never on a daily basis as in Canada. I saw them everywhere mainly just a single country flag outside properties, but now and then I'd come across a war memorial flying three flags, the Nations flag, the Province flag and the Union Jack.~~

We sat for a while talked about many things and soon the best part of the day had gone. I reminded Dave that he had wanted to watch a game of hockey, bidding farewell to Allan and his wife, we headed back home. Back at the homestead we passed the tractor at the sheds. Just for conversation I happened to mention the fact that I used to work on the old grey and red ones back home. Before I got the words out of my mouth Jarred said that it had been there a few years, it used run but would not move and it would be handy to use for clearing the logs and trees. Cunningly, whether he knew it or not, he had sown the seed within me. Back in the house Theresa had made some sandwiches and we settled down with a couple of beers to watch the hockey. The game was interesting as an American team were playing a Canadian team and as luck would have it the maple leaf team won. Celebrating with the boys I took one final beer with them before heading to bed.

The following day was Sunday so I wasn't expecting for much to happen. How wrong I was! The guys would be going out and I accompanied them in their pickup to a disused quarry where we loaded some small gravel with shovels into the rear of the truck. Once loaded we head back in the direction of the house me thinking the gravel was for concrete or something like that. Ha! I was wrong, we soon took a turning and stopped part way up one of the many tracks, turning the truck round we climbed out and started to fill pot holes. To me it was just a track that went nowhere. I couldn't see anything from where we worked. I was puzzled but carried on filling pot holes. Almost out of gravel we had nearly reached the top of the hill, but I still could not see anything of interest,
I asked the boys if I could take a walk further on over the rise. "Sure" they said, "carry on we are going back to get another load of gravel."

Turning round I made my way to the top of the crest before coming upon a church. A little stunned I stood for a while just wondering how long it had been here and what was its history. I was soon to find out. On looking at the first of many gravestones neatly in lines, the names started to appear, MacDonald, Mackenzie, McCrae and Stewart just a few of the many names dating back to the 1700 and 1800 hundreds. I stood frozen for a while my mind running wild thinking is this for real? The proof was there lying in the ground, these people had been pioneers crossing a huge ocean in wooden boats. It all became a little too much for me and I turned and headed back to the pickup, trying to put myself into the shoes of the forefathers of this new world. On re-joining Dave and Jarred I told them I would like to take a look at the tractor tomorrow. Feeling pleased that I might be able to do something for them in return.

The following morning, I arose, washed and headed for breakfast and pancakes were my start for the day. It was just me and Jarred, mum was staying in bed and Dave had gone out to visit a friend. As we headed over to the tractor, I asked Jarred a few questions about the tractor trying to get some history and background at what I had let myself in fore. It turned out it had been sitting there for two years and had not moved. It had been running back then, but now it just would not move. I enquired if he had a good battery and he said "I'll take the one off the pickup it's not very old."
Before going to get my tool box from the Minivan, I told Jarred the only other things I could do with was some clean diesel and a strong chain, as long a chain as he have, He looked at me with a puzzled face and took off to get the battery and fuel. Returning I could see that he was dying to ask what the chain was for. I was keen not to tell him. "We may not need the chain just leave it on the floor please."

Digression
I have always worked better on my own and can't stand being watched by others, even more so if they have hands in their pockets and can't stop talking, that's how it is with me.~~

I said I would do some checks to the fuel system and generally look for problems. Jarred checked back to see if I was ok and if I needed anything, I was to give him a shout should I need help. He had some trees that needed cutting down then cutting into shorter lengths. Left on my own I now set about the much-aged tractors fuel and electrical system. It's basic and uncomplicated and I was soon getting to the point of fitting the battery into its box and hooking both main wires to the terminals on the battery. I switched the key on and got a red light. Now to see if the single preheat plug that was located on the air intake was working. With a short wire running from the battery direct to the heater plug, I could feel it heat up.

Focus now turned to the fuel system that too is reasonably simple. Jarred said that tractor had run albeit some time ago and my thought was to check the fuel filter, always a weak point and prone to dirt and water. Removing and refilling with fresh diesel I bled the system to draw the air out and opened up one of the 3 injector pipes on the cylinder head. Checking the tractor was in neutral on the main high gear range and also in neutral on the low range, which had a safety device that stopped the tractor from starting, I pre warmed the inlet manifold for about ten seconds then turned on the key to the start position. The engine turned, followed by a cloud of mixed coloured smoke from the exhaust. The battery was holding up to the job in hand. It took a little while but it started running but not on all cylinders. I jumped off the tractor and grabbed my 11/16 spanner and tightened the one injector pipe I had undone, and sure enough the engine revved up and ran smooth. I stepped back to listen, it sounded good. The next job was to try the assorted gears and see if I could get it to move. The tractor has four forward gears with a high and low range giving eight in total, dipping the clutch I tried them all. Nothing was happening, it would just not move. Checking the clutch pedal shaft that goes into the side casting of the gearbox was turning ok when you depress the pedal then the clutch action was working ok. I had over the years come across this strange anomaly once before and if my thoughts where correct I might just have the answer with the chain that had mystified Jarred. As fortune would have it there was a large tree by the shed so I set about tying the chain about the base of the tree and fixing

the other end to the rear axle of the tractor. I climbed back on and restarted the engine engaging both high gear and high range on the two levers, then increasing the throttle lever for higher working revs. That done I casually stepped off to stand and watch for a while. Now happy to leave the tractor to do its own thing, I went looking for Jarred and eventually found him with his home-made mobile hydraulic log splitter working hard at clearing trees. Turning round he stopped the engine to welcome me. "Is that the tractor I can hear?"
"Yes" I said.
"Well done did you have any luck with the clutch?"
"No not yet, thought I would take a break and come and help you for a time." "We can stack these logs on the trailer if you would like" said Jarred.
Half an hour had passed when Dave came walking over shouting the tractor's going and that must be a miracle. I said I was trying to get it warmed up and we carried on quietly loading the trailer.

Suddenly there was a huge bang from the direction of the sheds then total silence. Instantly dropping everything the three of us rushed towards the tractor, stumbling over tree stumps and roots and all the while I was hoping the tractor had not taken off and destroyed a shed. I was first on the scene, the sheds where still intact and the tractor stood motionless. I took a look at the chain as the guys arrived asking what had happened. I explained I wasn't sure. The chain was tight so I climbed onto the tractor and started her up. This time I selected reverse and lifted my foot off the clutch and the tractor made its first move in two years under its own power. I was well pleased, as for the guys they couldn't believe what they saw.
"What the hell did you do to make it work?" they asked.
I told them the problem had been the clutch plate which had stuck and bonded itself to the flywheel and once I got enough heat in that area it came free. That's what the chain was for Jarred.
"We owe you Dave."
"No, you don't, let's finish and go have a beer" I said.
That evening I ate well and downed a few beers and while on a high I told the guys I would be leaving next morning; it was time for me to move on once again.

It would be close to lunch time before I started the van. Theresa had made up a bunch of food for me and the boys had put a few beers in a white plastic bag, just like the ones I'd seen a week earlier. As I waved goodbye Jarred shouted be sure to come back. Maybe I will one day.

Re-joining the road, I was once again on the Celtic trail driving clockwise, peeking first at the most northerly point of Cape Breton before turning downwards along the eastern seaboard onward past English town and onto North Sydney and a ferry which I figured was a day and a half away. That afternoon by pure accident I found myself very close to a sandy beach and pulling up I stopped to take a walk and explore the dunes and coastline. I stepped onto the deserted beach where I spotted a couple of wooden notices above the high waterline and went closer to take a look. I could also see a big stone that lay on a grassed area with a table and seating close by. On the stone was a stainless-steel plate with the name of John Cabot. It read, having set sail from Bristol England early in May 1497 and after fifty days at sea in his ship called Matthew, he had landed here to claim this new land for England.

Cabot was born it Giovanni Italy but was hired by King Henry VII of England to seek new lands afar. When Cabot first landed, he thought he had found Asia. That evening I set my camp up to sleep on the dunes, drinking a beer and looking out to sea trying to imagine what this place must have looked like to the crew of the Matthew al those years ago.

I was up early the next day and soon on the road to try and make the port of New Sydney and my sailing to Newfoundland aboard the MV Caribou. On a crossing that would take six hours. I arrived in plenty of time having pre booked my passage and cleared check in with no problems. I joined the many lines of traffic and boarding soon started. I found my vehicle attracting the usual interest, mainly from the deck crew. At one point I thought the whole ships company was giving it the once over only to be told by one of the crew the captain will be down to have a look while we are at sea.

Making sure I had plenty to keep me occupied on the long crossing. I headed up several flights of stairs to reach the lounge and a power point to recharge my electric items. I joined the queue for food and settled for good old fish and chips, but the chips turned out to be frits, or French fries. A long blast on the ships horn and we were underway. The sea crossing was calm and about an hour into the voyage the captain came and joined me to chat for a while. He was fascinated with the mini and my travels. He told me I would love the people on the rock, as it is known and finally wishing me a safe onward journey before he returned back to the bridge.

Now on my own I fell asleep for some time only waking to the sound of the ships horn again warning us of our approach to land and the shores of Newfoundland and its southerly tip of Port Aux Basques my next launching point on this unbelievable adventure.

Chapter 6

Life on the Rock

Disembarkation from the ship was swift and as I drove off the crew waved and I blew my air horns in response, then I was straight onto Route One of the Trans Canadian Highway with its starting point some 1000kms away in the capital of St Johns on the far east of the Island, the Highway finally finishing in Vancouver on the western seaboard of Canada. Back on an island felt good and this was Newfoundland known locally as the Rock, there would be much to explore and am keen to see how many Newfoundland dogs I would get to see having owned one.

Digression
The Newfoundland dog is a wonderful pet for a family with children, especially if you lived close to water and the white sand of Calgary Bay on the island of Mull as we did. The Newfie is a gentle giant who loves the water. Their life span is only eight to ten years, but it is a dog that can leave you with lasting memories. ~~

Traffic was heavy from the boat and not far along the big trucks would have to pull over to be checked and weighed. The road was in good condition so I settled down to a steady speed of 40 to 50miles an hour. One of the laws in Newfoundland is that you must drive with your head lights on at all times.

Digression
I was well aware that in some counties it is the law that you must drive with your vehicles head lights on at all times. During the van build I sought a way to cover myself a little from being caught out by this law. All minis come as standard with the sidelights built into the headlight bowl. All I did was to adapt the indicator lights below and incorporate a second sidelight into the same unit, still leaving the sidelights in the headlight, so the headlights always looked turned on, be them a little dim having forgotten not put the main lights on.~~

Sticking to my speed it was not long before I could see headlights in my mirror and with a bit of good timing on my part and knowing what to do, the next hour was spent letting the big rigs, of all shapes and sizes go by, most running double trailers (pulling two trailers) sounding their horns and flashings their lights. It looked like a scene from the film Convoy 10/4 good buddy.

The day was moving on and ever aware that I needed to find a base for the night I turned off the Highway at River Brook where I spotted a sign to St David. Being a left turn the sun was now in my eyes and a short drive brought me to a T junction with a store and petrol pump. I pulled up to get some milk and bread and while paying for my goods I enquired about camp sites back up the road. The lady gave me the information I required and thanking her I decided not to back track but to carry on along the coast, stopping a couple of times to take photos of the sun setting and looking for a possible place to camp. The problem now was I had too many choices on where to make camp. A further short drive brought me to a pub or inn with a small shop.

I pulled up and stopped. Staying with the vehicle I could see life in the pub. Deciding to drive a little further and would come across an old wooden house that looked like it was falling over. Confident that it was abandoned I parked up on the safe side using the side porch to store my plastic boxes from van. Doing this saved having to put the tent up so I laid my sleeping bag out.

As the pub was only a short distance away, I decided to go for a beer. There were a few people at the bar that I could see through the glass window in the door, and sure enough as I turned the door handle, the heads turned in synchronisation just like my local pub back home. Making my way to the bar a one young chap stepped back to let me get to the counter and order. I had barely paid for the drink when a lady that had been sitting at the side of a man at the far end of the bar made her way over to me. Are you looking for a room for the night at the inn? "No thanks" I told her. You only had to look into her eyes to see she had been and was still drinking.
"Where're you staying?" she asked. This was to be twenty questions while the rest of the pub looked on and listened.
"I have my own sleeper that I'm staying in."

"But where?" she persisted.
"Down the road" I replied. After that she got fed up and went back to her seat. It seemed the night's entertainment was over, and the locals went back to what they had been doing. I finished my drink and headed back to my camping spot smiling and thinking no matter where you are, in a small community in any part of the world human nature is the same.

There was a good chill in the air after a day of sunshine and back at the van I turned the night heater on and climbed into my sleeping bag, I lay back and in ten minutes I was warm and cosy. Good planning had made it easy for me to reach the heater controls and sleep was not far away.

I woke next morning and pushed open the single rear door that I had to support with a four feet stick. You could feel the warmth and hear the birds. It was spring heading for summer, and I could not be in a better place. What was I going to do today? I did not really care, my Matty stove and breakfast were more important. Breakfast over I washed and repacked the van with my boxes.

Re-joining the Highway for the day, I travelled 220kms to Lark Harbour which is located in the Blow Me down Provisional Park. On the days travel I passed through Corner Brook, quite a large town with a paper mill. I got lost here and had to ask the way out of town. Back on route I passed so many place, with names like Frenchmen's Cove, Halfway Point, Wild Cove and Humber Arm, how did all these place names come about? I turned off the main highway, but the road was bad with lots of holes, so I didn't rush. Part way I came upon a lifeboat station at York Harbour, and I decided to pull in and take a look. Calling at the office to say hello I was met by Ian. He told me a little about the place then took me down to the boat that was tied up alongside the jetty.

It was a four-man crewed boat and the crew do two weeks on and two weeks off. The engineer joined us, and I told them about our lifeboat back in Tobermory. I stayed for about an hour then finally head out for my destination that evening at Lark Harbour.

I arrived at the harbour, which was tiny, I had expected something bigger. Deciding to check in at the café I had a cup of tea and some cake. I chatted with lady who served me and found out her name and not long after her husband came in to the café to join us. We shook hands and he told his name was Llewellyn or known as Junior to the locals. As usual I asked about camping.
"Would you like some dinner with us" asked Junior, "it's only spagbol but you're welcome to join us, then I can take you to a good spot to camp on the headland."
After a really nice dinner in great company I left with Junior for the headland. Thanking Marlene and telling her I would call back tomorrow; Junior led the way in his four by four vehicle up this well rutted track and on reaching the top we both found ourselves impressed with "my steed" as Junior called it.

After the usual morning breakfast and washing I hung out my sleeping bag to air on a makeshift line. So far on this journey I had not felt any fear or found any reason to hide or lock my vehicle and this way would continue for some time. Armed with my camera I set off on the foot path Marked Captain Cooks Trail. I walked for a while, admiring some lovely views, unwittingly thinking that having seen the Captain Cook sign I might come across nautical or interesting things from the past, but I was to be disappointed.

About lunch time I packed up and headed back to the Tide Watcher café. Marlene welcomed me and in no time produced a pot of tea on the table. I wasn't hungry as I had a late breakfast, so I just asked for a piece of cake with my tea. The café had a few tourist items and looking at the post cards I came across one that had Newfoundland dogs on it. That reminded me of a text message my daughter Louise had sent me after I had landed on the rock. The message read "Well done bring me back one of those little black fluffy things." However, she would have to settle for the next best thing, a postcard. Just as I was leaving, Junior came in and gifted me a present of a rather large lobster. I would eat well tonight; again I had been blessed with meeting some wonderful people.

An hour would see me back on Highway One. Once on the Highway I pulled over and stopped for a group of runners dressed in blue shorts and white tops all carrying buckets. As they got closer, I could see they were naval girls and guys. Happily, they stopped, and we chatted. They told me that for the last ten years, part of the ship's crew is landed at the port and would have to run the full 1000kms of the Highway to St Johns, raising money for underprivileged children. They were only assisted by a back-up car containing food water and medicine. On completion of the run they would meet up with their ship in the capital. I wished them well and dropped some money in the bucket. Before parting they said." Be sure to come and see us in St Johns if you get there."

My route would take me through the town of Deer Lake, at that point I could stay on the Highway One in the direction of St Johns or head north on the 430 route then take the 431 to Trout River and the promise I made a month early in Halifax to Chris Reid, from the customs and border agency, to call on his sister at Crocker Cabins. The drive was about 60kms to Trout River and I arrived early afternoon. Finding the cabins was easy as they were located at the end of the road and almost on the beach. The promise to Chris had been well worth the journey and if possible, I would like to stay a while. Pulling up at the cabin marked office I made my way to the door and was greeted by a young girl. I proceeded to tell her about Chris and how we met. "Yes" she said "Chris is my uncle, moms out just now but will be back later." I asked if there was a spot where I could camp, she told me up by the cabins was a good place to set up. I offered payment and not for the first time on this trip I was told there was no charge.

I got back in the van and drove the short distance, past a couple of cabins. All seemed quiet and deserted; I picked a spot out of the way ever conscious it might get busy as I would be staying a while; so I set up my full camp. That entailed unloading everything out of the van which would give me ample space for sleeping. With the kitchen set up in the tent, and a lobster for dinner my biggest pot went on the Matty stove to boil some water, while I sought out the lobster from a wooden box that had been packed with ice and paper earlier on in the day. Dropping the lobster in the water I sat back to watch the transformation from blue to pink.

Digression
Back home on Mull many types of wild life was available, be it the odd river salmon, mainly found at night time on a full moon while trying your best also not to disturb the plentiful deer on the hill, on occasion they could be found hanging in my garage, accompanied by two guys on a Saturday morning whilst I did a bit servicing on their pickup. Local fishermen would not let you down and over the winter months it was not unusual to find a mysterious box left outside the pub door with prawns, crab or the odd lobster. It was custom to just help yourself to a couple. I always felt that lobster was overrated and crab had more taste. ~~

Finding my biggest plate and a pair of long nosed pliers I removed the lobster and waited for it to cool down. Improvisation is the name of the game while on the road and this could be found in my tool box in the form of a hammer that made access to my supper easier. I settled down to enjoy my meal and was soon paid a visit by a gentleman who introduced himself as Russ Crocker, the owner of the cabins. We chatted for a while and he told me that his wife Ivy wouldn't be back till late, so would I pop down to the office in the morning and see her. Checking again that I was ok to camp in the spot I had chosen Russ told me the site wasn't busy yet but as it was Friday there were people coming for the weekend and would be staying in the two cabins, but I was fine to stay where I was. I washed the dishes and laid my sleeping bag out. I decide to walk the mile back to the junction and the paved road where I'd turned off.
I was surprised to see a small store and petrol pump. How I had missed them I was not sure, but it was handy to know they were there.

The area was mainly flat with a few sand dunes. It must have been about 10 o'clock in the evening, the sky had some dark clouds but once the moon popped from behind the moving clouds, the light was good. I started to head back to my camp, passing the odd wooded house most of which were in darkness and none of them with a garden of any sort.

My pathway back was the sandy road and on approaching the last building to my right I was surprised by the sudden appearance of an outside light at a door. The door opened and a man stepped out and said "Hello."
I responded with "Hi there" and walked in the direction of the light in the small porch. As I got closer, I saw an elderly man with a sweeping brush. Quickly I told I him that I was staying by the cabins for a while and that my home was back in Scotland.
"I've been to Scotland" he told me" When was that I asked thinking it was probable not to long ago. O back in 1939, to work cutting trees down." He went on to tell me he had signed up with nineteen other guys from around the area and that they would all be away for six years, to help in the war effort. This elderly man was just eighteen then, and I found it difficult to hold back my emotions. He said he would love to go back to Scotland as the people there were so kind and friendly. Turning to his door his last words to me were "It's getting cold I should go in now." I wished him well and thanked him for his support all those years ago.

It took me a while to get to sleep as I was reflecting on the elderly gentleman I had met and all the things I had heard and seen so far on this trip. I marvelled at this part of Canada and the lengths that people went to in the war effort, all on distant shores, and which should never be forgotten. Little did I realise that evening would not to be the last time that I would come across brave stories about people from the Rock. Late on that evening I heard a couple of vehicles pull up and people unloading items into the cabins. It sounded like a lot of people and it took a while for things to quieten down to muffled sounds once they were all inside.

The morning brought good weather again so I made my way down to the office in the hope of meeting Ivy and chat about her brother who had insisted I should call and say hello. Ivy told that she had not seen Chris for some time and was hopeful he and his family would make it over this summer. Russ came into office and I hooked up with him for a couple of hours, first calling to look at his boat before heading to a small sawmill he owned, telling me times where quiet in the mill, but his main work came from the forest with his harvester and skidder.
We got back in the afternoon and I met up with some of the party of people who were staying in the cabins. I was invited to join them in the evening for dinner which went on well into the early hours of the morning. The group of ten people was made up of two families, brothers and sisters who had become great friends over many years, and I would keep in contact with them for many years.

The following morning, I decided I should move and I called into the office to let Ivy know that I would be packing up. "It was good to see you Dave" she told me "and next time I speak with Chris I will tell him you called in and stayed a while. Be sure on your way back to the highway stop at Woody Point and call at the coffee shop and say high to my sister." I gave her my thanks and made my farewells.

With a deep heart I fired up Silent Wish and set off back on the road. I've said before how difficult it was to move on each time, but that was eased in the knowledge of what could lay ahead. I did as I was asked and called at the coffee shop and spoke with Chris' other sister. Whilst there I tucked into tea and cookies. My favourite biscuits. On leaving the coffee shop I offered to pay, but like so many times before my offer of payment was dismissed and waived to one side.

My aim today was to crack on and cover as much mileage as I could. This was helped as I was back on the TransCanada highway making for Bishops Falls and by the end of the day, I had clocked 333kms, the most I had done on any day. I was well pleased having made it to the campsite early in the evening. Calling into the office I paid for a night's stay and was told I was the only one on site and was welcome to use all the facilities, which included the showers and laundry room. It was late by now but I still decide to boil up a tin of meat balls before climbing into my sleeping bag.

Morning came bringing again with it sunshine. My site has 110 volts so armed with my multipoint lead of four connections, the laptop camcorder and camera were plugged in to recharge. My mobile phone is a Nokia 6310Iand sits in a rechargeable hands-free unit on the dash board. Loaded with a bag of washing, my soap and towel I went to find the showers and laundry room. The laundry work kept me going till just after lunch time, where upon I packed up the Mini and headed east for a short way before I turned at a place called Notre Dame for Twilling Gate.

Being off the main highway can get more interesting and, on the way, to Twilling Gate I stopped at Lewis Porte and the small store there to buy an extra 5ltr can for diesel, as there were fewer gas stations. The store had a large area for guns which were on display. Guns are not my scene and I soon moved on to the camping department to find some mosquito rings to buy. The drive to Twilling Gate was stunning, taking me in and out of small bays and coves with wonderful names. Time and distances seem to fool me and on getting to Twilling Gate I found id covered a 100 kms. Most towns had the towns name and the Lions and Round Table emblems on boards as you entered the outskirts.

Digression
Lions are an international organisation and I joined the Mull Lions a few years back. We totalled between eight to ten people at best and represented like-minded people. There was nothing secretive about us and we would meet once a month to talk and try to come up with fresh ways to raise money, alongside two or three fund raisers we did each year. Any money made went back into the community and for me and others the highlight of the years had to be the Santa run just before Christmas. This involved setting up the grotto in a van with Santa and his elves, accompanied by sacks full of presents. The journey would take best part of the day to cover the half dozen different villages on the island. ~~

I drove through Twilling Gate deciding to look for a camping spot for the night and reaching the end of the paved road, once again I turned onto a dirt track that finished at what seemed like an overgrown parking area with lots of old machinery set out on the grass verges. It looked as if I had found a good spot to set up camp for the night. The end of day meal was from a tin of spiced chicken with boil in the bag rice. The evenings where getting much lighter so after dinner I took a walk through some trees and bushes, picking my way to what I believed would become the headland, I soon came across more abandoned machinery. Stopping to look at one of them I tried to understand what they were and what they could be used for? Finally clearing the bushes and reaching the cliff top I was stunned to see icebergs below me in the cove. After taking some photos I sat down to look at these graceful marvels in the sea, sitting for hours trying to see if they moved, I also noticed across the bay, what looked like rows of caves here and there in the cliff face.

Next day I headed into town and while I was there, I tried to find where the Lions Club met. Finding a notice board outside the community hall, a small listing showed that a meeting would be taking place that evening at 8.00pm. On joining them that evening, I was welcomed and I sat and listened to their talks and topics. At the end of proceedings, I was asked to give a small talk on life back home which I willingly did. I stayed back after the meeting and managed to talk to one of the older chaps, I told him where I was camping. "You're at the old mine by Crow's Head."
What type of mine?" I asked. It's a very old copper mine that ore was extracted from a long time ago. The man turned and pointed to a painting of the cove. The painting showed a boat being loaded by men pushing box type trolleys on rails. The engineering that had gone into the making of the wooden pier so deep draft boats could be loaded was amazing, and added to the pier were sheds and rail tracks so that carts could be winched up and down from the top of the mine shafts. Winches also lifted the ore from the bottom of the mine shafts. Due to costs and lasting only two years it was closed and abandoned. The painting was twenty feet long and six feet high and when I looked closer it was dated 1908 to 1910.

The following day I looped my way back in the direction of Gander and Highway One with the possibility of finding a good beach location before the end of the day.

Digression
The airport at Gander was used during WW2. Its size and location was the closest aerial route to Great Britain and would find itself widely used for the war effort in Europe. The airport has sat quiet for many decades until 9/11 when Gander ended up receiving thirty-eight diverted flights in one day in the wake of the September 11 attacks on the USA. Gander was second only to Halifax Airport which to received forty-seven diverted flights. The number of passenger and crew accommodated at the small town of Gander were about 6000. The population at the time was fewer than 8,000. ~~

My plan was to drive back to the highway and head for Eastport on the edge of the Terra Nova National Park, always keen to find that special spot to stay. I pulled up at the gas station at Eastport to fill up and asked a few questions about places to camp. The attendant told me I could camp anywhere here, in someone's back yard if I wanted to. I moved on to a place called Sandy Cove were finally the road stopped, this time with a huge sand dune bringing me to a holt, I was disappointed. On looking to my left, I saw a couple of large high chain fenced gates that were partly open, wide enough to get a mini through, being one never to down to find somewhere a little different to camp, I decided to take my chance and have a look at what might be there. I drove through the gates and stopped at the office taking a look through the window where I could see packed boxes on the floor. I decided to drive along what looked like a row of beach huts, after the third one I spotted a vehicle parked down the side. I got out and walked to have a look, but the place seemed totally deserted. My thoughts told me the car must be local and the occupants may have gone fishing. Time was getting on and I had to make a decision whether to stay or find some other place. Deciding on my first option I continued to drive, counting a total of twenty-four beach type huts by the time I reached the last one. They were all very nice yet empty. Time was getting on so I slid the van down the side of the last building to hide it, and set up my van tent. My meal that night was sliced potatoes fried, follow by yogurt, tea and cookies. Popping out in the dark before bedtime I went for a quick comfort break I gingerly moved my head round the corner of my hide out behind my beach hut, only to spot two lots of dim lights at the far end of the huts in what would be numbers four and two huts. Heck I thought it feels a bit like Colditz camp, I shall have to watch my step and leave early and be quiet doing it. So with that in mind I head back to the van and a slightly restless night.
Rising early and not bothering with breakfast I managed to sneak out of Colditz, it was a little worrying to find the gates closed as I approached, but luckily not padlocked so myself and the van creped out slow and quite.

I covered the 45 km back to the main highway in good time, and looked for somewhere to get breakfast; I pulled up at the first gas station I found that it had a Diner so I ordered pancakes with bacon and maple syrup. While waiting for my breakfast I picked up a brochure about the Burin Peninsula and read about three islands off the point that are French owned. I was interested in going there, but the 600km round trip on the peninsula put me off the idea.

Digression
The three islands are Great Miquelon, Little Miquelon and St Pierre Island. They are French owned and lay about 20km off the Burin Peninsula and are accessed via a small ferry from the mainland. The population is approximately 3,000 and mainly French, and should you wish to visit, you would need your passport. One interesting fact is that it was used by Al Capone to transport alcohol from Canada to the United States during the prohibition. ~~
Having enjoyed my late breakfast and made my final decision to give the French islands a miss; I travelled a short distance on the Trans-Canadian Highway before coming upon a naval vehicle. Thinking it might be to do with the runners I had meet when coming off the ship at Port Aux Basques I stopped and got out to have a look. It was the same group of guys and while talking to them I learned this was the last change over point on the run before the finish at St Johns. As I left, they again invited me to their ship based in the capital.

Digression
I was keen to get to St Johns for a couple of reasons; one of the reasons was to meet up with fellow mini enthusiast Paul Malone. Paul's name had come to me in a roundabout way from fellow mini enthusiast Rick Higgs who lived in Vancouver. For many years I had been getting the monthly editions of Mini World and Mini Magazine and on the back pages they listed the world's mini clubs and contacts. You would be hard pushed to find a country that did not have a Mini Club. The first e-mail I sent was to the Vancouver Mini Club and it was Rick Higgs who replied and would become very helpful to me in many ways. I have since spent lots of happy times with Rick and his wife Elaine. Another great couple was Larry and Ann Sutton, Larry going out of his way to allow me to store the mini at his place over winter, before restarting my travels. Thanks go also to the guys and girls at the Vancouver Mini Club; having joined them many times on club meetings, home barbeques, and rallies where upon I was always made welcome.~~

Getting ever closer to St Johns and the thought of lots of traffic and people, preferring to be in less densely populated places, I took one last loop of the main highway and found myself at a town called Dildo. Stopping to take a photo of the oddly named town as proof that I had been there, I started thinking why not camp here overnight. For some strange reason, I found what I thought was a peaceful spot for the night only to have to fight off mosquitoes and flies all night. Even hiding in my sleeping bag just didn't work so a mosquito's net went straight to the top of my must have list.

Rising early to escape my winged enemies I was making tracks for Port De Grave when a noise suddenly appeared from the nearside front of the mini. Pulling up I stopped to take a look and soon found my first breakage. This turned out to be the bottom main shocker mounting bolt that is located through the top arm, had sheared off. I set about unloading the van to get the much-needed bits only to find the replacement bolts were a metric size and I needed 3/8 unf ones. The camp owner's son just happened to pass by and he stopped to see what my problem was. After explaining what had happened, he took me the short distance to a garage where the owner found me four 3/8 bolts be them a little short on the length I needed. Returning back to my vehicle I replaced the broken bolt with a new one having to leave out the spacer to get the lock nut back on. Happy that the repair had got me out of trouble I made my way to the fishing village of Port De Grave.

Arriving at the harbour pier I was greeted by some of the fishermen and spent a big part of the day talking and looking over the boats. They made me very welcome and told me I could camp and use the wash and shower unit on the pier. I set up my camp on the tarmac and on a hard standing for the first time, deciding to use the sea wall as shelter. This way I would be able to see the harbour and the town. As I made my evening meal I thought about my location and how I would like to stay or even to come back one day. Some of the boats were leaving and heading out to sea as the wind had subsided and the forecast was good. While on my guided tour earlier on I had been offered the chance to join one of the boats and her crew of five for two weeks dodging icebergs and catching crabs 200 to 300 miles out in the Atlantic. I often look back on that day wishing I had taken up the offer just for the hell of it.

I stayed for a few days on the pier to enjoy the pace of life there, during which time most of the village must have driven by or visited me. My last morning on the pier was warm and as I repacked the van, I experienced a lot of emotion hoping I would return one day. While I was finishing my packing, Dave the skipper of the boat called Conception Run pulled up to talk and told me he was on his way to get some crab for me. I told him I was heading to the shower block for one last time. On my return to the van, good to his word on my seat was a bag of crab but no sign of Dave.

Before leaving I went to the Harbour Masters Office to say thank you for so much courtesy being extended to me on my stay. The long climb up the ladder that is situated on the harbour cliff face has stunning views and inside I meet up with Bill Ralph, he was such a nice man and had lots to say. We were joined by Steve Anderson from the Fisherman's Museum who too had lots of stores from the past and present about life at sea off these shores.

Bidding my farewell, I turned out of the harbour when the knocking noise on the van returned. Driving a short distance to find a level place I stopped and removed the front wheel to find the new bolt had broken the same way the first had. I sat back on the wheel mystified why this was suddenly happening. The build had been of all new parts and I had not covered that many miles. It was all very strange why this would and could happen, only to have the same thing break twice on the same unit. I thought long and hard, but saw no logic to what was going on. I decided in the end to remove both front shock absorbers and drive without them, figuring I could manage. Due to the weight of my loaded vehicle, bounce and body roll was not a problem. Happy to carry on I would take a look when I got to St Johns. Before moving off I sent a text to Withnel Mafia base and my rally friends back in the U.K. to come up with a possible answer to the breakages. I spent the next couple of hours whilst driving trying to figure out what was making the bolts shear. Just before mid-afternoon I was 10kms from St Johns when I again saw the naval ship runners. Slowing down to wave, they shout to me to be sure to call at the quayside and our ship on Saturday for a drink.

Now in the city I headed for the centre and Pippa Park to find the camp site. Yes, slap bang in the middle they have a camp site that is well sign posted, unlike the rest of the city. I picked a site and booked for two nights then drove into town, getting lost several times before finding the docks and the location of the naval destroyer. As I pulled up close to the ship an officer came off and started to take photos of the van and ship. He told me it would be ok to leave it there and walk into town. I walked a short distance and found George Street; it would seem all the pubs were there. Finding an Irish pub I had one beer before picking up the van and heading back to Pippa Park.

While it was quiet I got my laundry done and again charged up all my electrics. That evening settling down with a beer I caught up with my log and decided that the following day I would make contact with Mini man Paul Malone. Climbing into bed the mind kicked back into gear, still trying to figure out what was causing the bolt breakages.

Having promised the ship's crew, I would see them today I was up early and did not bother with breakfast, just a mug of tea I then made my way into town. I had contacted Paul to tell him what I was hoping to do down at the docks and we agreed that I would make my way to his place after I had seen the crew. I found my way to the naval ship and joined the crew on board along with people to celebrate the runner's achievement on raising needed money for young children. After a look round the ship I said my goodbye's and took my leave.

I then found my way to Paul Malones, which was easier than I thought, pleased to see him and his wife Bev. Paul was soon looking over the van while I chatted with Bev. Keen to show me his car we headed for his garage. Inside was a mini that Paul had almost completely restored and was hoping to have it all done by the Mini's 50th Anniversary. The work on the car was impressive but not only that the garage was filled with all things mini and as for the floor you could have eaten your dinner from it. Bev invited me into the house for something to eat while Paul insisted that he would like to take me on a tour of the area. Early afternoon we left Bev behind, while the two of us took off with Paul pointing his finger in all directions as I sat back, happy to be a passenger.

The first main point we headed to, was Cape Spear the most easterly point of North America and the closest I would be to home for a while. This whole area of Newfoundland is full of history I had well forgotten about. Exploring the many gun emplacements we head to Signal Hill where back in 1901 Marconi made communication history by receiving the first ever transatlantic wireless signal. I thanked Paul for a great day and he offered to take me sightseeing again tomorrow which I eagerly agreed to.

Back at the park that evening I sat down to fill in my daily log and finish off the last two beers. I don't usually have beer in the vehicle due to the strict laws on this continent. Always In my mind, the itch to move on is never far away, so I did not want to be caught with beer in the van while on the highway.

Next morning after breakfast I headed back to Paul's house to join him and Bev, coffee for them and tea for me. Luckily the weekend's good weather was holding. We climbed into Paul's car and off we went, after half an hour of driving we arrived at another historic location. Getting out of the car I could see a plaque ahead of us. Being unsure where I was, I tried to figure out the strange outline engraved on the face.

The face of the plate had faded but I could make out the names of Alcock and Brown, I found myself standing on the spot where the two men had made the first non-stop transatlantic flight from on 14th June 1919. Little did I know, one day in the distant future whilst on the west coast of Ireland, I would accidently come across the town of Clifden and the bog where they landed.

Returning to Paul's we said our farewells, as in the morning I would go to the centre of town and the starting point on the Trans-Canada Highway. Turning my back on the city I would head west for 660kms to Deer Lake then turn north to reach the ferry crossing to the province of Labrador. Monday morning, I was out of bed and had my breakfast, packed up and showered, leaving Pippa Park by ten o'clock.

Not far out of the city I stopped and filled up with 43ltr of fuel. I settled down for the day ahead. It was not long before I came across red and blue flashing lights and on getting closer, I came upon police and ambulance vehicles attending what I thought was a general road accident. As I slowed down, I could see a damaged people carrier with the roof that looked like it had been peeled back with a can opener, two medics were working on the driver's side of the vehicle. Seeing no advantage in stopping I carried on trying to puzzle out what had happened, with no other vehicles seemingly involved. Why it came to me I don't know, but I could only think it may have been a moose. Sure enough, at my next stop it was confirmed that a lady driver had been killed. A stark reminder of what can happen in this part of the world. The rest of my day was a little sombre as I reflected on the accident, thinking about the lady, was she young or old. She had seen her day start, was she going to work visit friends or family? Then in the blink of an eye life had been taken away from her that morning.

Late that afternoon I arrived at Bishops Falls and on seeing a Lions sign reading Lion Max Simms Camp, I turned off the highway to my left, onto the dirt road not really knowing what I would find at this camp. About 15kms further on I started thinking, where does this track go and does it actually go anywhere? I stuck with it a little longer, eventually coming on a ranch stile open gate with a sign that read, Lion Max Simms Memorial Camp. I continued to what looked like the front door only to find it was locked. Disappointed at having driven so far down a dirt road I returned to the van to decide what my next move should be as it was now about six o'clock and I was getting hungry. Just as I was about to leave a car arrived, it was the night watchman. We spoke and he asked me inside for a cup of tea. A second vehicle then appeared and four guys came in and joined the conversation keen to learn about me and the little rig outside. Each of the men introduced themselves and told me that they were now retired, having all worked for the Aliant Phone Company.

Coming together they were now known as the Aliant Pioneers, a group of guys who gave their time for free to help others, they had been coming and giving there time for many years at this camp. Over the next ten days they would eat sleep and work at the camp. The project this trip would be a small timber building, built on the large lawn out front so people in wheelchairs could access a place to sit and get fresh air.

Sitting there listening I felt humbled by this group of men aged between sixty-five to seventy-eight, they so inspired me I asked if I could stay and get involved. The guys where more than pleased I had offered and agreed I could stay subject to Carina Anderson, the camp manager giving it the ok when she came in the following day. That night I set up camp out front in the car park and headed to bed after having spam and half a tin of potatoes for dinner.

Monday morning and the camp manager Carina arrived. I called into her office to introduce myself and to find out more about the camp and its history. She told me about the opening in 1981 after the effort made by many dedicated individuals and groups. The camp eventually became a place where challenged individuals can receive respite with an enriching and rewarding camping experience. After sharing some stores from back home I was given a room and was told she would be pleased for me to stay and join the pioneers.

Donning my work clothes, I went to find the guys to tell them my good news. I eventually found them at the rear of the camp in the workshop. Soon put to work I was ferrying lengths of timber with the camps quod bike and trailer to the front lawn. Over the next few days and with good weather on our side the building was beginning to take shape with the main job left, being the roof and felting. The days went bye as we all worked well as a team laughing and joking, constantly I reminded them I was the youngest there and should do any of the dangerous climbing.

Without warning a rain storm engulfed us. It was Friday and the work needed to be completed that day. The roof was now ready for felting and a collective shout rang out for me to climb onto the roof quickly, Robert joined me while Ron stood on the scaffolding at the side passing the felt rolls onto the roof. Dave was being passed the felt rolls half way up the ladder from Edmond who was doing his best to stop the ladder from falling. While Ernie and Jack Badock stood at ground level issuing orders to all on site.

With the job finished and completed we headed back to the main camp complex, most evenings we would have a beer before going to eat in the dining room. Dave gave me a couple of beers to drink while I had a long soak in the bath, now dressed in clean dry clothes I joined the guys back in the dining room where they were already seated. I just stood and looked at the table. A voice came to me asking, "Have you never seen lobster before Diddy?"
"Yes, but never this much to try and get through." I took the only seat left, which for some reason was at the top of the table, heck we dined well on lobster, salad and potatoes, with long drinks of rum and coke gifted to me aplenty and in the nicest possible way, It soon came apparent I did not have a great deal of choice to refuse their gifts. On the odd occasion I looked around the table at the faces of my new found friends and smiled telling myself these times do not come too often in life. I had been gifted to be amongst these Aliant Pioneers, a band of aged gentlemen willing to give their time for free to help and support others of the world.

Tidying up we retired to the lounge to sit back and reflect on the weeks work. Talk turned to me and my time on the rock, and I told them of my many great experiences, the places I had been and the people I had met while here. Nearing the end of the evening Robert asked me to join him at the far end of the room and take a seat on what looked like a commode, whereupon a yellow fisherman's sou'wester was placed on my head and I was given a salted cod fish and instructed to bite the head off. Duly done I was handed a glass of rum and coke and told to drink this down, soon finding out it was straight rum, whilst being read the rules and laws of the Royal Order of Newfoundland Screechers. I was then knighted by Rob with a boat ore and given the Certificate of Charter in one hand, while in the other hand was placed a large glass of Rum. Finally just about able to stand up to look about the room of happy friends, Rob or Dave and I can't recall which, read the following poem to me.

> A toast to Dave and his daring du
> In his quest to cross the sea of blue
> To see the world in his tiny car
> We wish him well in awe we are
>
> We wish him safe journey on the road ahead
> No flat tyres and maybe a bed
> As he meets the world and says hello
> We shed a tear to see him go
>
> We'll watch on line and wait for mail
> We'll hope to hear on each new tale
> As he flies along in his tiny car
> We are glad we knew him we are we are!

I woke up next morning feeling ok, yet a little surprised considering the amount of Rum consumed the previous evening. I went outside to get some fresh air and check the van over looking at the front suspension problem. I'd had a text back from the guys in the U.K. but no fresh ideas as to my breakage problem. Refitting both front shockers with new bolts I decided to raise the ride height a little to see if that would help.

Just before lunch time we all gathered out front to take some last-minute photos and say our farewells. I believe to this day that this farewell had to be the hardest on this whole adventure. As I waived my good bye I made a promise to my self, a promise to return and seek out this band of brothers one day before it is too late.

Now back on the number one highway I drove for about three hours before arriving at the junction near Deer Lake, I took the 430 north in the direction of the UNESCO World Heritage site of Gros More National Park. The views were stunning taking many photos, stopping at the empty beach at Cowhead, armed with my towel; I lay in the sun for a while, before my overnight stop at Deer Cove. The summer was well underway and so were the flies and mosquitoes I was always trying to make camp on the high ground or close to the sea to help to reduce the ever-present bugs. I had stopped at a store back down the road to get bread and milk, but the trouble was they only had 2ltr bottles of milk so cornflakes would be on the menu that night along with several cups of milk, the menu to be repeated again in the morning. Finding fresh fruit was more available I turned to buying more plums and pears which fitted well into the large door pocket. While eating my cornflakes I studied the tourist map that covered the North West corner of the island, and my point of departure further north to Labrador. Deciding to just pick on a couple of places to visit I made the drive to Rodington and passed on through to the site of the underground salmon pool I had heard so much about. Leaving the van, I took the boardwalk for about a mile until it reached the river. As I stood on the bank I could see the river and the direction of flow passing to the left, while the river from my right flowed from nowhere but a stone face wall. Bewildered I walked to take a closer look. Sure, enough the river was coming out from under ground somehow into a pool of bubbling water. Standing for a while thinking I might just see fish; my time was wasted as when they do arrive from the sea, they enter the limestone cavern at its entrance two miles away and swim underground to reach their destination for spawning.

My idea was to head for St Anthony and what looked like a large town, but just before getting to Rodington I spotted an iceberg off to my right, soon after I came on a small dirt road so I headed off to investigate to see how close I could get to the iceberg. Coming out of the trees I could see a cove with three or four icebergs. Driving on I passed a cigar shaped object looking like a piece of scrap metal enclosed by a rope fence, I remember passing it and thinking what the heck that is? My driving took me to the village of Conche with about twenty small wooden houses and on reaching the beach I got out of the van and walked down the sand for a closer look at my first iceberg. It was big and a little scary. Telling myself not to be stupid, it couldn't get me as it was stuck on the sea bed and surrounded by smaller ones that lay at anchor also. Pleased that I had made the turn I decided to camp there for the night.

That evening I was back on fried thin sliced potatoes with spam. Not having a chip pan, I was getting good at this cooking lark; name course was followed with a yogurt dessert. In the morning before packing up I walked to look at the strange object I had passed the previous night. Sure enough it was roped off, but by crossing a walkway I could cross the ditch and gain access to the roped area covered in stone on what was a peat bog. Looking over the rusty silver metalwork I soon figured out it had been the fuselage of a plane. To one side of the small open compound was a plague with an inscription telling the story of the plane? The writing told of the Second World War and how the plane had left Newfoundland from Gander early in 1942. The plane was a Boston Douglas DB7 with a crew of three. Its destination was the U.K. but on climbing from the airfield they hit bad weather and started having fuel problems. The navigator bailed out and was unhurt, soon after the pilot and radio operator crash landed in the peat bog, unhurt. After packing everything back in the mini I wandered one last time back to the beach to try and capture the blue and white colours of the icebergs, something that was nigh impossible to do with my camera.

Now being that bit closer to Labrador only divided by a ferry crossing I was keen to move on, making St Anthony in the afternoon stopping first at the post office to ask the staff if they would stamp my Scottish passport, and like most they obliged. St Anthony's would be my last major stopping place for some considerable time and with it a chance for stocking up on essentials such as tinned food, dried milk, fruit, bug spray and mosquito burn rings. It was my second to last night so I drove along the peninsula to find the furthest point north, calling in at Cape Onion Cove then Ha Ha Bay. The area is steeped in history as it is the historic site of the first Viking settlement in North America dating back to 1000 B.C. I set up camp by a Viking long ship that is six times the length of my mini and watched the final light of the day go down.

Digression
I find it difficult putting these places and sites I have seen into the written words. The truth is you have to see them yourself to capture those long-lasting memories and at times like this I wish I had brought all my friends along. ~~

Tomorrow I needed to cover the 160kms to St Barbe on the western side of the peninsula and my stepping off point from this incredible island and its people.

The morning arrived bright but very cold reminding me this would be the way for a while yet. The journey would take me north for some time, ever closer to the Arctic Circle. Arriving mid-afternoon in St Barbe I filled the petrol tank and a spare fuel can also, not being sure how far the next petrol station would be. That done I went straight to the port harbour office. The ferry was due to leave at 10.00 a.m. the following day, so I booked and paid for my passage asking the lady if I could park on the pier in a quiet corner. She assured me it wasn't a problem adding "Sir you will be fine as it does not get busy till about 8.00 a.m."

My month on the rock had passed too quickly and I was keen to top it off. Happy to leave the van I walked a short distance to find a restaurant and treat myself to a T bone steak and a glass of wine as it maybe some time before I could do it again. With a skip in my step and excitement in my heart for tomorrow and the unknown once more as I would be taking on Labrador and its never-ending dirt roads not fully knowing if the new road to Happy Valley Goose Bay had yet been completed and was it officially open for traffic as I had been given yaw's and nay's to it being open. The thought of having to turn back and retrace my tracks was a little worrying.

Chapter 7

Dust and Dirt

All I had to do was make it round the world with no planned route and in no fixed time, as that was my ace card. Things so far had been easy with my route, tomorrow would be the start of something so different as I head more north out into an empty wilderness, well that's what it looked like on Goggle Earth for this part of the journey when I checked it out back home, and on seeing this route I wanted to challenge myself to take it on.

The sea crossing from Newfoundland to Labrador is about one and a half hours and while on the ship I spoke with a couple of truck drivers about the road conditions ahead and if the new road from Cartwright Junction to Happy Valley Goose Bay was completed and open. The reason I asked about the new road was I had looked on a map in the UK and the proposed finish was in the spring and I would be arriving in summer, thus my thinking would be that it had been completed. The two drivers told me the roads were not too bad, the biggest problem was the dust and dirt along with wind. They told me they were going all the way to Cartwright and were carrying a liquid glue solution that gets sprayed on the road that helps bond the stones and dirt together. They also informed me that I would pass the start of the new road at Cartwright Junction and it could be opened any day, it looked finished but still had a barrier across as they could still be working at the Goose Bay end. It was a total unknown for us all.

The boat was not very busy with most of the traffic only going as far as the port. Excited but a little nervous I joined the two laden trucks and sat between them as we headed up the hill out of town on the paved road. Once we crested the hill and hit the dirt road our speed increased to about 60kms. The sky was bright blue with white fluffy clouds and we hugged the coast line for some distance, the dust creating large plumes of brown cloud that was blown sideways due to the onshore breeze. The road was now turning inland and we started to pass trees and an endless forest, the constant dust now had nowhere to go. The lead truck took off and left me fighting to see anything but dust. Now worried to slow up, let alone stop, his buddy behind me was now alongside blowing his air horns and passed in a flash. Gradually I slowed up and stopped, giving the dust time to settle. I pulled over to a safe spot and let the trucks put some distance on me. I got out of the van with my camera and stretched my legs spotting I'd stopped by a single-track rail crossing. I checked if it was abandoned and looking at the rails could tell it was still used. Standing for a while I listened for noise and even put my ear to the rail, but nothing could be heard for miles.

Returning to the van I could see the driver side front wheel arch was almost touching the tyre. Something was not right, so out came the jack and off with the wheel. A quick look told me the shock absorber bolt has again broken and the knuckle joint for the rubber cone as well. Still totally puzzled with the bolt breakage I removed both front shockers and placed them in the sin bin, and set about replacing the knuckle joint. The process took me about an hour and during that time nobody passed me. I placed the small blue tarp I use on the floor of my tent to cover the rear contents of the van as dust had started to get into everything.

Now back underway I stepped up the speed to 80kms to try and make port Hope Simpson 248kms away and a campsite with showers. The dirt road was great and well looked after with most of it better than some tarmac roads I have travelled on. Dust was still about but mainly from the tail of my van which I could see on long open bends. Keeping to the same constant speed for hours I only had to slow twice due to oncoming vehicles. This part of the journey was truly deserted.

Digression
For me every day was a new day, my mind was not clogged up with unwanted things and ideas and I was steadily growing into this adventure learning new things. Moose and their eating habits was one of the first things I picked up back in Newfoundland, being told they tend to avoid flowing rivers, but like nothing better than standing in still water such as ponds of lush green shoots dipping their large heads in to the bottom to eat. Mothers can be usually seen with a calf, but the bulls tend to stick to the forest where the most danger lay for me and my little vehicle. Canada has a lot of dirt roads built almost to the same standard no matter what type of ground or direction the road may take. Permafrost also pays a big part and can damage the paved roads, easily lifting it a foot high in places. The

gravel road is less prone to lifting because it's built higher than ground level, starting at a minimum of two feet that can level out as much as six to eight feet deep in an effort to maintain a level road. Huge stretches in the north are covered with forests which the roads pass through. The trees are also cut back thirty of forty feet on both sides of the road; this gives you a chance to see the wild animals coming from the cover of the forest. Occasionally the odd tree falls, and the cut back has worked leaving the road clear and safe. There is one big problem though; when spring comes new growth appears on small trees and bushes in the cut back safety area. The moose can now step out of the forest and enjoy miles of the fresh new shoots, most of this time the moose are unseen, hidden by the fresh under growth, should they start to move you might get lucky and see some branch movement. Should they decide to move a moose will just appear and walk taking four foot strides with each leg and no intention of stopping? Seems that they walk and never run, if the did them they look like a bouncy castle on the move. The shear size and weight could make mincemeat of the mini. ~~

The day was getting on and was surprised to come up on a small shed with a single gas pump and just down the side of the shed was a narrow track. Pulling in I filled my fuel tank and asked the lady was there anywhere that I could camp for the night. She pointed in the direction of the shoreline and told me I would find some showers which surprised me; I could see it was little used and that the area was well overgrown. I checked the showers worked first before setting up my camp, not too close to the shore, as the lady had warned me that a bad storm was to hit the coast to night.

Opening up the rear door of the van I was confronted by sand and dust covering every part of the inside of my vehicle, and somewhere under the dust was a blue sheet. Luckily the words "stay calm" came to me and I set about the daunting task of removing everything out of the van that even meant the well packed spares box hidden under the floor. This operation and the clean-up took me a good two hours and all the time I could feel the air changing. The final job was to set up the Matty stove as after the shower I planned to eat. Checking the showers early on I had spotted an electric point high up in the wash room. Grabbing my wash bag and rechargeable gadgets I made off for a much-needed shower. Once cleaned up and back at the tent I cracked on making a meal of curry and rice. I only have one ring on the stove and juggling two pans is difficult, three is out of the question. Room for improvement much needed there. The camp site owner's son came down to say hello and chatted for a while telling me that there had been an aeroplane crash the night before in the fog. The pilot had been trying to land to collect someone and fly them to hospital but unfortunately the plane had missed the gravel airstrip and hit the hillside, sadly the pilot lost his life, a stark reminder of life off grid. The thunder and lightning arrived in the early hours, doing its best to unsettle me in my nice warm metal van, and in doing so left me reflecting on the day and the dust that had taken over the inside of my vehicle.

The plan after breakfast was to pack everything up and again spread the blue sheet over as much as I could in the van, then to seal the doors with 3inch gaffer tape. At the start of the days drive the dust control was helped as the damp roads kept the dust down till about lunch time when the sun took over, making the rest of the day very hot.

Not wanting to travel too far I would make it to another cove called Charlotte Town early in the afternoon. Stopping at the grocery shop I walked up the wooden steps where an elderly man was sitting in a rocking chair, we both said hello and I walked on and through the open doorway. Once inside I could see the post office counter so I called there first to get my Scottish passport stamped. Interest was soon shown to me as the new stranger in town, and after buying a few things I headed back outside. The van again was a magnet to many and as I got to the bottom of the steps the shop owner followed me down the steps and gave me a book titled A Dream That Came True. It was about the town and the man who had founded it back in 1950. The elderly man sitting in the rocking chair was that man, now aged ninety-two, I stayed with him for a while and he chatted away telling me how he had come here as a youngster and lived in a tent and had built his log home by himself, I was the first to do it, now take a look around you he said. I thanked him and wished him well as I walked away with a smile on my face and a tear in my eye. I have to say I was also a little jealous of him, the man for me was a pioneer.

The foreshore was not very big with just a few wooden singe storey houses and a small wooden jetty, I decided to camp just past the jetty. I removed the tape from round the doors and was pleased to see the vans interior had stayed dust free. With camp set up I took a walk back in the direction of the main highway passing a caravan on the way with a bench seat and a table out front. That seems a bit out of place I thought and I wondered if it had been a beach bar or something similar. Continuing my walk I passed a sign saying No Stopping. A little further on I could see the trees had been felled back, a lot more than usual, a wind sock could be seen flickering in the night breeze. This was a landing strip as well as the main highway.

Again, I had learned something new. Turning back and getting closer to the caravan I had passed earlier the top half on the side door was now open with a lady leaning out. As I approached, she said "Hello you still here?" it just happened to be the Gas station lady." Yes, I'm here for the night I told her. With that she handed me a menu, "I will have the chicken and chips please." With my order in, we passed the time talking and I was keen to ask her why she went to so much trouble to cook from her caravan with only a couple of houses about. Simply she told me if you walk just round the corner a little way there is a seafood processing factory that works twenty-four hours a day and employs a hundred people. Stunned by her reply I had seen nothing other than a few houses. A huge smile came to my face as I told her how pleased I was for the community in such a remote area. Thanking me the lady handed me my meal, nicely wrapped in paper.

Digression
Several deep-thinking thoughts would come to me over the next 1500kms. Labrador would teach me a lot about spending days on end behind the wheel, preparing me to take on the vast emptiness of the interior with huge distances and the possibility of breaking down. Along with that was the distinctive lack of vehicles and people, all this was new to me. As the days passed my confidence grew with the mini and my ability on handling the conditions, we had both taken on. ~~

Next morning, I awoke a little nervous as I was getting ever closer to the end of the road and the town of Cartwright and the worrying possibility of having to turn round and retrace my tracks. Bidding farewell to Charlotte Town I stopped at the highway junction and looked left then right to check for any incoming planes. A couple of hours had passed and I started to wonder if I would ever see the link road apply named Cartwright Junction. The new road will enable road traffic from the east to take an unbroken route across Labrador to hook up with the exciting road that runs west of Happy Valley Goose Bay. Another hour passed and I finally came on a couple of red and white marker boards lying on the road which had been blown over by the wind. Stopping I got out to have look round. The new road looked great so I stepped over the boards and took a walk hoping to see some form of work happening and possible confirmation that it was open for traffic. I kept telling myself I could navigate it if anybody can do it I could. Uncertain what to do I headed back to the van and stood for a while trying to figure what I should do next. I figured I had three options; one was to turn back, something I didn't want to happen, or continue the 100kms to the end of the road at Cartwright. My last option was to drive the new road hoping all the time that 260kms of construction had been completed all the way to Happy Valley Goose Bay, in doing so would give me any chance of getting out of the Province by road.

Having convinced myself months ago all would be ok and that the link road would be open in time for my arrival, I now found myself having to roll the dice, something I do not like to do. Now back in the van I decide to wait a while in the hope a vehicle of any sort would come along, an hour passed and nothing had moved. Before making my final decision I got out of the Mini to pick up the fallen boards and take a toilet break.

Making my way through the trees I spotted a board lying upside down. Turning it over I began to read the information, it described the project and how the scheduled opening was for the spring as I had already thought. Unfortunately, two black lines ran diagonally across the board with the words, Now Opening in autumn.

Now pleased that one of my three options had been removed I would not now be chancing the new road. It still left two choices and my thinking was that as I had travelled this far north then I must carry on to Cartwright and the end of the road. Feeling annoyed, I pushed on to cover the 100kms to Cartwright before nightfall. The late afternoon would see me getting closer to the coast as on occasion icebergs started to appear to my right. The last few miles were mostly downhill and with journeys end in sight I could see the many icebergs out at sea and with that my spirits lifted.

The town was bigger than I had expected to find being this far north. A short drive round would find me at the harbour front with a couple of fishing boats tied up, the harbour looked like many I had seen over the last few weeks. It was now about 9.00 pm and very quiet outside, I soon found a corner on the harbour front to set up camp and make my bed. I didn't feel like eating that night.

Getting up next morning took a while and it would be 9.30am before I stepped outside, the mornings were still cold as I pushed north. Firing up the Matty stove the smell of bacon was soon wafting round the tent as my appetite had returned and I was hungry. Not long after finishing breakfast a vehicle pulled up and a chap I half recognised got

out and said "Hi Dave its Tom, Tom Barret, we meet in Newfoundland." While talking I started to remember when summer's underway he runs a kayak business in Cartwright. "I'll come back in an hour if you're interested and give you a tour about in my truck."
"That would be great" I told him, and sure enough Tom was back in an hour. We headed straight out of town and after about twenty minutes we reached a rusty wire gate lying on the ground. A high fence surrounded the scrub like area as we drove on past the gate slowly climbing a long narrow dirt road. As we got higher I started to pick out a large half noon shaped object that I couldn't identify properly, on getting closer Tom told me it was called Blackhead Hill. Tom went on to tell me that it was once an American air force base used for radar operations, checking out the Russians back in the 1950s till it closed in 1968. Standing on the top of the hill the view was stunning especially looking out to sea where I spotted all those big white floating ice cubes.

Returning back to town Tom asked me about my plans, and I told him I wasn't sure, he suggested we grabbed a coffee back at his office where I could access the internet to catch up with people. Tom is from Newfoundland but each year he drives to Cartwright and stays to run his small adventure business, taking people out in kayaks, so his office doubles up as his bed sit also. While Tom was outside prepping his equipment in readiness for the season, I spent some time catching up on my daily log and firing e-mails back home. Ready for another drink I put the kettle on and made coffees for us both, there is a lack of English tea bags round this part of the world.

Outside Tom and I chatted, he asked if I had made any plans to go back or take the ferry? What ferry I asked? The one to Goose Bay that sails at 8.00pm every couple of days, it will return tomorrow morning he told me.
With those few words my day had suddenly taken on new possibilities. You are welcome to stay Dave as I have a few friends coming round tonight to play some music with their guitars. Excited at the possibility of taking the ferry and being able to continue on my route, I headed down to the harbour to seek out the ferry ticket office and establish if the cost of sailing was within my budget.

Digression
A budget Ha, costing for this adventure now that's a laugh if the truth be known. Yes, I had some money but not that much and most of it went on the van build. That's when I thought I had better look at shipping costs across the Atlantic to Canada. The cost came back at about £900 which I thought was not too bad when you considered the cost of a holiday in the sun by plane. The fuel was going to be cheaper than back in the UK, I would also eat less food and I would be sleeping in the van and not hotels. I started my adventure not knowing if I had enough money to complete the journey, but what I did have was a determination to complete it. ~~

The pier was again quiet and it didn't take long to find the ticket office, but unfortunately it was closed. A notice was posted informing people it would reopen at 4.00 p.m. I hadn't slept well last night and my neck had been itching for most of the time and right ear which by now had gone red and felt hot. The van was still set up on the pier so I found the medicine box and applied some cream to my neck and ear. That done I returned to Tom's place and offered to help him. He set me the task of washing the kayaks, which I did until 4.00 p.m. where upon I returned to the ticket office to check out the sailing cost. The total price came to £80 for the twelve-hour sailing, including a cabin which delighted me. The down side was I would be first reserve, being told to check back at 7pm for an update. I walked back to Tom's on a high knowing I could afford the ferry and that I would now be truly heading west. The staff at the office hadn't asked me the size of the vehicle but I was confident of getting on the ship. Come 7.00pm I thanked Tom for his help and support finally wishing him a busy season. Be sure to come back if you don't get on the boat tonight Dave.

Back at the ticket office the lady told me I had a place on the boat so I paid her and was told to be in line to board at 7.30pm I walked back along the pier to start repacking the mini and set aside the most needed items for the long passage. Vehicles could now be seen lining up so I joined them, and soon after we started to load and by 8.00pm the ship was underway. I went to the upper deck to take some photos of Cartwright. The light was fading but the sky was very clear and as we turned at the headland the ocean opened out before me and I could clearly see icebergs in the distance. Smelling food, I headed to the cafeteria and by now people were sitting down and eating. Seeing I was the only one at the counter I talked with the chief for a while and eventually deciding on two pork chops with mash and gravy. My new found friend filled my plate to the maximum, followed by dessert and tea, all for $7. That would certainly set me up for the night. The only traffic on the boat was cars, seemed it was very rare to get any big trucks on the passage to Happy Valley Goose Bay as it can be accessed from the west quicker and cheaper. The length of the days was starting to fool me as I headed further north. It was now about 11.30pm and still bright outside. Deciding to take one last look outside before bed I climbed up two steel ladders to the outside open viewing deck.

The sky was cloudless, the full moon turning night into daylight, disturbed only by the stars and icebergs all around the vessel. Rushing back down to my cabin and collected my camera and returned to watch how the Captain was navigating our route. Confident he knew what he was doing, I took some photos of the icebergs, occasionally a whale would come up and breech, I tried for ages to capture a shot of the Whales against a clear sky and the moon. All this for £80! I stayed outside till well past 2.00am before turning in for a nights sleep, happy the ship was in good hands manoeuvring round these white monsters.

Next morning, the ship's paging system woke me at 5.45.am for breakfast, with the information we would be making our approach into Goose Bay for disembarkation just after 7.00am. I decided to take a shower as it might be some time before the next one, then down to the cafeteria for breakfast and my favourite meal of pancakes and bacon while maximising on cups of tea.

Back down on the car deck the crew gave me the thumbs up to move out and by 8am I had cleared the boat and the town only stopping to take photos of the huge log shaped welcoming structure to Happy Valley Goose Bay. This also allowed the traffic to pass and hopefully give me a dust free run as the dirt road looked good and smooth.

If I intend to do a full day's driving it usually tops out at 300kms or 200 miles. My aim today was to make it to Churchill Falls 330kms away. I pushed on even though the dust returned, the road surface was good for about 100kms then it started to change mainly on the bends due to the wash like ruts, which chattered the steering endlessly, so much so, it was not long before the front offside knuckle joint broke and I had to stop and change it.

This operation could take as little as half an hour to an hour; a lot depended on how quickly I could get the broken ball end out of the plastic socket in the top arm. Repair done and back to driving this quite road my driving average still looked good. After covering another 50kms I could see some distance ahead of me what looked like the tail end of a truck which I thought was still moving only to come upon it quickly. In fact, it was stopped and I could see it was loaded with a big oversize excavator. I slowed right down and drew alongside finally stopping at the tractor unit part to find that all twelve drive tyres had burnt out and the steel rims and hubs where sitting on the road. The wings and most of the sleeper cab had gone or twisted in the heat of what must have been an intense fire, leaving only the two front tyres and the main cab intact. Checking in the cab I found there was nobody there. The place was deserted, so after taking a couple of photos I moved on as I still had a way to go.

The problem with my neck and ear had come back again so I stopped to put some more cream on the problem area, I was now a little worried as I had heard so many stories about the black fly in Canada. I wanted to get somebody to take a look at it and if necessary, treat it.

Digression
Now having been on the road a while there was a couple of thinks that I didn't have the answers to and they were bugging me. So, what came first the town or the dirt road and if the dirt road is 200 or 400kms long were is everybody? I only seam to drive through towns at the beginning and the end of the road. Back home towns and villages are never far apart. Before the end of the day I would get the answers to both questions in my eagerness to make camp at Churchill Falls by night fall. ~~

Today's driving was hour after hour of grey dusty gravel roads in a tunnel of trees and hanging dust, broken only by what I figured were fire breaks off to the sides. Occasionally I would make out a weather worn sign informing me of No fuel for 220kms or more. This continues type of driving makes you a little fixated and if you are not careful you will start to loose your observation and focus. The day was now getting on and there was no evidence visually or by sign for the town of Churchill Falls, what made me look up this particular fire break that turned out not to be a fire break was pure luck. I could have easily passed at speed what was the missing town. Turning of the main dirt road I drove up the short climb only to crest the top to see about 60 wooden houses hidden in the forest clearing.

A short drive away was the grocery store and gas station. Mindful of running out of fuel even with the long-range tank I filled up my tank. Driving a little way further on I came to a police station for the Royal Canadian Mounted Police. I decided to stop as there was an officer outside cleaning his vehicle. I got out of the Mini and we chatted, I told him how lucky I was to find the town, as you don't have big blue or green signs on the highway pointing into their hidden town.
"That's probably why we don't get too many visitors" he told me. I smiled and ask if I could camp. "Yes" he told me "Just drive on round this road and you will come to a flat area and a couple of hook up points that are free to use." Thanking the officer, I moved on to find the spot and set up my camp for the night.

Digression
Setting up camp each night had become a simple routine to me by now. First thing to do is find level ground, climbing out of my seat I would pick up two, two-inch-long thin bolts located in the small side pocket of my Volvo driving seat. Going to the back of the van I lift the lid on the roof box and take out the two five-foot tubular bars that are threaded at one end with a three-inch fixed round base plate on the other. Next out of the box is the tent cover, this is laid on the floor till needed, and it has been folded the same way each time for ease of fitting onto the bare frame. Pulling out the two internal eight-foot parallel tubular roof bars and the three roof loops for the canvas tent. The two thin bolts are inserted into lined up holes that keep the horizontal tubes in place, now screwing the two five-foot upright threaded tubes into the other end of the extended roof bars, support for the tent frame is now completed. This done the tent can easily be rolled out over the top of the tube frame then clipped to the van by means of toggles, side entry into the tent can be opened by the heavy-duty zips. Set up time is about ten minutes maximum. I now have a choice of sleeping in the tent or the van. If I feel I need the safety of the van to sleep, I just lift out the half dozen plastic boxes and place them in the tent. ~~

True to the Officers word I soon came across the free electrics in what was an open exposed spot that might help with keeping down the mosquitoes and flies should there be any wind. The ground was tarmac so setting up my full camp was easy and I opted to sleep in the van as my thinking was it could help keep down the bugs. Before starting to cook my evening meal in the tent I lit and placed an extra mossy ring in the van. It not the best thing to do because of the fumes, but there were so many little flying bugs, I hated them. This time of the year there was no shortage of bugs, mainly because of the wild animals, and it would seem that old friends from back home had followed me to this part of the world, yes the dreaded midge, over here they are called no see-ums.

Not feeling my best after dinner, I bedded down in the van quite early; lying there telling myself I must seek medical help when I get to Labrador city. My situation was not helped by the fact that the evening was so light and hot.
Just as I was dropping off to sleep I became startled by a wupp wupp noise. I turned over and sticking my head out of the sleeping bag I saw the State Troopers vehicle. "Just thought I would drop by and warn you Dave there is a bear loose around the town so just be aware. Seeing your tent set up I thought you might been sleeping in it." Thanking him I lay back; thinking it was going to be a long night.

I must have slept, but for how long I wasn't sure, the trouble was I had become desperate to make it to Lab City as both my heck and ear had become very swollen, and with so much dust both in the van and on me, it was getting me down. Decamping was fast as I wanted to get going so I decided to skip breakfast and to drink lots of water. Back on the highway I speeded up a lot which made the run into Lab City more like a rally stage, occasionally having to have a short conversation with myself due to the overloaded van making it tail happy, something the mini is known for but it sure kept the mind of my swelling problem. Getting ever closer to the city the road at last changed from dirt to paved and it wasn't long before a sign for the hospital was advertised. On arrival I reported to reception were upon I was sent along to a waiting room and told the doctor would see me soon. There was only one other person ahead of me so my wait was not too long. Once with the doctor I explained what I was doing and what my problem was. I was checked over and in no time a prescription was made out and a charge of $130 for that privilege. On the way out of the hospital the lady in reception gave me directions and I soon found myself again relieved, this time of $30 for two tubes of ointment.
Now with my bag of medicine I headed back to the van where upon I was greeted by a gentleman named Jack O'Brien. We struck up a conversation and I told him about going to the hospital and that I was looking to find a bed and breakfast place for the night. "You're welcome to stay with me and my family for a few days, just follow me back to the house" he said.

A short drive would find us at a small housing complex. Pulling into the driveway we where met by Karen, Lisa and her young son Keno. I thanked them all and was shown to my bedroom that had a nice bathroom connected to it. It wasn't long before I headed for a much-needed shower, something I had not had for a while. Looking down in the shower tray I could see a sandy beach and it was some time before I stepped out of the shower. That evening I enjoyed a lovely meal and later on a few beers with the family, while watching a DVD I carry in the van about life back home on Mull.

Next morning waking at 9.30am I felt so much better, I went down stairs and apologised for being late getting up. Lisa told me it was ok as they were all going out for breakfast and I was invited to join them. We all piled into Jack's truck and went to down town Lab City where we pulled up at a diner. Before we even got in, I had decided what I was having. Once round a table big enough for us all, we ordered a mound of pancakes and a mixture of other things to go with them. It took about fifteen minutes for the order to come which when it did was massive. What did blow me away was the size of the jar of maple syrup. I just love the atmosphere of a proper diner it's full on action with waitresses that are so busy and polite; nothing is too much trouble for them. We spent a good hour eating and talking before taking a drive round the town before going back to the house. Jack insisted I stayed another night to make sure my health had improved enough to travel, I agreed, thanking him for the extra night. After the evening meal we talked and had a few beers till way past midnight, my new friends were good company. My last night again had been a great sleep for me, indicating I was a lot better, giving me the confidence to get back behind the wheel. My last morning here, and too soon I would be in that awkward position having to say my farewell to another group of kind and generous people.

After breakfast I said my farewells, before leaving Jack asked me if I would like to see a mine that employs most of the city and was not too far of my route. More than happy to, I followed him out of town on the paved road for a while before it reverted back to dirt with my body language telling me I was starting to head in a south west direction and civilisation. After about ten kilometres we turned off the highway to a viewing point high up on a ridge. Once at the top I could look down into this huge bowl that seemed to go on forever. The mine had been running for a long time with the rock being hauled by some of the biggest trucks in the world, the site was huge. I shook hands with Jack one final time and thanked him for generosity that had been shown to me in my hour of need.

Climbing back into the mini I set my speed to 80kms and sat back to enjoy a different type of scenery, as the trees had gone leaving bare mountains. My instinct was telling me I would not make Quebec tonight; looking out of the window I could see the surface ahead would be dirt for some time yet. The days driving had passed well and with the late afternoon approaching I would have to start looking for a spot to camp. Still on the dirt road I dropped my speed as the odd house started to appear more often and with that the thought there may be a camp site available. It may be interesting to say at this point that I never fitted a radio or a disc player and that might seem strange to some people, I am more than happy not to have that company with me, content to listen to the harmony of forward motion. That peace and quite was soon to be broken with a noise I had not heard for some time coming from my Nokia 6210 phone that had just picked up its first signal for about ten days, as it proceeded to cough out endless text messages. Unknown to me till now my travels were being followed round Canada by a few Mini minded people and a website about my trip had been set up. Going through the text's I picked up an e-mail about going to see Keith and Deb from Mainly Minis of Montreal.

That evening I stopped and camped at Forestville with my normal evening routine done and the few dishes washed, I decided to try and make contact with Deb and Keith by phone, but unfortunately did not succeed. Making a rough calculation on the mileage to Montreal I was a little staggered that I still had 1000kms to cover. Next morning, I rose at 5.30am and by 6 the dust of the day was following me and no matter what speed I did I could not shake it off. I was now covering the miles as the road was really good and I would find myself descending hill after hill sometimes getting overconfident in my driving skills, the van tried several times to swop ends while running down hill. To try and suppress my exuberance, I would tell myself think moose and bear. The weather and temperature was going from one extreme to another and I was glad to have lots of water. The day ran trouble free with the surfaces changing unexpectedly from dirt to paved, and back to dirt. This part of the drive was exciting not only because of the fun I was having with the Mini, but also the possibility of meeting new people in the coming days. As the day went on I thought the never ending up and down climb would never cease, eventually I came on the biggest dam wall that I had ever seen. The road ran along the base of this huge concrete structure, getting out of the Mini I looked up the wall and quickly got back in the van, the thought of all that water the other side sent shivers round my body. The next 30kms was again a very memorable decent down to sea level and the St Lawrence River. By the end of the day I had clocked up 730kms and was not best pleased with myself for doing so, this adventure was not a race.

Digression
As most of you know the mini does not have air conditioning and my answer to that was the vent scoop on the front part of the roof, it could be opened and closed from just above my head. What I had failed to do was to fit mesh on the scoop entry which allowed dragon flies the size of helicopters, and bees and bugs the size of Barnes Wallace's bouncing bomb to join me in the cockpit, it was though a useful item to have. ~~

By the end of the day I felt as if I had driven through the desert as the dust and heat had become so bad, I had taken to drive with no shoes and only underpants. Grateful to have recovered from the painful neck and ear, my moral was a bit low when I took a look at myself in the mirror and the dust that covered me. That evening I skipped putting up the van tent, just dragging out the blue dust covered sheet as the van was now a disaster inside, opting to stack the plastic boxes outside for the night. Getting into the sleeping bag was out of the question as my body had turned to another colour. My final job of the day was to debug the windscreen and inspect the oil cooler and radiator grills for bugs also.

My bed that night was the van floor so sleep was not too good, so much so I started to ask myself what I was doing here among so much dust, dirt and endless assorted bugs.

The next morning breakfast was a bowl of cornflakes and with just the boxes to pack in the van; I was soon underway yet a little unsure of how hard to push on. I had still not been able to contact Deb and Keith, Montreal was now in touching distance. After driving parallel with the St Lawrence River for a while it once again turned inland and back into the mountains for a couple of hours. After a while I started to descend more than climb, on occasions I would cheat a little and free wheel for miles on end out of gear. It was while doing this I picked up a noise coming from the rear of the van and straight away I knew it to be a noisy wheel bearing. Stopping I jacked the van up to spin the wheel, the unit felt firm be it a little noisy. I decided to just undo the bearing nut to pull the wheel hub and brake drum off as one piece, leaving the bearing exposed to be cleaned and repacked with fresh grease. I would check the bearing when I got to Montreal and if it needed replace it.

It was now about lunch time and can I remember quite clearly this part of my journey. It's difficult to try and explain. I felt as if I had been in some sort of bubble over the last few weeks and what I was about to experience felt strangely new to me. The experience was short lived as it turned out to be lots of traffic, proper paved roads with traffic lights a plenty. Turning right at the T junction I ran parallel with the St Lawrence River once more and was now having to adapt to a different style of driving, taking on large amounts of traffic and a province of mainly French people. It felt a bit like stepping out of one world into a totally different one.

Digression
It's interesting the information I would pick up going forward on this journey, not least about what I should do before getting into the Province of Quebec and what I should do when I get there as told to me on a couple of occasions. Simplified, don't stop unless you have to and fill up with enough fuel to get through the province. If you do stop have the right money and don't open your mouth unless you can speak French. ~~

It wasn't long before I saw a proper campsite. Despite looking distinctly like a hobo and in need of a clean, I paid up and was let me in. The site was huge and I felt quite out of place with Winnebago campers of every size, not to mention the articulated trucks that had been converted to campers. It would seem the summer and the cavalry had arrived. Opting to choose a paved slot alongside the biggest camper I could find rather than being on the grass, I paid the extra cost to have some fun and make a point with my minuet vehicle, well some times in life you must create your own fun.

The inside of the van now looked second hand, with the dust covering everything. The inside needed time spent on it to but that would have to wait for a couple of days. I set up the van tent first, usually if there are people about they tend to get interested in the van and it's little add on tent. Not tonight though, there wasn't a sole about and I could count at least forty camper vans about the place. Once the tent was up, I made the effort to try and clean the inside a little as I wanted to bed down in there this evening. With the tent now turned into a kitchen my night time meal was soon underway I could now relax a little. Stepping out of the tent to stretch my legs there still was not a soul about. The camper rig next to me was about 30ft long with a big car attached by an A-frame to the rear; it looked really nice but not my cup of tea even though I would have liked to take a quick look inside the camper.

Meal finished and dishes washed I collected together any rubbish I had and along with my fresh water container took a walk to the garbage area. When I got back to the Mini the door of the camper next to me sprung open and a man stepped out, on looking up and seeing me he became a little startled on seeing this small thing parked next to him. We both said hello, it didn't take me long to figure out he was American and after a few comments on the size of my transport comparing it to his, he insisted I should come and take a look round his pride and joy. Just before we started the external tour, he reopened the door and shouted "Pass me the auto box honey," thus started the evaluation of his box on wheels, a large bed room appeared on one side and a shower room on the other. "Come on in and get some coffee." Inside I introduced myself and met his wife Jackie who was very pleasant and told me to take a seat. "Make coffee honey while I show Dave around." Eventually we sat down and talked. Well mainly Ron did the talking as I sat back listening to his stories about being on vacation, having travelled 500 miles to get here and by the end of the trip they would have covered about 2000 miles. We sat for some time as several cups of coffee were consumed, the thought of asking for a cup of tea could start a whole new conversation so I stuck with the coffee thinking I would be hyper soon and not be able to sleep. Ron's wife had tried a couple of times to ask me questions and eventually she got the chance. Her Interest turned to me and with it she wanted to know where I was going on my vacation. O I'm heading back home. "So where is home" she asked? "The UK" but I have to get to Alaska then Russia first, which got Ron's attention. So how did you got here then? "I shipped the vehicle across the Atlantic two months ago and have been on the road since." Jackie was keen to listen and ask more questions. I think Ron had got a little over whelmed at my exploits and had taken a back seat in the conversion. Summing up I just told them that the world is about twenty-five thousand miles round and that I should clock up a lot more than that before I got back home in my little rig. Thanking them for the coffee and a pleasant evening I shuck Ron's hand then turned to Jackie and thanked her for her interest in my journey, we to shuck hands and she gave me a thank you mod as I stepped out of there door. Back in my camper I settled down to send an e-mail to Keith and Deb letting them know where I was and I had been unable to contact them by phone. That evening I had a remarkable sleep, so much so, that I had not heard my next door neighbours to move on.

Packing the van and completing my log, I joined the highway stopping shortly after at a gas station to fill up one last time in Labrador. While at the Gas station I received a text from Deb telling me she will ring me in about an hour and Keith would give me directions to their house. Now happy we had made contact I pushed on getting ever closer to Montreal.

True to her word the phone rang and I spoke with Keith receiving directions on how best to avoid the city. With the phone call finished I set about the task of finding them, which in the end turned out to be a nightmare having travelled up and down the freeway a couple of times. I did make it in the end, but it an hour later than we thought it would take. Give me the loneliness of the open road anytime and not these concrete jungles at rush hour. Eventually I had escaped the big city and in the suburbs, a lovely small peaceful place with just a few houses. I soon spotting the right house, as the garage was open where I could see lots of mini things, I pulled in onto the empty drive and stopped the engine deciding to sit for a few minutes to reflect on my achievement of getting this far. Getting out of the van I stretch the legs and take on much needed water. The temperature was now in the 80s. Just then a car pulled up and Keith got out and introduced himself and his two nieces telling me to stay where I was, he would be back in a minute. He returned with two cans of ice-cold beer we walked the short distance to the river and sat on a log. Sitting down I took a huge sigh of relief and cracked open the beer. Bless him Keith knew exactly what I needed. It is a memory that is etched in a special place in my heart. I had found myself an oasis on the edge of a big city that is overseen and hosted by two welcoming people.

Chapter 8

Get out of my town

Now back in the land of the living and amongst people, my hosts did their best to make me welcome. Deb was now back and showed me to my bedroom saying that Keith usually had the use of it, when he came over. Wondering what she was saying and still confused as to what she meant, she added when Keith Calver comes to stay. Then the penny dropped as Keith Calver was well known in the mini world for his knowledge on minis and engine building, when he visits this side of the pond he stops with Keith and Deb. That evening after dinner we talked while down loading my videos and photos onto my lap top. I also managed to up date my Grandson Sam who was back home on Mull and had been following me on a large map on his bedroom wall. This took till about 1.00 a.m. then we headed to our beds.

Next morning, I came down having slept well in a proper bed for the first time in ages. Keith was making breakfast and Deb had gone off to work. At breakfast niece Catharine joined us and while we were talking, I learned she was keen to be a mechanic, so I asked Keith if I could do some checks on the mini and Catharine could help if she would like to.

Keith was going out for a while and he would leave the garage open in case I needed anything. The weather was good so Catharine and I started by unloading the entire contents of the mini with Catharine offering to set about washing down everything in sight. This left me to get on changing the engine oil and filter followed by replacing the noisy wheel bearing and adjusting the brakes. Catharine was great and just got on quietly, hoovering and washing in every corner; she was a hard worker and seemed happy while doing it. My final job was to remove the winch from the front of the vehicle as this would help the airflow on the long drive across the hot prairies.

That evening Deb brought back a Chinese meal, something I had not had for a long time and Keith produced the beers. I was keen to learn about their interest in the mini as I had seen lots of mini stuff in the garage, along with a Riley Elf. It transpired that Deb ran mainly the mini site with the help of Keith who had a race car. Before the end of the evening I told them, I would have to start making my way west.

Next morning after a good breakfast we said our farewells. Once more I had been gifted to spend some special time with great people. How long before this would happen again, I was not sure.

Fully gassed up I was now on the main artery across Canada, The Trans Canadian Highway known as the Number 1, last time I had seen this road was in Newfoundland. With a fully paved road under me I was now heading in the direction of Alberta and the city of Calgary 4500kms and several time zones away. Taking most of the day to exit the Province of Quebec and dip my toe into Ontario, a place that would take me four days to travel across. I now settled down to enjoy a different looking landscape to Quebec. The roads now are wide and flowed up and down left and right, more like a good A class road back home. I found no need to stop as the driving and views around me urged me onward. That evening I pulled into a truck stop to take a look at the big rigs spending some time with the Guys and Girls in the café, I had a nice time with then and they showed me a lot of respect that day. That respect followed me in the coming days as they were only too happy to sound there loud air horns as they sped past me and away into the vast beyond. That night I set my camp up on the concrete pad amongst the trucks feeling happy and secure.

Next morning was dull and overcast so I decamped as quickly as I could to miss the rain that looked like it was heading my way. The next town I came to was Wawa where I gassed up and bought some fruit before going on the hunt for a new bed. I needed something better to lie on than the air mattress that had tortured me for so long with its tendency to deflate in the night. I eventually found a Wall Mart store and purchased a three-inch-thick piece of foam plus a large box of mosquito rings. That evening once again I found myself at a truck stop. I made camp, as there was no charge and I could use the showers for free. Most of the camp sites would now charge about $25 to $30 a night and not the $5 or 6 I'd been charged on the Eastern seaboard of Canada, it didn't seem like much, but it soon adds up Next morning, I woke up feeling pretty good, the three-inch foam must have worked, and I headed to the washroom then into the café to have a trucker's breakfast that cost me about $6, with as much tea as I could drink. By 9.30

a.m. I was back on the road and driving in the direction of Sault Ste Marie along Lake Superior, one of the three great lakes and on this route. I would eventually reach what was called the water shed; this was one of the few places that water runs either into the Atlantic Ocean or the Pacific Ocean. After taking a few photos of what was just a sign I moved on. I wanted to make it to Thunder Bay at the westerly end of Lake Superior and a camp site that was a must to visit and stop, I had been told.

The Trans Can Highway was becoming flatter and the road ahead was more visible for greater distances, by evening I had made it to Thunder Bay. After stopping to ask directions to the Terry Fox Camp Site I was told it was about twenty minutes further down the highway and that I couldn't miss it. Sure enough a great big high statue appeared and with it I turned off the road along a very neat and tidy drive eventually coming into a car park and what looked like a museum. It was about 7.30pm and I thought everything would be closed up, but on trying the door of the building I found it was open.

Walking inside I took a look around and read up on who Terry Fox was. Sums Terry lost his right leg to bone cancer at the age of eighteen. The loss didn't diminish his drive or his courage, in fact it inspired greatness. Once recovered he set out to run across Canada east to west on what he called the Marathon of Hope to raise money for cancer. His journey started in St Johns Newfoundland and his plan was to cross Canada from East to West. After one hundred and forty-three days he was forced to stop and finish his run at Thunder Bay as his cancer had returned, soon after he died leaving a legacy of over $750 million raised in his name.

A huge area had been made into a park and I saw a notice explaining that should you wish to camp then find a quiet corner and enjoy as it is for free, but you are welcome to make a donation when you leave. Taking the advice, I drove a little way round and found a spot to set up my full camp. If there were more people about it was hard to tell. For me the evening's big dinner was sausage and beans on toast made on my Matty stove, followed with half a tin of tangerines and carnation milk. Carnation milk is ideal for the traveller as it tends to last longer than the luxury of ice cream. After dinner I went on a walk about the park keen to take a look at the Terry Fox statue and the very pretty garden where his monument stood. I found this very much a place for deep thought and reflection.

Up at seven the next morning, I only had cornflakes for breakfast, as I was now in the routine of eating more fruit throughout the day leaving me to have something a little more filling at the end of the day when I stopped and made camp. Pushing on out of Ontario, passing Winnipeg and across Manitoba, the drive was easier. The roads were now dead flat with just green fields as far as the eye could see. Moose would not be a problem to me on this part of the journey, just the odd deer to look out for. Now running a bit late in the day, I was surprised to see a Tourist Office open this late. Pulling up at the front door I went to ask about campsites and that was when I spotted a clock on the wall telling me it was just coming up to 7.00 p.m. Unknowingly I had crossed two time zones it was not 9.00pm as I had thought. My clock was wrong so I set it back two hours. The good lady in the Tourist Office helped me out and told me about a site 8km down the road. I thanked her and laughed to myself thinking, had I gained or lost two hours of my life?

Twenty minutes later I found the campsite a little way off the main highway and as pulled up at the office a chap came out to welcome me. "Go pick a site off to the right in the wooded bit" he said, telling me he would call on me later. I found a nice spot and set about putting up my full camp up as tomorrow was Canada Day so it would be pointless to be on the road. I was about to start cooking my evening meal when the couple from the camper next to me paid a visit and invited me to come and join them for dinner. Walking back, they introduce themselves as Dug and Mary. They were both teachers on vacation for six weeks and were heading for Jasper in the Rockies. Their camper was none too big and so unlike many I had seen. It was cosy and did the job for the two of them. Mary dished up dinner of stew and dumplings Dug got out three beers and we settled down to a night of good-hearted conversion and more beers that finished up with me finding my way back to the mini close to 1.30am, well I think it was. As it was Canada Day it would be a lazy start to the morning which was just as well as I didn't raise till about ten thirty. I remembered the camp owner had called on me last night to invite me, and all the other campers, to hotdogs and buns at the office at midday.

As I had time I went and showered and did a bit of laundry before joining the others to celebrate Canada Day. Most of us stayed around for about an hour after which I left deciding to take a walk in the sun across the fields and find a quite spot to take a nap and top up my suntan. I must have fallen asleep for at least three hours in that one spot hearing nothing.

On waking up I walked back to the mini and checked to see if my washing had dried on my make shift line, Sure enough it was perfectly dry, so I packed it away into my plastic box.

My thoughts turned to what might be my evening meal as I was none too hungry, eventually I decided on a small omelette and an early night. The camp owner had organized fireworks for ten o'clock and I elected to listen to them from my camp bed within the van. Once the fireworks finished I fell asleep only to be awakened at midnight by thunder and lightning with rain coming down in bucketful's for at least another hour before falling back into an uneasy sleep that lasted for the rest of the night. When it decided to stop, I got up and set about packing up my camp which was none too easy when the tent was wet. It's a great feeling when you can improvise no matter how big or small the task is. That morning was not the first time that I had to do this messy damp job. Using the Bug window scraper I removed most of the water off the thick plastic tarp then I towelled it down dry before packing it away.

By the time my camp was packed into the Van the sun had come out and I was hopeful of good weather. Re-joining the number one highway and the fastest way to get out of the prairies I was packing the miles in. Then disaster struck in the form of my brand-new Ohmmeter it had decided to stop working at 13.000km. Was this a sign of something to come? The speedo was still working fine, but I was gutted as this would stop me keeping the daily log mileage, plus the exact overall mileage figure. It took a while for me to put it to the back of my mind and move on.

Within a few hours I was out of Saskatchewan and into Alberta, now getting low on fuel I stopped at a garage to fill my tank and buy a sandwich and a small bottle of coke, something I had not tasted for some time. While sitting in the sun I reflected on the low price of fuel in this part of the world and with it some justification for making this journey.

Alberta was much the same as the last two provinces, flat but now I could see nodding dogs, well the wooden type that bring oil up from the ground. There was gas and oil aplenty and with it I could see a new pipe line being built to carry the gas across the plains. Driving on I was amazed how dry and hot it was in this Province, you could see vast areas of pure white which looked like salt flats. In the end I concluded it must be sand as areas were replaced with vast fields of green and water irrigation which was now turning into wheat with the coming months of sunshine. The best part of the day continued this way mile after mile of straight flat highway. Occasionally I would see a Canadian Pacific freight train headed up with three locomotives carrying 40ft containers with the names of every major worldwide company painted on the sides. The containers were double stacked and the length of the train could have been as long as two miles. This was just another incredible sight in this vast country, a country that I had warmed to so very much.

My drive for the day would soon be ending as the evening was drawing closer, in the far distance I started to see large mountains that I figured must be the start of the Rockies and with that I could see dark clouds with flashes of lightening. Incredible as it may seem driving so many miles came easily to me, and I enjoyed the many challenges that it brought. A huge part that also helped was not having any of life's external baggage. I could enjoy the day as it developed and occasionally reflect on a particular thought that would come into my head like the one I was about to have, as a sign told me 100km to Calgary. Now and again I laughed at myself for not sitting down and planning a route or even writing a list of cites to visit. I had not even planed what port I would exit Canada from if my journey was to be completed.

So yes, here was a sign telling me Calgary was none too far away. That pleased me as I had been to this Calgary a few times but only by plane, landing for a short time while some of the passengers got off, and we continued onto Vancouver. I also had a connection with Calgary back home on Mull; I had at one time lived not too far from the beach at Calgary. That evening while camping I learned the Calgary stampede was starting the next day and that it lasted for two weeks. It would be stupid not to go and take a look

That evening I camped at a site called A Place with No Name. In this side of the world you would come across these strange place names, so after dinner I managed to borrow a map of western Canada from the campsite manager. Laying the map out I started to realise just how big this country was, having just reached this particular point of the journey.

Digression
For the first time I sat down and planned a route and wrote a list of places to visit, Places like Crow's Nest Pass, Revel Stoke, Lake Louise, Banff, Jasper, Grand Cache, Grande Prairie and Peace River a journey that would take me South from Calgary to the Canadian border with the USA, then North to the very top of Canada to Inuvik in the northwest territories a distance of 4500km through some of the most diverse and best locations anywhere. ~~

The next morning, I was back on cornflakes and milk while it was still fresh. I did have a problem keeping certain items cool as I had no means of keeping things cold for any length of time. The clouds that gave a picture of pending bad weather last night had gone and the day was looking good for the run into Calgary which I gauged I should make by lunchtime. The drive into the centre was easier than I thought, but parking would be difficult and I finished up outside a bank opting to put money in a meter that would give me an hour to do a quick recce and find out where the biggest show on earth was happening. With the van locked I walked a couple of blocks and by now I could hear noise, and as I got closer, I could see a parade. Finding a stairway, I stayed and filmed as I watched an endless convoy of horses, wagons with cowboys and cowgirls, intertwined with police, fire, ambulance, medics, military and every other type of float you could think of. Somewhere there was also brass bands and pop singers, country and western bands, scout groups, and girl guides, nothing was missing, there were even bin Lorries and road sweepers. I stayed well over an hour expecting to get back to the meter and find my van towed away.

Opting to go and try and find some where to park for the rest of the day I got back in the van and was about to restart the vehicle when a man passing by stopped to take a long look at the van. I could see him in my side mirror beginning to walk away and then suddenly return. My instinct made me open my door and say hello, he replied with hello and said, well done whilst passing me a twenty dollar note. Now standing face to face I thanked him for his kind gesture of the money. I have to say I felt a little insulted by his gesture right at that moment and as hard as I tried I could not revoke his insistence that I must take it. Finally he gave in and told me that he wanted me to take the money as I had travelled and achieved so much by getting to Calgary. I thanked him and accepted his money, before parting I felt the urge to tell him that I lived in the real Calgary back on the isle of Mull Scotland. I went on to tell him how his forefathers had made that dangerous journey across the ocean to start a new life. So in the end he had his way and I got to keep the twenty dollars. With a smile on my face and the thought that the kind man had learnt something new about his city I went in search of a car park that would be safe to leave the van.

Things had settled down the procession had finished and I was soon able to find a parking lot and on pulling in a young guy came out of the pay box. We chatted a little and I told him that I should move as I was blocking the entry. He told me they were full because of the stampede, to which I replied it was a pity as I had hoped to get parked and go to the show.
"Drive in and find a place for your tiny rig to then come back and see me."
Thanking him I drove round a few minutes and came on a position that was close to the road on small grassed area that was possible to drive on and park in safety. Calling back at the pay booth I informed him what I had done with the mini and offered him $40 to pay for the charge, to which he handed me back twenty dollars. I thanked him for his help and generosity.

The show ground was only a short distance away and cost me fifteen dollars to enter. I joined the many people inside and soon noticed I must have been the only one not wearing a white cowboy hat. I walked around a little, not really knowing what to look at as there was so much to see. I decided to sit down with a beer and enjoy people watching for a while. What I did find amazing was the fact that all of this was in the centre of the city and I could see skyscrapers all around. Eventually I came across a large canvas tent, so big it housed about twenty locations of red-hot fire furnaces with anvils, horses and Ferrier teams from all over the globe competing in the world horse shoe championships. The tent was so big it had elevated seats inside so you could sit and watch. I took up a position directly in front of team Scotland and watched the craftsmanship and speed that went into the work of firstly making the shoes then the shoeing of these big horses against the clock.

My final big watch of the day would be the wagon train racing. Four teams of four horses and covered wagons raced round an oval track. Like any event that involves speed acceleration off the line is important. Trying to get past an opponent took it to another level as they pushed their horse teams so very hard, all the while trying to keep the wagon upright on four wheels or two wheels on occasion in the bends.

It was late in the afternoon before I left the show ground and headed out of Calgary southerly on the cowboy trail. The good road made the drive easy with fields of green as far as I could see. The sun was starting to drop behind the distant mountains to my right, making for a mix of colours on the mountains and in the sky, darkness was descending. Even in the bright sky the fight was on between the sun and moon forcing me to light the road ahead with all my lights that helped me pick out the occasional Elk as it attempted to cross my path.

My destination was Crows Head Pass just short of the American border which meant taking a westerly turn parallel with the border to enter the by now darkened pass. The welcome relief of a campsite run by the Lions found me setting up camp by sporadic moonlight, as it became hidden by the odd grey cloud. Payment was a donation in the honesty box. Not realising it was now 1.30am I finally climbed into bed surprised that it was still so hot.

Awaking at eight I could already feel the heat of the day on the vans metal sides. As usual I had left the rear door open when I have the tent connected, this helps with the airflow. Breakfast now on the go with the Matty stove I made bacon sandwiches and decide to stay another night giving me time to explore the area a little. After tidying up my camp I set out to walk the short distance into the village and seek out the Tourist Office, once inside I chatted with the two ladies who made me a coffee as they looked at my book of pictures showing Mull through its four seasons. I was well pleased spending time with the ladies gaining lots of local history from them, they finally told me about what is claimed to be the smallest church in North America. Taking an overgrown pathway, I came on a wooden building that looked as though it had stood the test of time. No bigger than a six by four shed, painted white and with a short green bell tower. Trying the door, it was open and even with my smallish size I had to stoop to enter the inside which was very confined. The simplicity of it I loved. So much so I sat on one of the only two seats in complete silence reflecting on the loss of two special people and why I was making this journey.

Rising next morning to another bright and warm day I started to make my way through the pass that made the Cheddar Gorge back home look like a model. After about an hour the landscape flattened out and with it the drive became more relaxed. Having left Alberta, I was now in British Columba. Soon I would be turning north to start dipping my toe into the Rockies proper but before that I would spend my final night close to the American border where again I found a campsite run by the Lions. As I pulled up onto a grassed area a guy came over and gave me a beer before I had even got out of the van. I thanked him and we talked a little before he went away. Getting out of the Mini I picked up on noise coming from beyond a line of trees, so I decided to walk over and find out what was going on, once through the trees I could see a group of guys playing baseball and drinking the odd beer. Sitting down I watched for a while before returning back to the van to update my log. I wasn't sure if I was up for cooking tonight or should I go out and eat, I needed to make the decision as once the tent is up then I was stuck for moving. Realising that I had not paid yet I went in search of the camp office. Finding the office I met with a lady inside who took fifteen dollars of me as a night's payment for the use of the showers and electric. We talked as fellow lions and I was interested in picking up any new ideas I could on how money could be raised for our communities back home. Before I left the office I asked her if there was somewhere in town to eat. She told me of only one place that served food and that it had a bar also. Thanking her I decided to put off putting the van tent up, but go out and eat first.

The town wasn't very big but did have a few shops on Main Street, none of them served meals so I took to driving round, I eventually drove up a hill and just before I got to the T junction at the top there was a sign outside a large glass fronted building. Food was now being served. I pulled up and parked on the steep hill. Walking in through the open doors I was surprised to find it completely empty but for one young girl at the far end of a long bar, I could see her cleaning glasses. I walk over to say hello and asked her for a beer and a menu. We talked while she pulled my beer and I commented on how quite it was. That is because it's mid-week and nobody comes out in this warm weather. Find a seat and I will bring your beer over, I could pick any of about forty seats so I opted for a window seat, not that I could see much as I was overlooking the tops of trees due to the steepness of the hill.

The girl brought my beer and took my order for fish and chips, with bread and butter. With the lack of company or people in the building there was not much to do or hear once I had scanned the room a couple of times while sipping my beer. The place was dead but for the return of the waitress and my meal which was plentiful.

Picking up my knife and fork the buildings silence was suddenly broken by screaming and ranting from behind me. Not taking much notice of the noise as I was sitting at the far end of the room and hungry, I figured a couple must have come in and kicked off. The rant did not let up, and I started to try and make out what the female kept repeating. Finally picking out the words, "It's your fault, it's your fault" and not before long she arrived at my table looking like a trembling wreck catching me completely off guard. I was trying hard to understand as there was no let up in her rant. I was helpless, unable to respond so in desperation I looked round the room for support from any of the staff. Things were not getting any better and by now her hands were on the table and she was screaming. "Why are you here? You have to tell me why are you here? I tried hard to break in and make conversion, but this was not possible. All the time I was doing my best to carry on eating my meal, thinking, where is this all going? The rant had been going on some time before two guys from the kitchen came over and spoke to the girl trying to calm her down. That only made her wilder and she changed the words of her confrontation to "Get out of my town, I have contacts that can take care of you." On hearing this, the two men escorted the girl out of the building and down the stairs. After a couple of minutes, the chef came over and apologised for what had happened asking me if I was okay.

"Yes," I relied. "A little shaken but would like to have been given the courtesy to respond to the one way out burst."

# Chapter 9
Mile zero

Next morning would see me up early looking forward to a direction now firmly fixed to the north. I drove till about lunch time, the weather was so good I decided to find somewhere and stop to do some checks on the van. Finding a small turn off the highway I took a chance and drove a short distance through overhanging trees that eventually opened out to a gravel area that looked ideal for me to set up camp and work away on the vehicle. Before unloading anything, I walked around just to make sure It was safe. I soon become aware that it was an old abandoned mine of some sort and the spot fitted the bill. Back at and the van I opted not to put the tent up but unload everything out to make working on the van easier

Digression
Being someone who believes in the words "A place for everything and everything in its place," being like this has always given me a sense of pride. Having said that I can also remember being told that it would probably hold me back in life with wasted hours that could be used to do other things. ~~

With the van unloaded and armed with my tool box I made a start on the rear wheel bearing that I had repacked way back on the dirt roads of Labrador. It was still working okay be it a little noisy, but I decided to change it. I had two spares but would keep the old one for back up. One of the good things about the back of the mini is it doesn't take long to check, even stripping the brake drums and adjusting the brake shoes and finishing off by pumping some grease into the radius arms, was quickly achieved. Next, I moved to the front and started to take a look at the business end of things. The engine had been running fine but I decided to change the oil, leaving the filter and oil cooler till next time. The water temperature had been running higher and I put that down to a couple of things, the long mountain climbs and the summer weather that was now full on. Happy with what I had done with my checks I decided to stop and take the rest of the day off and leave checking the drive train and underside until tomorrow.

Cleaning myself up I relaxed and sunbathed for a while. Unfortunately, that did not last long as the evening brought the mosquitoes back out to dine on me. Lighting up a couple of mozzie rings I set about cooking a couple of pork chops with sliced potatoes in the frying pan, as quickly as possible. I had bought a mosquito net to sleep in and tonight I would try it out. Getting away from these little pests was virtually impossible and the discomfort made for many a disturbed night. My trick had been to light a mozzie ring and put it in the van for about half an hour then climb into the sleeping bag, quickly zipping it up and taking full cover inside. The down side to that was I soon ran out of air and I would have to take the chance of just exposing my head. That worked for a short time but sure enough soon I would hear that unmistakable sound that meant trouble was back. Sweating inside the sleeping bag also added to the discomfort and helped prolong the lack of sleep. Something that did help a little was to place shoes and socks outside at night.

Hanging up a large size mosquito net in a mini was not easy when I had to make sure I could find the entry in a hurry, once in I grow in confidence that the net might work.

I had better sleep and awakening at 5.30am I decided to get up and have a quick breakfast to get started on finishing the jobs on the mini in the hope that I could get the work down before the heat of the day started. Jacking up the front of the vehicle on the sump guard I checked the steering and ball joints for any play or unusual movement. All was fine considering the work they had done so far, sticking with the decision I made to take the shockers off some time back all looked good. Well that was until I spotted what I first thought was oil on the sub frame below the radiator. Sliding under for a closer inspection it turned out to be from the inboard drive pod and a cracked boot that had been throwing out the black grease that keeps the ball bearings lubricated. Taking the few spare wheels and tyres I set about supporting the van with them so I could remove the extra-long sump guard to gain access to have a proper look. With the guard now removed I lay my blue tarp down and was rather startled to find the poor condition of both rubber boots, the pods were new ones fitted on the build. I spent some time underneath trying to figure out what my best option would be, I was in no rush to set about fitting new units or a new boots, both of which I had in my spares kit. The whole boot was perished, it almost looked 50 years old, I was not happy at what I had found so early on my travels. I realised it had to be substandard rubber of the type that was starting to appear in the UK from distant parts of the world. It was now time for me to use some initiative.

Digression
Working for my self I would find everyday was a leaning day and I was happy to embrace that most days. Then one day I got a phone call from a friend asking me if I would be interested in joining a small team to work in Kazakhstan as an Engineer? The plan was to take two large Hovercraft and trial those for the Oil Industry on the Caspian Sea through both summer and winter mainly because the Caspian is very shallow so large ships could not be used and Helicopter use was unpredictable because of weather.

During our time there we would trial many new things including oil spillage response, crew change and carrying of 20 feet Containers out to the Rigs that had been built on rocks and concrete, doing so we would rewrite and set new standards for health and safety on more than one occasion.
For me one of the most enjoyable and interesting times was winter and travelling on the frozen ice with a 30 ton cushion of air and no brakes. All the time that the trails went along we would be watched and also having to report to the big chiefs of the oil industries European headquarters back in Belgium.

Next was an interview for Antarctica, also working as an engineer. The interview was held in Cambridge and armed only with a few photos slipped into a folder I turned up at the British Antarctic Survey Company headquarters a little nervous about what I had let myself in for. I will never forget the moment I walked into the interview room and being confronted by three people sitting at a large wooden half-moon shaped table. Two strides in and the man in the middle said "I see you come from Mull; do you know Peter Witty?" yes and so the ice as they say was broken, I sat and joined them at the table. Once I had shared my photo evidence from working in Kazakhstan, the interview of fifteen minutes turned into an hour-long chat. What I found interesting was the questions; each one was focused on what I might do should there be a problem while working in extreme conditions thousands of miles from spares. I soon learned they were looking for experience and not a folder of qualifications. I drove back home well pleased with myself on how I had given the right answers, thinking I don't remember being taught that while at school. ~~

Sliding from under the engine I got my Matty stove out and lit it up so I could heat a screwdriver in the hope it would bond the cracked boot together. After a few attempts I gave up, it was never going to work. Finally, I decided to try araldite and leave it to dry for the rest of the day while I carried on and cleaned up the sump guard. Deciding that I would not be putting it back on during this part of the drive and in doing that it would help with the engine cooling. Space to store the Guard was found in the roof box. As I would be staying here again tonight and with my checks done, I settled down to enjoy the sun before the bugs started to come back. Soon the peace was broken by a vehicle approaching through the trees, stopping close to me a guy asked me if I was okay. "Yes, all is ok I've been doing some checks on my vehicle." His name was Brian and looked like a hippy. We talked for a while and he told me that the place I had stopped at was place called Slocan and through the trees was the deepest lake in Canada. He was an interesting guy and he went on to tell me about the area and its many mineral deposits, seems that a little further on was Upside Down Mountain. With that comment I started to believe he really was a hippy and may have been happy to take the odd smoke. In all fairness to him he went on to tell me that the Dalai Lama had visited the mountain. It would seem the oldest part of the rock formation is near the top and the youngest is at the bottom. Before leaving Brian told me of some hot spring further down the road and that I should stop and call in as the hippies go there and the woman don't wear any tops. Just the tonic I thought I needed with some nice hot bubbling water for a couple of hours. As he left I thanked my new found hippy friend, I then headed back under the van to check on the drying process of the araldite, sure enough the glue had dried so I became confident the temporary fix could work.

Rising next morning I felt refreshed and reassured, having spent a couple of days checking the van over, and with that I could now settle back to take on the famous Rockies. Once more back on the highway I was now running parallel with the lake to my left and with that I felt sure I would find the hot spring somewhere to my right, but as time passed I soon found my self at a small ferry crossing. I joined the tail end of the stationery traffic, without any hope of finding the hot springs. The next hour was spent sitting in the ferry queue while two boats seemed to take forever to reduce the traffic length; deciding to sit it out as I reckoned the alternative route could put three days on the journey. With so much time on my hands, I brought my log up to date and eventually spent time taking to a group of Harley bikers. Two of them were husband and wife Peter and Petra Hak each on their own bikes. They were originally from Holland and where now living at the end of the lake in Revelstoke. Not long after we boarded the ferry that would take about twenty minutes to complete the crossing.

Just as we are about to reach the other side the Dutch couple invited me to call in on them and camp in their garden if I made it to Revelstoke that night. Once off the boat I was now following the lake on the other side at a steady speed and the town was only a few hours away. Now and again I was passed by the many bikers who gave me the thumb and small finger wave.

Just before 5.00pm I had made it into town and decided to visit the grocery store and get some chops, milk and bread along with a roll of Kling film.
Back in the van I soon find Peter and Petra's home. Peter was outside getting the barbeque ready and he told me I could use the spare bedroom to sleep in and just leave the van at the side of the house on the big lawn. I had a shower and Peter told me they had some friends coming round and I must join them. Offering to give the chops I had bought Petra thanked me but told me to keep hold of them as there was more than enough meat on the grill. The weather was good and soon I heard the distinctive sound of Harley Davidsons approaching in numbers, I have to say I was well impressed with what I saw.

Digression
Motorbikes have never set me alight, maybe it's because they are two wheeled and the thought of an accidental death has never excited me. I can recall from my teenage years the time when I was seconded onto the back of a friends brand new Triumph and told to hang on. First all seemed fine until I looked over my friends' shoulder at the speedo which read 110mph and thinking I am not in control of this moment in time. Since that day to this I have never sat on a motor bike. Having said all of that I do have huge respect for the riders, well for most of them. ~~

Back at the get together the company was great and most were keen to hear about my travels as we sank a few cans of beer till the early hours when I told myself that's enough and headed for bed at 2.00 a.m.
I was awakened at 7.30 a.m.by a knock on the bedroom door from Peter telling me that coffee was on the go and Petra would soon be on her way to work. Having a quick wash, I joined them at the breakfast table and chatted for a while before thanking them and finally saying farewell to Petra. Peter told me I did not need to rush as he had work to do in his workshop today. After breakfast, as usual I was itching to get going, but I was grateful for having slept in the house. The weather outside had changed dramatically and all I had to do was collect my wash bag as the van was fully packed just as I had left it last night. Before leaving Peter gave me information about a route that would take me east a little along the 1a Highway then onto the Transcan for a short distance, finally taking the 93 in the direction of Banff and Lake Louise.

Over the next few hours I found it very, very scary driving due to a combination of things, one being the upgrading of the road through the pass and the way the weather had brought huge landslides of sand and mud combined with the odd big boulder tumbling down the mountain side onto the road. The traffic was very much in a hurry to get out and away from what looked like becoming a real disaster. I plodded on as best I could with wipers that couldn't cope with the water. All of the time I was trying to keep control of the van as it aquaplaned its way round the ever-changing road works.
Making it to highway 93 the weather settled down and now I was heading for Lake Louise and hopefully to fulfil a promise I made to myself having flown over the lake many times from Calgary to Vancouver. The promise was to visit the lake one time in my life and today was that day.

Now getting closer to the lake I had hoped for better weather and for it to clear properly. I pushed on determined to also call and take a look at Chateau Lake Louise. Finally driving from a line of tall trees I got my first site of the building, with that came a surge to not miss a once only opportunity so I headed for the main entrance of the Chateau with my little vehicle. I pulled up outside only to be greeted by the concierge. "Is sir staying with us tonight? If so, can I have your vehicle keys and I will get someone to park it for you" Asking if I could take a photo of him with the mini, he quickly told me "I don't do photo's" to which I responded, "I have decided then not to stay."
The concierge turned on his heels he walked off in a huff in his Swiss looking robe and hat. Just then the key boy walked out in our direction whilst giving me a reversed V sign as he walked past the retreating concierge, all much to both our amusement. I could see the posh cars where pulling up and expecting attention. The key boy told me not to worry just park your vehicle over that side and take a look around. I shook his hand and thanked him.

Now finally here at the lake this was for me a special moment and nothing was going to take it away from me. I walked off through the main entrance making a bee line for what was the rear of the Chateau and the view that people pay for while staying here. I walked the short distance to the edge of the lake and found myself looking over the lake that even in this weather was blue. At the far end of the lake could be seen the Glassier and the snow and ice-covered mountains. I did wish that the weather could have been better and that the sun would come out but this was not to be. The sheer beauty kept me there for the rest of the day making it very late for finding somewhere to camp. I did at one point consider spoiling myself and book one night at the chateau but what would that do for me other than empty my wallet some what. My alternative was to spend a night under the stars, and with that in mind I reluctantly turned the key in the ignition and headed back along the 93 that take me in the direction of Banff and Jasper through the glazier ice fields park.

Congratulations must go to the Canadians for what they have done in trying to preserve this delicate part of the country. The road was as big as any highway I have travelled but on approaching the park they had tastefully brought the highway to a halt which made me turn onto a single road and not long after I came upon a pay booth. Stopping I was greeted by a young lady who said "Hello" and asked me if I had a pass." No, I am on a world tour." "Okay I won't take payment from you" and she bid me a safe onward journey. As I returned to the main highway the afternoons rain clouds started to disappear with the evening getting brighter. I was now deep into the heart of the Rockies and the Ice Fields on a road that was almost abandoned to traffic with views that were stunning. Tonight I would be camping in one of the many forestry run Wild Camping Sites. The camp sites are very simple to spot as the camp signs stand out on the side of the road and on seeing my first one I decided to drive in and along a well-maintained gravel track eventually coming to a small area and a notice board giving instructions on what to do.

My first job was to drive round and pick a spot and make a note of the site number then return and fill out one the envelopes with the site number and pay the five dollars before popping it into the honesty box. On all the forest sites toilet facilities can be found. Wild camping sites are kept so very clean and on some of the bigger one's there may even be a covered barbeque area with seats and tables with a big grill that can be fired up, wood is available ready cut and you just put five dollars in the honesty box and take a bundle. Some of the numbered plots may also have a table and seats complete with a fire ring dug into the ground. I loved these sites as they were usually remote, simple and clean. The forestry people had such huge areas at there convenience that they made the sites so good that you didn't get to see or hear a soul due to the way the plots were laid out.

I remember that night in the park, and being under the stairs amongst the trees and mountains thinking back to my childhood of watching TV and Yogi Bear. The seed for that thought had been sown back at the notice board early on where I read the Ranger will be round later. Now trying to set up camp I kept looking over my shoulder. Well you would wouldn't you, just in case you had a surprise visitor in the form of a bear, added too that I had heard so many stories on what you should or should not do, if encountering one like don't run don't look them in the eye just clap your hands to make a gun like sound. I don't do guns but the thought of party poppers came into my head.

Why I don't know but I slept well and awoke to an overcast day at 9.00am. Breakfast was on the go and Mr Ranger came by on his bike. He stopped to chat a while before moving on leaving me to decamp from my peaceful spot. It was almost mid-day before I moved and by then the weather was back to blue skies.

Re-Joining the park highway I could start to see the white of glaciers appearing in between the slits of large black mountains and within the hour I was at the ice field centre stopping for a coffee and a look round before returning to the van and the short drive to one of the glaciers. Arriving at a small car park where a notice told everybody that ice had once covered this spot less than a hundred years ago. Deciding this may be my one and only chance to walk on a glacier I set off on foot to climb the well-trodden pathway that was long and uphill to reach the glacier face. I stopped at several intervals to read the signs that gave the year that the ice face was at that point and how it had receded to its present position. The walk had taken me well over an hour to get to my destination, it was well worth the effort to come this close to a living moving Mass. I stood and listened to the strange noises coming from within the Ice deciding not to walk too far on the ice as the dangers where all too well documented. Thankfully the walk back down was a lot quicker and easier.

The weather was holding out and the beauty of this scenic route continued for the next two hours only to be disturbed by the odd wild mountain goat stepping out onto the road and by 7.00pm I exited the park to see buildings and the small village of Grande Cache.

Spotting a Motel, I readily thought why not stop if it's not too expensive and make it a first. Checking in at the office the lady told me the rooms cost sixty dollars and I decided to take it hoping they had changed the bed sheets. The room was basic and clean, so I ran a bath of hot water while unloading a few clothes along with my electrical items that needed recharging. Internet was not available, so I was again unable send any messages back home. Bath now full I soaked for half an hour and drank a couple of beers before dressing and heading over to the restaurant to order a beer and pizza. I found I could only eat half of the pizza due to the size, so the waitress took it away and put the rest in a box for me. Having one more beer I chatted to a couple of people who were on their way into the park the following day, so I gave them a bit of information on what to expect and at 10.30pm I bid them good night and headed back to my room climbing into bed with real sheets and pillows, and on closing my eyes I made believe I was staying at the Hilton Hotel.

Waking next morning I opted not to go to the restaurant for breakfast but to fall back on my box of cornflakes, which I was more than happy with as I had found I was eating less but eating better on most days and the benefit was I had lost weight, and in the right places. By 10.00am. the van was packed, and I was underway trying to figure out what the weather would be like as it seemed to change so quickly in the mountains. Driving on I could see the river was high with lots of logs floating down stream, so much water was flowing and with it the possibility of more rock and mudslides came to mind.
Thinking the weather must be bad ahead I pushed on while the road was good and clear, by 4.30pm I had reached the junction at Grand Prairie in Alberta which gave me the option of either heading north to Yellow Knife or North West into the Yukon and Mile Zero, the true start of the Alaskan highway at Dawson Creek.

The decision was not hard as my thoughts turned to those men and the challenge to build the ALCAN in the depth of winter as quick as they possible could during World War 2 to connect the contiguous United States to Alaska across Canada starting in Dawson Creek through the Yukon to Delta Junction a distance of 600 miles.

Front view in Paint

Rear view in Paint

Front foot well with safe and Diesel Tank for Heater

Engine Bay

View of the Cockpit side

Multi storage

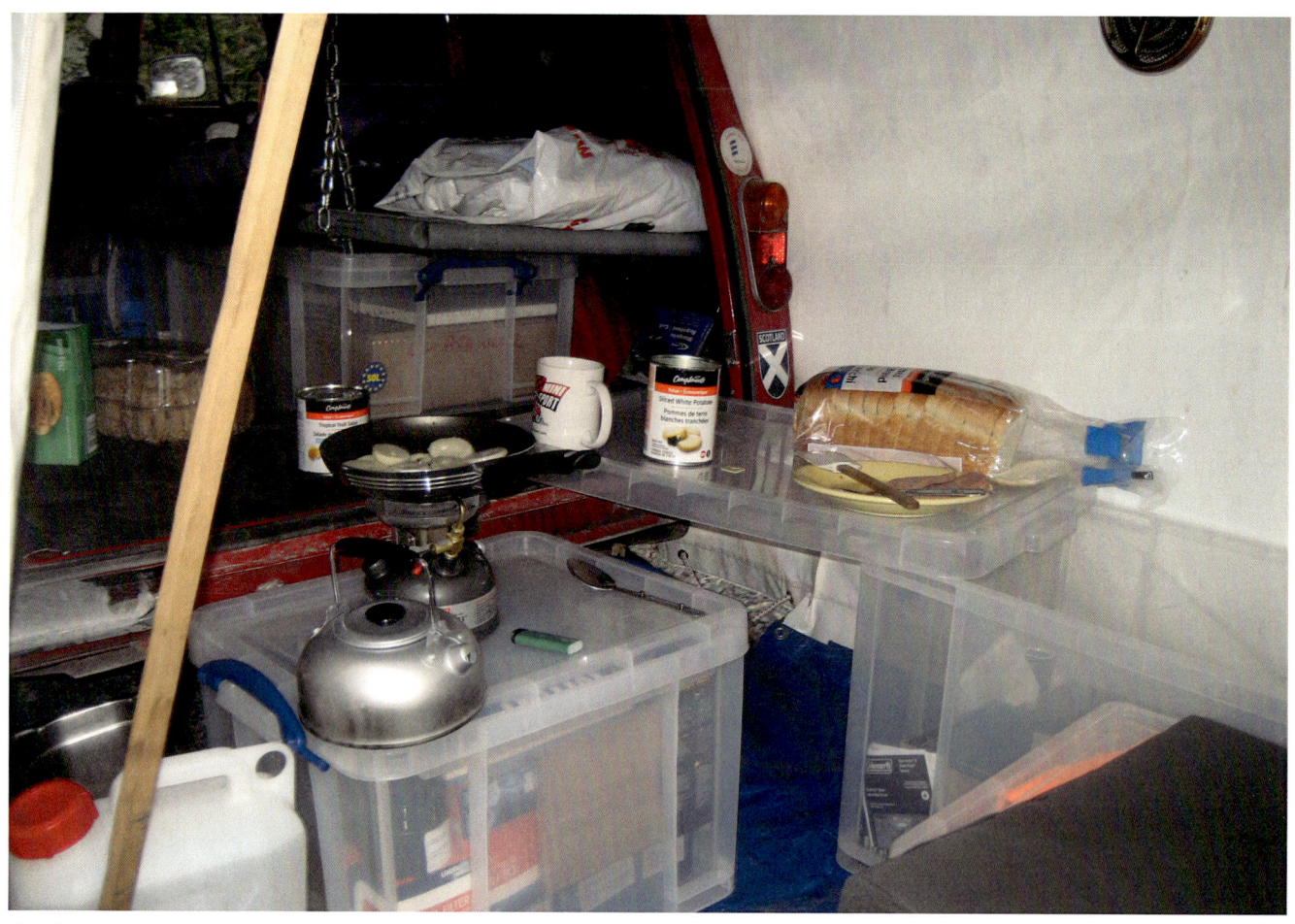

Cooking undercover

Some tail gate reading

My extra accommodation

We're did you come from?

63

Yes it all fits in

Repairs in the Arctic

Again dirt road repairs

Serious problem in the Desert

Start of the Canadian Ice road

Hiding for a few days in a Quarry

Small works for me Guys

Mystery graffiti?

I need to slim a little

San Francisco and that Bridge

Dirt road and Airstrip all in one

Going North and the fuel costs also go up

I must be crazy, 735 miles to a dead end again?

Enough said

70

You can see the North Pole from here on a clear day

Not what you want to see

71

Avoid this place if you can, I should have

If you go down in the woods today

Guess these guys have right of way

Working my Magic on an old Tractor

RCMP's at the Calgary Stampede

The Haul Road to the Ocean

Driver waiting for a ladder

I saved this for all the tree huggers

Found a good road in Siberia

Always beware of Solid Obstacles

Love these Arctic Roads

One of the two River crossing in the McKenzie Delta

Friendly Native People. NWT.

Japanese Police sending me on my way

My Volatile new friends aboard ship.

Sound Advice

My travelling Companion at rest in the Arctic.AK.

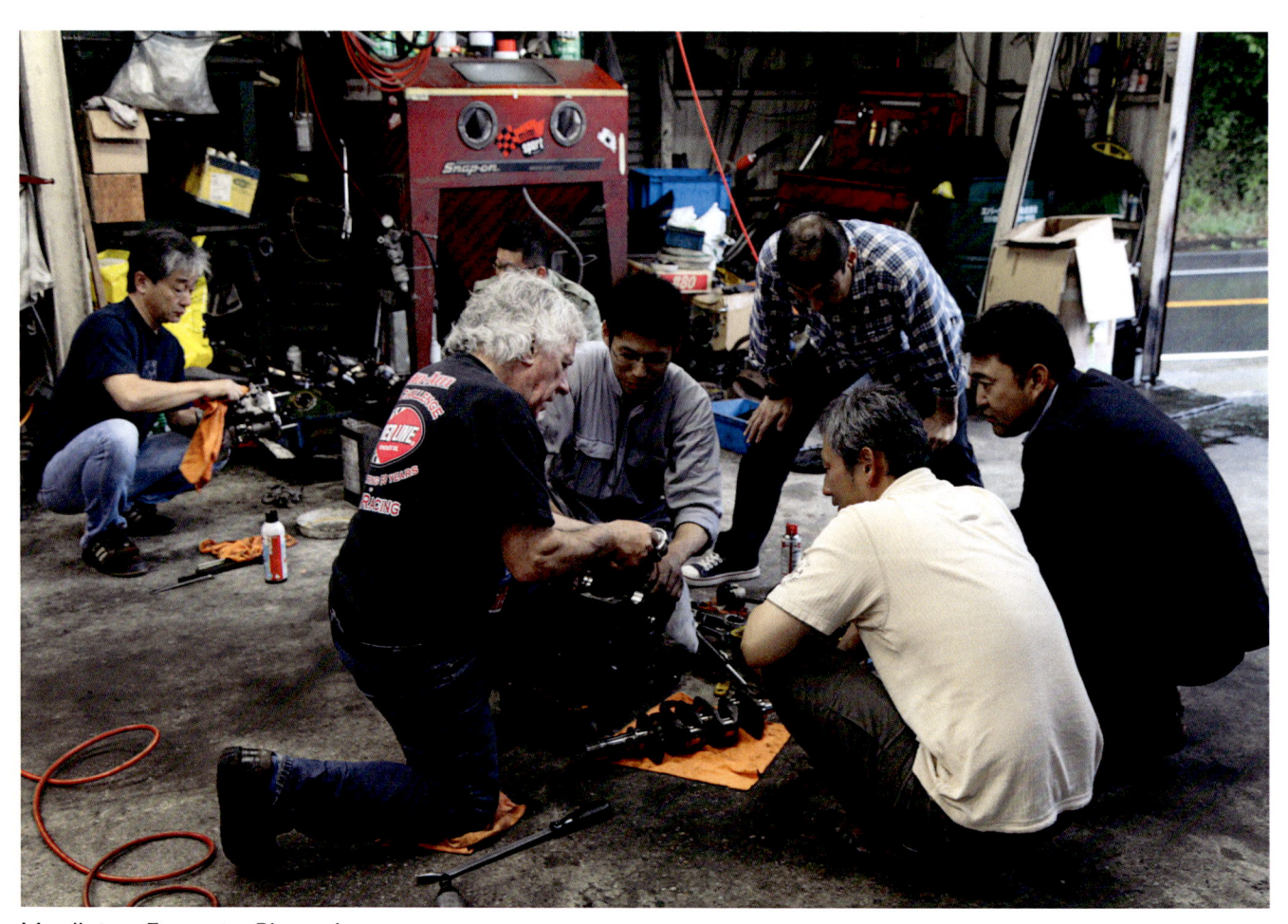

My all time Favourite Photo. Japan

Rick and Elaine Higgs. BC.

Larry and Ann Sutton. BC.

Shinobu and Hiroko Kitani. Japan.

Jack, Robert, Edmund, Bill, Ernie, Ron. Pioneers. NFL.

Bill de Creftt and Mike McCann with Mini. AK.

Next stop... the ice road to the North Pole

Chapter 10

Making for the Arctic

Driving long distances gives you lots of time to think but you have to be on your guard mainly for wild animals. Latter in the day I would start to think do I have enough fuel where will I camp and most of all will it be safe especially as animals were starting to outnumber people?

Getting ever further north I was starting to get a little more excited and felt that I was travelling back in time with place names such as Fort St John and Fort Nelson on my radar and wondered were these places still circled with wooden poles and men camping in tents guarding them with guns trying to keep the Indians out? I would have to wait a day or two before finding this out as more up to date history was just an hour away in Dawson Creek.

I arrived in the outskirts of Dawson and spotting the tourist office I pulled in and was welcomed by a nice girl called Becky. She told me about her travels to the UK and Europe and after a while asked me if I would go to the main office and do an interview and an article on my travels. I said I was not really up for that but would call into the main Visitor Centre if only to tell them that she was good at her job. We chatted a while longer and Becky told me where the best campsite was and the official start location of Mile Zero. As good as my word I did call at the main centre, but little did I know, Becky had rung ahead and warned the staff that I might turn up. In the end I gave in and did an interview and had some photos taken for the local newspaper. After the interview I took a look in the small museum that was attached to the Visitor Centre which gave the history of the Alaska Highway that became known as the Alcan and was built during WW2 in 1942 by the US army of engineers who worked through both summer and winter to complete the project. After thanking and saying my farewell to the staff I drove the short distance to check out Mile Zero and take a few photos before my overnight stop at Mile 0 Camp Site.

The rain returned as I set my tent up, I then headed to the laundry room to catch up on my dirty washing. While there I engaged in conversation with a lady and gentleman who had driven from the Lower 48, their destination was the army base just outside of Fairbanks and they would be there for the next four years. With them were there five fantastic children and as much of their belongings as they could carry. The introduced themselves as Bill and Jane and before long invited me to join them in an hour time at their camp for burgers and beer. With the invitation accepted I head to the shower room before dressing in some well travelled clean clothes.

Walking across the camp site I could see the whole family sitting round getting ready to eat, joining them I sat and we started talking about each other's experiences on travelling. I was very surprised to learn they had been to Scotland and had managed to make it to Mull, while there had also paid a visit to Tobermory. It was now getting close to bedtime so I made my excuses and thanked them for a lovely evening before making my way back to the van. During the night the weather turned dramatic with heavy rain and lots of thunder and lightning that lasted most of the night.

Next morning, I woke and looked out of the van window; my friends had been under canvas and where packing up as best they could with all the wet items they had to deal with. The rain had stopped so I went over to my American friends only to find that disaster had struck them in a big way during the night. The rain had completely washed them out and they were attempting to dry as many items as possible at the laundry building. It was so interesting and heart warming to see how these two people took on the challenge of a big clean up with five children to cope with at the same time, perhaps that's why Bill was a Sergeant with the army. Wanting to help I offered to entertain the children, so all six of us headed back to the van and set about taking down my small camp, with the promise of giving each child a run round the campsite in the mini, finally driving past their camp where Bill filmed the event which went down great with everybody.

Midday was not far away and with the weather improving I bid farewell to this lovely family Now back travelling and in the direction of Fort Nelson the scenery started to get back to its old way of trees and more trees. The drive was good and the weather had changed to sunshine which nearly made me miss a black bear that was barely visible lying in a ditch at the side of the road. Deciding not to stop suddenly, I carried on a short way then turned round and headed back to drive past what I guessed was the bear's position, turning once more I coast quietly to the bear's position. Stopping the engine, I sat for a couple of minutes to put a plan together to try and film the animal. The road was long and straight in both directions and was completely absent of any traffic. I gingerly opened the van door and stepped outside with my video camera then crept round to the front of the vehicle leaving the van door open, while all the time listening for traffic that would automatically stop to take a look at what was going on. This could possible chance things by disturbing the bear, who I had by now figured out must be eating. Slowly I could see a set of ears through the green grass and as I got closer the head appeared. Sure enough it was a bear and he or she was lying in a freshwater ditch eating something, what it was I couldn't tell. Now shaking with fear and excitement I turned the camera on and started filming while keeping my right foot in the sprint position and my ears fixed on any approaching traffic for sound. The bear seemed quite happy as it was eating its favourite meal of blueberries, occasionally lifting its eye to take a look at me. I filmed a short while longer until I heard the sound of an approaching vehicle were upon, I packed up and returned to the mini very pleased with my experience.

The rest of the drive was simple, and I made Fort Nelson by 3.30pm only to find that it didn't have a fort or any cavalry anymore. I thought I would carry on for a couple of hours, but as I was exiting the town, I spotted a line of old bulldozers and construction equipment that my dad would have been well pleased to see. I pulled up and paid five dollars to wander round for the next two hours taking in this incredible collection of equipment that included houses, workshops, tools, and everything from teaspoons to massive earth moving equipment. The site covered every aspect on building the Alcan.

The time had passed too quickly so I decided to camp in Fort Nelson for the night with a dinner consisting of beans on toast washed down with a mug of tea with carnation milk, I finished of the day by writing up my log on the day's events before bed backend me.

There was further rainfall in the night but not too much and by the time I got up the sun was out helping to dry the tent. That morning I fancied bacon on toast, so I loaded the frying pan with all the bacon I had, thus making for a mega sandwich. While packing up my food box divine intervention came to me on seeing the roll of cling film. Taking the jack out of the van I raised the front and crawled underneath with the cling film to have a look at my temporary glue repair to the inboard pod joint rubbers. They seemed to be holding up well, with only a small amount of grease loss, and more surprisingly water had not got in. Armed with the cling film I set about wrapping both boots with four layers of the wrap wondering to myself why I had not come up with that idea before. Cling film would now go into my emergency box alongside gaffa tape and araldite. Job done I took a moment to contemplate what might lie ahead as I was getting ever further north making for the Arctic. Sitting for a while I thought about the remoteness that it would bring. Figuring that It would take about three to four days travel to get to Dempster Junction, the road to Inuvik would then take me a couple more days to complete just one-way, so food and fuel would be essential to have should things go wrong in any away.

Saddened to be leaving the interesting town of Fort Nelson, I filled the petrol tank and checked my spare fuel reserve. That done I went and paid for the fuel and asked the guy at the counter if there was petrol available before Dawson City, "Yes there are two open, as its summertime." Thanking him I settled back into the mini and before long the paved road changed to gravel, and that afternoon belonged to me, as I spotted moose, caribou, bears and mountain goats. Late in the afternoon I came upon a sign at the side of the road, Hot Springs. Surprised to see this sign I pulled over to read the notice that told me it was Liard Hot Springs and If wanted to use them just pay the ten dollars and walk down the boardwalk to get there. I decided to pay the ten dollars charge, and placed my money into the honesty box. I grabbed my towel and trunks and walked the half mile along the boardwalk just as spots of rain started to appear along with the return of mosquitoes. I arrived at the hot springs where there was a small wooden divider where I could hang my towel and change. The damned bugs were well and truly back, not helped by the dampness of the surroundings. I took the wooden steps down into the steaming water and my first experience of immersing myself in the natural environment. I stayed for some considerable time because of the bubbling hot water felt so comforting, the only thing that was going to spoil it would be the mosquitoes when I have to give in and dry myself while being attacked by them from every angle. Getting back to the Van I decided to skip the evening meal and headed straight to bed at seven.

Rising at 6.30 a.m. next morning I made myself a big omelette and boiled the kettle up to make a mug of tea and by 7.30am I was back on the road and heading for Watson Lake.

Making good progress I covered the 220km to Watson Lake by lunch time, on arrival I spotted lots and lots of wooden poles about eight feet high covered with signs of different shapes and sizes. I spent an hour looking at them, and I finally gave up as it would have taken a full day to get round them all. Seems this small community holds the world record for the most signposts in one place.

Ever weary of running out of gas even with my extra large tank and spare can I would not pass a gas station this far out into the wilderness on a little used road like this. The afternoon was creeping by and with it came the feeling of loneliness about the day, something I had not felt before. Come 4 pm and I came on a gas station that wasn't easy to see as the building was surrounded by trees and looked deserted apart from the two fuel pumps. I stopped and got out to take a look only to see the door to the cabin boarded up and a sign saying closed this summer. Disappointed at not being able to top the tank up I climbed back into the mini and set off back on the road not too worried as I still had fuel and been told that there was another fuel stop on the road before Dawson City.

Not far down the road I came on a couple of bison walking towards me along the road, I grabbed my camera and managed to get a picture of them as I was driving. Not long after I came upon another bison standing on its own in a small clearing, I pulled up slowly and stepped out of the van to take a couple of static photo of what is my favourite animal. Now only about thirty feet away, I started to get brave and I walked slowly closer to the motionless bison which was now about twenty feet away. I took a couple of photos and still with my eye in the lens I spotted the bison's short tail starting to move in a circular motion and he turned his head in my direction. That's when I remembered being told if a bison starts moving his tail, they're not safe to be close to, so I backed off gracefully and got back into the safety of the van and drove off happy I had got some good photos.

The road I was travelling on was called the Robert Campbell Highway and it had to be one of the quietest roads I had been on in Canada. A quick look down at the fuel gauge and a cold feeling swept over my body, I started to worry about fuel for the first time on this adventure of mine. Not long after the van ran out of fuel so I added the five litres from the spare can, hoping this would get me to Ross River and the chance of fuel. I carried on and as the day passed into evening, I was now cruising every downhill section out of gear in an effort to save fuel, things got that bad I even turn the ignition off till I started to climb back up hill. Added to my stress was the continuing lack of signposts or information about civilisation and I had not seen a vehicle for the last couple of hours. Finally, at seven forty-five in the evening I came to a halt at the bottom of a large gravel dip that went over a narrow ravine. The gravel had been piled up by the tons rather than build a short bridge to the point that the trees in the forest were only eight feet high with the bottom of the tree hidden in the cut below.

Getting out of the van a loneliness came over me one that I had never experienced before and for the first time I felt helpless due to the lack of fuel, something I could not produce, I did not have a fix for that. I took the spare empty fuel can from the van and placed it on the ground to the rear of the mini. Well its something you seen to do automatically in the hope that someone will come by and save the day. I was hopeful a vehicle would soon come along and rather than sitting back in the van I decided to get out of the vehicle and listen for any approaching vehicle in the still air while leaning against the front wing and staring straight ahead into the tree tops

The light was still good as I stared into the tree tops, half an hour must have passed when I was suddenly became aware of something moving to my left. I turned my head very slightly and slowly only to see a large cat like animal appearing from below the gravel cut and attempting to cross the road directly to my left behind the van. It looked neither left nor right and within minutes the last thing I saw was its long curled up tail disappearing down the other side of the cut. I remember standing there, everything happened so quickly as I tried to figure out what type of animal it was, was it dangerous and should I stand still, and if I moved would I startle the beast, all the time wishing I had my camera and was I brave enough to get it. As quickly as the animal came it had gone, I had witnessed my first cougar.

Deciding to sit back in the van I started to resign myself to the fact I could be sleeping in the pilot's seat tonight but if there was any good to be had about my situation it had to be that daylight lasted till late in these parts. Some fifteen minutes went by and I heard my first vehicle approaching. The vehicle stopped with the man offering to help, but unfortunately any fuel he had was diesel and his vehicle ran on diesel as did the next one that came along some twenty minutes later. It had now been about two hours since I had run out of fuel and I started to think I would have a better chance tomorrow.

Now having almost given up, a big black pickup with a quad bike in the back stopped and the driver got out, I asked him if he had any gas. "Yes, in the back, help yourself." His name was Joe and he looked like a native to the Yukon. Filling my spare can I thanked this kind man and pushed him to take the twenty dollars I had offered. Joe stuck around while I put the petrol in the vans fuel tank then restarted the mini. Before leaving he told that in about 20km there was a turning off to the right and if I drove another 10km it would bring me to Ross River and a small fuel station that would be open tomorrow. Shaking his hand and thanking him he climbed back into his truck and sped off with me following in his dust enjoying whilst enjoying the relief of being rescued.

The day had almost gone when I came on the turning Joe had told me about; trusting him I turned off the road I had been on and took to this single track narrow road. I eventually came to a river that had a small boat type raft operated by wire ropes, it looked like it could carry two cars. With not a sole about or a building to be seen I was unsure if the gas station was this side or the other side of the river. Daylight was still good so I decided I would camp here with my back to the river as this would give me more safety. The reason for this was because I had spotted a couple of large concrete trash skips a short distance back that had bear proof steel lids on. My problem was they must be on the edge of town as cabbages lay all round, you could tell that unsavoury animals had paid a visit already to investigate. With one side of the van and tent to the river and the other facing back up the dirt road I had just driven down, I settled down with my Matty stove to boil the kettle for a quick cup of tea and biscuits before heading to bed. Sitting there and reflecting on the days travels while hugging my warm brew a wolf like dog appeared from my right and stopped to take a look at me, it then disappeared to my left and out of sight. Deciding I could do with a good wash after the dust of the day I put my biggest pan on the stove to heat some water. While doing this I was revisited this time by three dogs that stopped to look at me. Now feeling a little nervous as to what their intentions were, I picked up some stones and threw them at the dogs which eventually made them move on. Pouring the first pan of hot water into my wash bowl I refilled the pan and set it back on the stove while I started to look around for my soap and towel in the back of the van. As I leaned back to sit on my makeshift seat in the van tent, I was startled to see a bigger collection of dogs which I had not heard approaching the tent opening.

I counted six dogs this time and again they just stood and looked at me. I could feel the hairs on my arms start prickling and with it the thought that I needed to set some rules in place. After pouring the second pan of boiling water into the wash bowl I stood up expecting the dogs to at least back away, but no they did not, and with that I made the decision to pick up the bowl of hot water throwing it over the dogs in a fan like wave which made them run off. I sat up a little longer to see if they would return, it stayed peaceful so I zipped the tent side closed and climbed into the van and lowered the rear door. I tried to sleep for what was left of the night before rising the next day at 8.00 a.m. to have a good size breakfast of eggs and tomatoes on toast.

First job after breakfast was to take a look at the drive pods and happy that my cling film fix was working before a quick look round the vehicle to make shore nothing was hanging off, from now on I would be travelling on miles and miles of gravel. Repacking the van, I went in search of the village and the gas station, eventually I found two pumps on the side of a wooden house that was in desperate need of work along with the rest of the building that appeared scattered around in the under growth. Eventually someone came out and I filled up with fuel. To all intent and purposes the place looked deserted, except for old cars, snow machines, and quad bikes that had passed their sell by date. That's when I realised it had to be a native village that was trying to survive on very little as it didn't have any infrastructure. As I headed the 10km back to the main highway I could not stop from thinking about the many native people that live a poor and lonely life with very little chance of their lives ever changing in these parts.

Now on the Klondike Highway I had a 420km drive that would get me to Glenboyle Junction and Klondike RV Camp site, the only place for miles that had everything for the lonely traveller like gas, food and a camp site with showers and laundry. First task was to fill the mini and the spare fuel can to the brim and then a spot to set up camp. That evening I cleaned as much dust as I could from the van and I was as ever thankful that most items were in the assorted sized plastic sealed boxes. Once I had cleaned away most of the dust I then put anything that was loose into black plastic bags knowing that the next four or five days could bring the return of the dust if the temperatures remained the same. That evening I settled for celery soup followed by pears and carnation milk, a sure winner in the hot conditions.

Last thing that evening was a shower before climbing onto my bed as it was far too hot to survive inside a sleeping bag. I had now found that I slept better with a black mask to cover my eyes from the prolonged daylight. Next morning would have to be toast and marmalade as the milk had gone sour and with it any chance of cornflakes. Van packed I turned onto the Dempster and read the notices posted at the start of the highway, some of them interesting, some of them scary all of them warnings for the traveller. From this point on I would be travelling due North and at some point I would cross that line on a map that says the Arctic Circle, the thought of it excited me I was making for the Arctic.

Inuvik is 700km up the road and sits close to the Beaufort Sea. I had no intention of pushing too hard as the conditions could change so quickly on these roads and I had two rivers also to cross in the Mackenzie delta. The road itself was not good and for a big chunk of the day I dogged the trucks carrying stone for the road repairs. With that also came the graders and rolling equipment that had their own agenda, making it obvious that you had to avoid them by running on the wrong side of the road at times.

Concentrating on all this movement and disturbance helped the day to pass more quickly and at times I found it quite interesting when coming on one of the graders from behind, knowing that I had to overtake it by changing to the other side of the road having to climb the stone spoil that comes from the side of the graders blade causing a large gravel ridge for the mini to climb over. My pre adventure vehicle preparation would now be tested as I turned the steering wheel in the direction of the stone ridge, with a bit of speed followed by some sledging with the mini's aluminium full floor tray we were over. Then for some strange reason the minis ohmmeter restarted on of all days July 13th having sat at 13.000km for months. Once passed the road works I pushed on to Eagle Plains just south of the Arctic Circle. That night, I would camp there as following day was my birthday and I wanted to cross the line that is known as the 66 Parallel.

Digression
Driving back in the UK our roads are usually made of tarmac, now driving the roads of Canada is totally different. Take the Trans Canadian Highway or the number 1 that runs from St Johns Newfoundland in the east to Vancouver British Columba in the west, this road is paved for a distance of 8,000 km. Above the Transcan as they like to call it and the further north you go roads change to gravel (dirt), the main reason for this is the cold weather and permafrost which can lift and split a solid mass like a concrete road that then can become very dangerous. A similar thing can happen on the gravel roads but they tend to sink and flex. Most long roads are given a name such as Glenn Highway, Denali Highway, Top of the World Highway, Pan America Highway and the Dempster Highway. My favourite is the Dalton Highway and on many occasions, the dirt roads could be found to be better than the paved roads in places. ~~

As far as dirt roads go the road to Inuvik was quite busy at this time of year with extra traffic, such as camper vans and trailers along with the big trucks that usually have the road to themselves over winter months while running on the ice road. Much of the traffic was coming from Calgary and Edmonton.

My overnight stop at Eagle Plains was good and I mixed with a group of travellers who were running in a convoy of six vehicles towing larger than life camper vans. Everybody was nice; trouble was they kept giving me beers to drink, so I ended up staying in bed and not getting up till about 9.30 the next morning, yes feeling a bit fragile. Helped by some cornflakes and a shower I was back to feeling normal before the end of the day. Keen as ever to get back on the road I was desperate to reach the Arctic Circle to try and find the line across the road like the demarcation one on a map. Gassed up I set off after the convey had gone and within the hour I reached a wide turn off with a nice big wooden sign telling me I was now at the Arctic Circle. I backed the van up and parked it tidily, why I did that I don't know as the parking area was large and there wasn't a sole or a vehicle in sight. Having made it this far I walked over to check out the large stainless-steel plate that showed the North Pole and the top of the world with the countries the Arctic Circle runs through. I took a couple of photos as a reminder before returning to the van. On the way back I spotted the suspension had collapsed on the van's offside front.

I concluded it had broken within the last couple of hours and was unknown to me as I had not heard or felt it brake. I wasn't too bothered as this had happened a few times now and I was getting good at changing knuckle joints so I decided to change the broken joint straight away.

What puzzled me is to why this was still happening as I had many weeks of this type of travel to cover before getting close to a paved road. With my spare replacements now down to three and with the tools packed away, I climbed back into my seat started the engine and moved forward to re-join the highway

It was now getting close to midday, so I needed to push on if I was to make Inuvik that night. The dirt road was now well surfaced so I upped my speed and could keep rolling with the Speedo reading at about 90km.

I soon reached the first of two river crossings. I had to wait while a bulldozer made a gravel ramp for the small ferry to be able to load me and two other waiting vehicles. Once on the boat I talked to the two crew men who were native people. One of them pointed at the van and said, "The Italian job" I shook there hands and took a couple of photos just before the skipper dropped the boat ramp onto the shale beach. Now off the boat I had 75 km to get to the next river crossing, my problem was that two other vehicles on the crossing were big smart camper vans and why people take such expensive items on these roads is beyond me. So now I was taxed with either staying behind them and getting covered in dust or worst, getting paint balled with stones. Once the two vehicles in front of me had set the pace I decided to make my move and opted for the over take, but not before checking a few things.

Digression
Different tactics come into play when driving on these endless dirt roads and overtaking must be taken seriously. First is to check for oncoming traffic so be patient and wait as there are plenty of straight roads. Dust is the biggest problem and if there is no wind it can be really dangerous especially driving through a corridor of trees. Most dirt roads are a good width and in this part of the world, the van is left hand drive and this helps me as they drive on the right. In most cases you can see an approaching vehicle if the dust is being disturbed giving you time to check on what direction the wind is blowing the dust away. If the dust can be seen blowing from your right to the left then in most cases the on coming traffics dust should not cause to many problems for you. Having said that should the dust be seen to be blowing left to right then that can be outright dangerous as I found out a couple of times. Whilst slowing up is the sensible thing to do, stopping could find you being rear ended by a large truck. Finally as for the road surfaces you must try to judge its make up as the type of stone can change quickly and make for handling your vehicle very unpredictable at times be it wet or dry. ~~

Safely passed the two vehicles I enjoyed the drive across the Mackenzie Delta. I was in ore of the work that must have gone into constructing this road between two rivers on such a huge flood plain by using stone that had to be transported from a man made Quarry's. Arriving at the Arctic Red River Crossing I drove straight on to the boat and chatted with the deck crew. The crossing took a little longer than the last one and when we got close to the other side it took the skipper a few attempts to find the right spot to drop the steel ramp so we could drive off and up the shale to find the road. Now off the boat the rain started and continued for the next hour turning the road into mush in places that made the drive very interesting after so many days of endless dust. Finally pulling into Inuvik late in the afternoon my first stop was the Tourist office. Way back in Nova Scotia I had told myself to make contact with these information centres not only for local maps but more importantly for safety reasons, the town would then have a record of me having been here. The Tourist office in Inuvik can be found soon as you arrive and that made sense as the road would soon come to a dead stop with the Arctic Ocean calling a Holt. The building and contents were stunning with so many first nation items on display, I stayed and talked to the two native ladies for about an hour.

As it was my birthday, I decided to stay two nights next door at the Nova Inn at a cost of forty pounds a night all in. Once in my room I unpacked some clean clothes and soaked in the bath for a while before going down to join a guy at one of the tables for dinner. I introduced myself and he told me his name was Garry and he was a book publisher. We ate and talked for an hour or so occasionally being disturbed by people coming in off the street to inquire about the strange vehicle parked outside. After the meal I decided to go my room and try to send e-mails off to friends but that turned out not to be impossible. Disappointed, I turned in and had a really good night's sleep in the land of the midnight sun achieved by the very dark curtains that covered the windows. I woke at eight in my nice clean white sheets forcing myself to get up and wash before going down to have my continental breakfast. On going out I saw Garry and he told me about the Great Northern Arts Festival that was on in town for three days. He went on to tell me that in reality it can go on for a week due to the distances that so many of the native people have to travel, a lot of them come from as far as Tuktoyaktuk on Quad bikes along narrow tracks.

After breakfast the internet seemed to be good so I managed to send a few e-mails before heading outside to the van and check the oil in the engine which was down a little. I walked round to the back of the van to get some oil out, and I found that someone had gone to the trouble of drawing the outline of a polar bear in the mud on the rear window. It looked so real and it was a total mystery as to who had done it or when it had been done. I did not want to wash it off so I left it on the rear window. Now feeling relaxed I went in search of the ice road that I had heard and seen so much about on the Ice Road Truckers TV Program. Knowing most of the ice had gone this time of the year there was no harm in taking a look. I drove down the main road with a mixture shops and houses on both sides finally reached the working end of town. The drive finally led me to a row of Kenworth trucks and assorted trailers. I turned in and pulled up at the office front of North Wind Industries, instantly recognising the name from the TV program, thinking to myself, you've come this far, so get yourself inside Dave.

All buildings this far north stand about three feet off the ground on steel poles because of the permafrost, as I walked up the wooden steps my van had already attracted a few people to the window. Once inside I was welcomed by a staff of two Guys and two Girls were upon I was signalled to come inside the main office for coffee and a chat. Eventually we where joined by Aiden Dunne the head man for the operation. We talked about my driving experiences with the van and where well taken with the Mini and the tyres that had not as yet had any punctures, seem they run the highest ply rated tyres you can buy for trucks in this part of the world. Aiden was also keen to hear about Kazakhstan and my time with the hovercraft in an environment of two extremes that could be very similar to what they have to deal with in this part of the world. Before leaving I was given a tour around and was able to take lots of photos of the ice road trucks. Finally, Aiden handed me some keepsakes of my visit. I thanked him for his time and he told me how to get to the road that would in winter be the starting point for taking them and there trucks onto the ice.

With the afternoon left, I visited the Arts Festival and had a look round the village hall at the many native exhibits that had clearly been handmade, all on view and for sale. There was a large range of items from native clothes and moccasin footwear to huge moose antlers carved to depict an animal such as salmon, polar bear or a picture of there native ways. The whole hall was full of such beautiful items the likes of which I had never seen before. I would have loved to have bought something, they were quite rightly expensive and as luck would have it I had no space in the van, well I kept telling myself that.
Outside was equally as interesting as I watched the men carving in stone, wood and antler in the traditional way without the use of machines or electricity. I had an enjoyable afternoon mixing amongst these people and listening to their stories, how some of them had travelled vast distances taking days sometime to get here for the yearly event. The stories they had to tell were so interesting and mind blowing. I was very pleased with my day and had really enjoyed mixing with so many warm interesting people.

I decide to return back to the Nova Inn to shower and change before walking the short distance to the restaurant and the chance to choose a proper meal before leaving tomorrow. Finding a table, I settled down with a beer and ordered prawns. When they came, I couldn't believe the size of them, think small lobster, and that will give you a sense of size. Finishing them left me with just enough room for a small dessert, but yes you guessed it they don't do small portions this side of the world.

Back at the Nova Inn I joined Garry for a night cap telling him about my day, and he told me of his plans is to leave early tomorrow to get to Dawson City a journey that will normally take two days which Ralph planned to do in one. I wished him good luck and told him I was leaving at lunch time and would drive only as far Eagle Plains on the return drive. We shook hands and he left saying he hoped to run into me again and that I should write a book about my travels. That night I made the most of my comfortable surroundings knowing that tomorrow it would be back to miles of driving in the dust, providing the temperature and weather held out.

Next morning after breakfast I drove back to the North Wind Industries depot to give the van a reluctant power wash, as this would wipe away any trace of the polar bear outline on the van's rear window. The guys in the workshop set up the steam cleaner for me, and in no time I found a brand-new vehicle under a layer of mud. Happy with everything and fully gassed up it was now time to head south and start the return journey back down the Dempster to the first ferry, Now on board I spotted the smiling faces of the deck crew who told me they had not sailed yesterday due to bad winds and a heavy current in the river. While crossing the guys said I had to see the captain, climbing two steel ladders I made it to the wheelhouse to say hello. He told me his name was Douglas and I laughed telling him I have a friend back home called Douglas, Douglas Ingram and that he to is a skipper on a work boat be it a little smaller than this one it does have a drop front gangway and hydraulic crane. Back down on the deck I thanked the crew and bid them farewell as I drove of the steel ramp and back onto the gravel.

The drive to the next river crossing went well with only one 4x4 vehicle and no big trucks speeding up the crossing and my onward journey to Eagle Plains with a night's stay back in my own bed. Dinner that night was back to tinned food, stuff like beans on toast followed with a quick catch up on the daily log and bed for the night.

Next day the views were spectacular on this part of the return journey, and at one point I came to a stop to stand and look, eventually focusing on what looked like stones stacked on each other. Curious to know what I had seen I drove a little further on and found an old track. Feeling confident and with a mini that in my mind was built for the job we picked our way round stones and shrub to make it to the top of a small plateau. Out of the mini I walked about and found a mixture of stones, most of them having succumbed to the wind and the elements lying about the dusty floor. I could see that at one time they would have been carefully placed on top of each other. Looking round you could see a couple of make shift shapes still standing and these where made to look like animals such as dogs. Before leaving I make my own stone sculpture, I then took some photos and found my way back to the dirt road and a drive of 90km to reach my destination for the night back at the Klondike RV campsite once again. A few days later I learned that stones placed like that were meant as good luck and would be a special place to the people of Indian origin who had built them.

My evening was much the same as it was several days back, first making use of the showers and the laundry this time as I wanted to add my dusty sleeping bag to the list of washing. Dinner was a tin of Campbell's chicken noodles that I bought from the camp shop along with some bacon and bread for tomorrows breakfast treat. Digging out my Dick Turpin black eye mask I slept well through the night and would be awake by seven to make a start on my bacon sandwich, now feed and watered I would clear the campsite by eight. I drove the short distance and turned off the Dempster onto the Klondike highway, I now had a 90km drive to my next stop the capital of the Klondike gold rush Dawson City.

About 20km before Dawson I started to run parallel with the mighty Yukon River to my left, finally arriving in Dawson just after ten in the morning. The main street had approximately fifteen to twenty buildings of mainly shops on my right hand side opposite the river, also could be seen a couple of bars and a gold agents. A little further on and standing alone was an old paddle steamer which had been placed on dry land alongside the river and was now used for functions. While in town I decided to take a drive round and check some of the old buildings in the few back roads, the history here goes back to the height of the gold rush in the Klondike and the only modern things around where the vehicles. What excited and overwhelmed me was the buildings and the rawness of the place. For me it was like going back a hundred years as I kept getting visions of stage coaches, gold miners and ladies of ill repute. For those who have seen the Film, Paint your Wagon and that great actor Lee Marvin then this place reminds me of that film.

More recently, reality TV has been getting in on the action with programmes like Gold Rush that has featured the area and the town. My drive took me by many buildings, all of them made from wood, with some of them very dated and falling down. One building that did stand out was the Masonic Lodge with the biggest masonic symbol I have ever seen standing at five feet high on the front of the building. Knowing I had to cross the Yukon River I ventured to check where the Ferry was to beach to pick up traffic. The instant I pulled up I recognised the spot from the TV Gold Rush programme. I returned back to town but via the dump I had spotted in the trees, driving in I would find it full of old mining equipment including heavy plant that must still have some use for spares. I could see it was a great place for finding possible replacement parts for a much-needed fix if you where mining in the area. Now just after 1pm I decided to park up on Main Street and stop at one of the bars to grab a bite to eat and a beer. Like most bars this side of the world they can be interesting and also the people within. Taking up a place at the bar I enjoyed the company of the guys sitting along side me while I ate and drank. An hour past and reluctantly I got up from my chair at the bar and thanked the small gathering of people then headed back to the mini that was parked outside like a horse tethered to the rail by its reins.

Outside I talked to a few people who were looking over the van and told them I was heading for the river crossing and onward to Alaska. Now ready to move on I climbed into the mini and started her up selecting reverse gear, suddenly I heard and felt a great thump on the back of the van. Looking in the mirror I saw Garry the guy I had spent some time with back in Inuvik at the Nova Inn. I jumped out and walked to the back of the van where we embraced each other. It transpired he had seen the mini and stopped. We talked a little longer and then for some reason I turned round and looked at the back door. The mysterious polar bear had returned to the back window and the mystery was now solved as I hugged and thanked Garry for stopping. The crowd now was quite big and I asked someone to take a photo of us together with our polar bear. While taking to Garry he told me about the music festival that was starting tomorrow where upon I said that I had already decided to move on and go for the river crossing. Climbing back in the van I wished farewell to Garry and Dawson City. Tomorrow I would be heading for Alaska and the United States border crossing at Poker Creek, I was a little bit worried because I did not have a visa to get me or my vehicle across the border.

Chapter 11

The last frontier

Here I was at another river crossing this time the mighty Yukon River that starts in Canada and flows for 3.200km and finely empties into the Bering Sea off the west coast of Alaska. Little did I realise on this day that I would return many times to this river and enjoy many adventures, those days were a few years away with a whole different set of stories that could fill another book.

The drive to the border was 90km from the river with the first half a steady climb on what is called the Top of The World Highway, the drive had stunning views and a definite lack of traffic. As I got closer to the US Border the nerves started to kick in as to whether I would be allowed into Alaska. What little research I had done back home informed me I could obtain a green card at the border to enable me to enter Alaska? Any pre travel plans I had made did not include going to the lower 48 so I never applied for a visa. As I came round the last bend I see the next crest and a small green cabin that looked totally lost in this wilderness. It was then that my heart really started pounding as my driving slowed to a walking pace, in the end coming to a standstill. Sitting motionless I was trying to decide if I should carry on or turnabout. It's a no brainier I told myself so man up and take your chances with the nice border people. I moved on with the mini turning on the video recorder just before I pulled up at the barrier post. I could not see into the buildings windows, I was unsure what to do. Luckily a lady came out and spoke to me asking if I had a visa to which I replied "No." She told me to "Drive the vehicle round the corner and come to the office with your passport and we will do some paperwork."

Now in the office I handed over my passport and the border lady flicked through the pages asking me different questions and commenting that I had travelled a fair distance to get here. It seemed to take forever and the longer it took the more uncertain I became of being able to gain entry.

"There you are sir" she said, as she handed me my passport back.

"What happens next?" I asked. "You give me six dollars and you're good for ninety days so enjoy your time here." Thanking her I walked outside a free man very happy that I could continue my journey into the biggest state in the Union.

Back at the van I turned off the video camera then found my ordinary one as I wanting to take some photos of this out post at Poker Creek with a population of two that both work at the border crossing. I learnt that it is closed in winter and only open from 8am till 8pm during the summer months. Whilst taking my photos the lady Officer came out and asked me not to take anymore, as taking photos was not allowed on government property. I apologised and got back into my van before she decided to deport me back to Canada.

Time to get out of Dodge as they and with it another time zone; it took me two hours to get to a place called Chicken on a road that was in very poor condition being used mainly by gold prospectors and their equipment. Just before town I came upon Chicken Gold Camp, an outpost that looked just like an oasis in the middle of nowhere.

I decided to book two nights stay and set up my tent as the cost was only ten dollars a night for a place that was well equipped with everything I needed. The site turned out to be the cleanest of any of the many sites I had stayed at to date. I set up camp that night in a quiet corner and settled down to peel some potatoes and slice them into flat fries or scallops as we call them. I was missing the taste of chips so frying the spuds flat and making bread butties was as close as I could get to taste the real thing. After washing up and laying out my bed.

I set off on a walk to the site of a large piece of mining machinery called a Pedro Dredge that had been left and abandoned after the Gold Rush. The dredge did not look to bad for its age considering it was built back in the middle of the nineteen thirties and transported in pieces from California to Pedro Creek in the Klondike where it was rebuilt and worked for a number of years before being disassembled and taken to Chicken.

These Dredges are huge but I was reliable told there are bigger ones to be found. I spent a good couple of hours looking round at how it would have operated with it's endless chain of buckets that scoops up stone and dirt with any Gold that may be mixed with the extraction from the pond the that the Dredge works in. Tailing, which are the unwanted part of the operation can be seen all over the Yukon and parts of Alaska. These days with modern equipment gold miners are recycling the Tailing and finding good Gold left by the old prospectors from back in the day.

Having slept well and had breakfast I decided that I would like to visit a place called Eagle for two reasons, one was because of the name the other was that it sits at the end of a long road in the middle of nowhere, for me that is enough to make it interesting. The problem I have should I wish to base myself in one spot for a couple of days and nights then I have to pack away the Van tent each time. It's just a little inconvenient having to pack all my travel items back into the Van. Before leaving the site I checked in at the office just to let them know I would be back later.

On the way to Eagle I came upon three wooden buildings and on getting closer they looked like they had come straight out of a cowboy movie and been dropped onto this spot. I couldn't see anybody but I stopped to take a look. To my amazement the small buildings were active, the first one was a café the middle one a gift shop and the last one a bar, so I tied up my horse and went in for a drink and to explore. The inside of the bar was no bigger than fifteen feet square and came with no seats, just a short bar of six feet. Ducking my head, I walked in to the room which had a ceiling covered in memorabilia from all parts of the world, including shorts, ties, shirts and even the odd bra. Fearful that I might have to leave something behind I drank my beer and went to take a quick look at the two remaining buildings that made up the town of Chicken.

Back in the van I started looking for the road to Eagle and after 10km came on a turning that was signposted. With about another hour of driving I eventually came to a halt at the Yukon River. I was pleasantly surprised by the town's size; I reckoned that there was about thirty plus dwellings which were here purely because of the river. The town of Eagle like many of these small places has come to exist because of the River; the river was once the only way of getting in and out of the interior, which is still the case to this day in many cases.

Not long after I found the post office, a small log cabin that also had to be someone's home. The place looked closed which was disappointing having travelled so far. I stopped and tried the door, but it was locked. While I was peering through the window a lady came and opened the door. On seeing the mini she seemed to relax and greeted me with "hello." then apologised for being closed. I told her about my Scottish passport and would she mind putting the post office stamp on it and become part of my passage round the world, step inside and I will happily stamp it for you We talked for some time, this can happen when meeting people who live off grid; the mini is a great starting point for conversation. We talked about my travels and as I wasn't in any particular hurry to leave, we continued chatting as I am always happy to hear new stories and learn of other people's experiences. She enquired how long I would be around, as in a few days she and a few friends would be going up river to a cabin and getting together for a party of music and I was welcome to come along. I made my decision after weighing up the good and bad options of the offer and gracefully declined saying I was meeting with friends in Fairbanks in a couple of days. Happy I had another stamp added to the passport I bid the postmistress farewell.

Back in the Van I make my way back to the campsite and set up for my final night in this friendly place. It was still early and there was plenty of light so I decided to have an hour on the van adjusting the ride height to give me a bit more clearance on these little used and poor condition roads.

Next morning rather than cook I went in to the café for breakfast and ordered tea and a Dredge sandwich that came full of bacon, egg, tomatoes and small square chips, this monster sandwich took a bit of getting through. Ten O'clock would see the Van repacked and back on the road. This part of the drive was at a much slower pace on this part of the Taylor Highway due to the poor road service. A couple of hours would find me to the Tetlin Junction and the Pan American Highway, turning west I would travel the short distance to Tok Junction where I filled the mini with fuel as it was over 200km to Fairbanks. While there I bought some fresh fruit and water to drop in the side pocket as the weather was really hot and I had been warned that interior Alaska can get very hot this time of year. The day was moving on and my initial thought was to get to Fairbanks and make camp. Just before the city there is a military base, figuring that was the location the American family I had spent such a good time with back in Dawson that this was where they would be heading to spend time whilst being in the army. I searched for some time trying to find a campsite but found nothing thinking it was probably down to having so much military movement about this area why I couldn't find a camp site.

The Pam American runs straight past the Army Base and Fairbanks on it's way to Prudhoe Bay, not long after the

Fairbanks turning I caught site of the Alaskan pipeline that runs from Prudhoe to Valdez so I stopped to have a look at the roadside pull off.

Digression
Oil was first found back in 1968 at Prudhoe Bay but the pipeline was not built till 1975 and took two years to finish, this all came about because of the oil crisis of 1973. The biggest problem was the permafrost, so to overcome this it runs above and below ground and zig zags in places to allow for movement. The pipeline runs for 1300km and what is interesting if the flow were to stop or the throughput was too little the line could freeze. Alaska was formerly owned by Russia but in 1867 they sold the territory to the USA for seven point two million dollars and over the last fifty years have tried to claim it back. ~~

Travelling the way I do finds me loosing all track of time because I do not wear a watch, added to this is the extended day light this far North this time of the year. Now 9pm and I have not found a place to camp for the night yet. I pushed on knowing I had once again turned my back on civilisation and was heading further into The Last Frontier. The road was quiet but for a few big trucks and I soon came on a large truck stop, I decided to stop and fill up with fuel, whilst there I would check for any campsites. The lady at the truck stop told me that there weren't any official sites and the next gas station was way up the road at Coldfoot the best part of a day away. Thanking the lady for here help I drove on and found an old disused stone quarry that made a great place to stop for the night. The evening was still warm and dry so I just lifted the plastic boxes out from the rear and staked them at the side of the van; I then decided to give my evening meal a miss and climbed straight into bed.

Next morning, I had a big fry up of eggs and bacon with toast and tea all of this again cooked on my single ring Matty stove. The weather was warm and dry and decamping did not take long.

As I pulled out of the quarry and stopped to turn right, a double trailer big rig came by and blew its horns as a mark of respect. He too was north bound just like me, my day now started to feel special joining up with these guys on the Haul road. 60km on I would reach the end of the paved road and with it the last turning for 700km. I pull up and get out of the Mini to read the signs and take a couple of photo. One of the signs tells me that off to my right is a place called Livengood some 15km away, sounds like an interesting place if only for the name. The road across to the left was sign posted to Manley Hot Springs some 80km away that to sounds interesting enough to make me think about a detour, but right now I just wanted to keep heading north. Little did I know at that moment in time one day in the future I would get to visit Manley on a totally new adventure into the interior? Two other signs could be seen, one was green and said the Dalton Highway the other was a white sign telling me there was no fuel or recovery for 380km. The latter sign made me sit for a little while thinking back to when I was just a youngster and how I had studied an old map of Alaska, this road was just a squiggly line with no information on what was here, something that has haunted me for many years. I was now starting to get excited as it felt that very little had changed and I was about to find out.

I could see ahead of me that the road was not only uphill but the dirt was back. The climb was quite long and full of oversized stones, the best place to drive being in the centre, the only trouble with that was both up and down traffic liked that position for as long as they dared and inevitably traffic would have to take to the outer limits of the road and a very uncomfortable ride. Taking my time I eventually got to the top of the hill, thinking if this is what I am in for then the drive is going to be a disaster as I reached the top the hill the road levelled out and the surface suddenly changed to concrete and I relaxed. Bad move, as not long after I nearly wiped out the lower part of the van as it leaped into the air as I hit the end of a concrete slab that had been lifted by permafrost. A big bang came with the impact so I stopped fearing the worst, that the sump guard may have smashed into the engines sump and I would lose all my oil. On inspection I could see that the bang or crack must have been another knuckle joint and this was the only casualty, the sump guard having saved the day. Knuckle joint changed and oil checked I was back underway this time keeping much focused on the concrete surface, occasionally I had to pick my way round dips and joints that could cause damage. Some time on I learnt from one of the truckers that the America's wanted to concrete the road all the way to Prudhoe and it wasn't till after they had started that they had a mistake in wanting to pave it. Seems head office down in the lower 48 had not worked out what an enemy permafrost is. Not long after the concrete stopped and we were back on good old dirt. I loved this drive sharing it with the odd truck and place names such as Wiseman, Oil Spill Hill, Cobblers knob and No Name Creek.

Just before the Arctic Circle I had another knuckle joint break, so I opted to carry on the short distance to a safe pull in and a small area representing the 66.33 parallel and the line that tips you into the arctic. As I pulled in there were a couple of wooden notice boards, one of them read Alaska the last frontier. These few words stopped me in my

tracks and I became totally emotional as my eyes filled with tears. My life suddenly went into a fifty-year reverse to when I was a youngster and that one centre page picture I had seen in an old commercial transport magazine dad had brought home. The picture was taken in Alaska at the Arctic Circle and showed the middle of winter and those pioneering truck drivers who were trailblazing there way through an unknown territory in the thirties and forties.
I sat for some time reflecting on my life and how that one picture from back then had filled me with curiosity, decades on and I was here. None of this moment was ever concisely planned by me. Some things happen in life that you have no control over, be it for better or worse. Certain things in life are down to you, things like passing your driving test, having your own vehicle, the ability to learn, mend and fix things are attributes in the path of life. Working a long side my abilities is an inner mind that guides me to push doors open and reach out beyond the horizon and to look round that next corner, all of these thoughts I truly be leave have brought me to this day in time.

Emotions aside I get stuck into replacing yet another knuckle joint. It was still a mystery to me why they kept breaking, this time I would be left with only one in the spares box and the two fitted on the rear that I could take off and use, be it with a little modification to the rear suspension.

Back in the mini and mobile again I reached the other end of the run out that took me back onto the highway. It was at this point I saw a motor bike with the rider sitting on the floor with his helmet hanging off his forehead and over the back of his neck. I pulled up alongside him asking if he is OK.
 "I'm fine" he told me "The piston on the bike has a hole in it and I am waiting for a lift back down to Fairbanks."
We talked for a while before a truck pulled up and stopped. The driver got out wanting to know what the biker's problem was, then in no time we had lifted the bike onto an already loaded trailer, once it was tied down the truck driver and the biker climb into the truck cab and with a couple of long blasts on the trucks horns they were on their way, south bound.

Job done, I pushed on to Coldfoot Truck Stop keen to see this place as I had seen it on the Ice Road Truckers program on TV. Arriving at 5.30pm I set up camp opposite the fuel pumps on the only piece of proper grass to be found in the Arctic. The odd truck came and went after filling with fuel; some of them would stop for the night to rest up in their sleeper cabs. Deciding I would live the life of a trucker I joined a group at one of the tables in the café for a dinner that cost ten dollars. I helped myself from a row of hot dishes, where I could eat as much as I wanted. That evening I enjoyed sitting with a group of very friendly guys and girls for three hours or more before bedding down for the night. During the night I could hear the odd truck movement and the sound of air brakes, but in general it was quiet and I woke the next morning feeling refreshed. I took a shower then dined on a trucker's breakfast with as much free coffee as I wanted.

I had about 400km to reach the end of the road that day and it seemed to be taking forever to make any in-road into the mileage. There was very little traffic, only big rigs, as most people don't come up here other than the odd motor bike. The road just felt hard going and sapped my energy. It wasn't late in the day but I felt tired and I needed to maintain my concentration as I was getting close to the Brooks Range and Atigun Pass, a climb that would take me to an elevation of almost 5000 feet above sea level in one go and in doing so I would be crossing the continental divide. Approached the climb I speeded up and started the longer than average climb that seemed to go on forever, only disturbed by the odd truck and the sound of its engine exhaust brake as it descended the long climb. Getting close to the top I found myself climbing through the clouds which had a magical quality about it. Now down to first gear the vans engine started to falter and with that I started to worry about making the top. A little further on I found a safe place to stop and have a look at the engine. On getting out of the Van the penny dropped as I realised and felt the lack of air at this height being so high and so far north. Deciding there was nothing I could do I got back in the van and continued my drive still in and out of clouds while checking for trucks coming at me or from behind me. Having a CB would have been handy to have. Eventually I started the descent off the North Slope where the engine came back to life. I was now starting to see the beauty of the vast tundra and with it also came a change in temperature and an ice chilled wind. Whilst the run into Prudhoe Bay is now flat off to my right was a low strange looking mountain range the colour of pure white sand? It was now defiantly a lot colder here with the sky grey and dense that seemed to blend in with the surroundings. Driving round I looked for somewhere to camp, eventually I came on the Arctic Ocean and taking one look at the sea I decided to try and find accommodation for the night. Driving round I found two places, but both were full. Eventually I came upon a huge oblong building of modular units that was doubled stacked and very impressive. Pulling up I got out and was looking for a front door or a way in when an oil worker greeted me and asked if he could help. I told him I was looking for somewhere to sleep for the night, to which he replied, "Go on straight up those stairs to the second level buddy, and they will help you."

Digression
Just before arriving at Prudhoe Bay I got to Deadhorse and the location for everything oil industry related. The place was entirely built of prefabricated modules, shipped in by sea in the summer months when there is little ice, or by truck all year round up the haul road from Fairbanks. About 3000 people work there on shifts of four to six weeks turn round, flying in and out on two 747 planes owned by the oil company. Everything there has to be shipped in and having driven round this huge complex I got the distinct impression when they order one, they get ten, and when they order ten, they get twenty, given the stocks and machinery that were parked up in different company compounds. Search as much as I tried, I couldn't find a house or a shop and alcohol was completely banned. There was a quietness about the place maybe it was the scale of this man-made facility and the fact that everybody had their head down and getting on with there work. ~~

The wind and cold was noticeable as I climbed the steel stairs and on opening the door a warmth hit me and I told myself whatever it costs I am staying here tonight. Once inside I could see how clean it was and as I walked down a long corridor where at one point, I could see that one of the pods was full of washing machines. Finding my way to reception I asked if they had a room for the night. They did and the cost to me would be £100 but for that I got my evening meal and a breakfast that was as much as I could eat and the use of the spike room as they called it The spike room was a self-serve place that was full of food that the workers helped themselves to and took out with them to their work station. The man at reception told me about the laundry room, and I was just to make myself at home. To heck with it, you only live once and today had been a tough one so I handed over my Dollars and headed to my room. The room was clean and warm so I showered first then changed into the cleanest cloths I could find before setting off to the dining room to sample the food. I joined a short queue and picked up a plate deciding pretty quickly that I would have a steak. The lady behind the counter took my plate and duly planted a very large piece of meat onto the plate then handed it back to me. I looked down at the plate then looked back up at the lady. She asked me if there was a problem to which I replied "No, but where am I going to put the vegetables? To which she responded" Just take another plate sir." Smiling I thanked her.

I joined a couple of workers at one of the tables and we talked mainly about my trip whilst plodding my way through a large piece of beef then finally managing to eat a dessert also. After about an hour I headed back to my room and set up the recharging of my cameras before collecting any dirty clothes I could find and going to the laundry for the next hour.

Digression
Oil workers are some of the best fed people in the world; I can vouch for that having spent time in the oil industry as a hovercraft engineer in the Caspian Sea. ~~

Today was the 22nd of July and a full moon that night, but that wouldn't make any difference as I was in the land of the midnight sun and the blinds on the window were struggling to keep the light out. I noticed I had the best signal on my phone for months and apparently the oil company had its own satellite connection, so I sat down and sent text messages to friends and family letting them know I was well and had made it to Prudhoe Bay. That done I settled down on my bed in the hope of getting some sleep, when suddenly out of the blue my phone rang and it was Tugs, one of my rally friends and someone who had put a lot of work into the building of the van with me. We chatted and he congratulated me on my achievement. I thanked him but told him not to stay on the line for too long as it would cost him a fortune. "Don't worry Diddy, it is worth it considering what you have done so far." I thanked him and we chatted for a while. Evan with the blinds closed it was bright sunlight and in the end I placed a pillow over my head to try and cut the light out and get some sleep.

Next morning on opening the blinds I could see the weather had changed to become misty and grey looking. Showering first I then headed for a mega breakfast before heading to the spike room to fill two brown bags with food. One I filled with fruit the other with milk and drinks which I took out to the van first before vacating my room and packing my cloths back in the mini. The only job now was to return my room key to reception before revisiting the spike room for one last time to get some salad meals that would keep for a few days in the cold weather. Well I had been told to help myself so the stopover was cost effective I felt in the end.

To get to this part of the world turned out to be very economical for me and was reflected by the kind words that had come in my surprised phone call last night.

By 10.30 I was heading on the return journey south to get back to Coldfoot for the night. Soon after leaving I broke another knuckle joint and had to stop and change it in cold of the wind that was now blowing, and so because of this it took me long to sort than normal. Back on my way I joined a couple of trucks on the tundra that soon took off faster than my pace and in doing so leaving the road well clear ahead for me. I eventually reached the north slope and the climb back over the Brookes Range, with this side being a longer climb but not as steep as the other side. Progress through Atigun Pass was slow as the cloud formation had blanketed the climb due to the cold wind blowing in poor weather from the Arctic Ocean. Once at the top of the pass the weather improved, and on my way down and on my way down the other side I saw a couple of cyclists standing at the side of the road, slowing as I approached them they gave me the thumbs up so I kept going. Progress was good till I heard a bang at the bottom of the pass and once again it turned out to be a knuckle joint, my fifth joint to let go, so I pulled clear of the road into an entry to one of the many pumping stations used on the pipe line.

Thinking I had used all my knuckle joints I suddenly remembered that I was carrying a brand new ride height kit in my spares pack so I was covered should I have another brakeage. This joint took some time to replace as I had trouble trying to get the ball part of the joint out of its plastic socket in the top arm. There was nothing to grip, but eventually patience paid off with the help of a chisel and a lot of positivity. Just as I was finishing the repair the two cyclists I passed earlier stopped to talk. They were students from Anchorage and had taken the train to Fairbanks and then decided they would cycle to Deadhorse and back to Fairbanks during their summer holidays. I told them I admired the challenge they had taken on and wished them good luck for the rest of the journey. Van repaired and tools stored back in the foot well I finally checked about that I was leaving the place as I had found it. Climbing back into my trusty stead and on the move I soon caught up with the cyclists. They waved as I passed them and I tooted my horn whilst thinking what it must be like for two cyclists to carry everything they need from food to a tent over such a distance, and all with no back up for them.

The run into Coldfoot took just over two hours and when I got there the first job was to wash the back door as I had collected so much mud it needed peeling off before I could access the rear door. That done I topped up the vans fuel tank then set up camp before eating in the tent with some of the food stock I had collected from the Prudhoe oil site lodgings. With little else to do bedtime came at ten, and I slept well till about six. I had a simple breakfast of cornflakes and milk before packing up and bidding farewell to the Coldfoot Truck stop.

Digression
Coldfoot truck stop is what the name says a place mainly for truck drivers to stop, eat and fuel up, half way along the Dalton Highway and is seen as an oasis in a part of the world that can take lives any time of the year. There are only six permanent residents all year-round. The place was formerly a mining camp at the begging of the 1900's and in its hay day it boasted several stores, a gambling house, and many saloons. The name Coldfoot was given to the place by the prospectors who went looking for gold in the Arctic conditions, but would only get so far then turn back. ~~

With still some miles to cover I settled down to push on and try to make Fairbanks that night, but unfortunately this was short lived as another knuckle joint, the third on this road, the vehicle had once again succumbed to the rigors of the haul road. Fitting a new one took under the hour as by now I had learned my lesson of keeping a spare joint in the door pocket. By doing this I did not have to remove most of the items from the rear of the van to access the floor box that holds the spares. It was early evening before I came off the Dalton, at the cross roads once again near Livengood. I opted to stop at the quarry I had used five days before and set up my camp for a couple of days. That evening supper was chicken noodles followed by English muffins and two mugs of tea, as I needed to use up the milk, I had collected in Prudhoe as it would soon go off because I was back into warm weather. Bed time came at ten and I lay there thinking how well the van had done having driven up and down what was a harsh demanding road.

The knuckle joint breakages did not make sense and as hard as I tried, I did not have the answer as to why it kept happening. Having gone through six units I was now out of spares, but the plus side was I had returned to paved roads. Tomorrow would be a day of checking over the van and its tyres, as the rear ones looked distinctly bald.

Breakfast was egg butties with tomato sauce helped down with black tea, making me think that I would drive into Fairbanks and do a shop later in the day then return back to the quarry. Not long after breakfast I set about looking over the tyres that had served me well, with not a single puncture to date. I put that down to the tyre liquid I used on the tyres. Removing the wheels and tyres it soon became apparent that the liquid had worked on a few occasions, as signs could be found on the inner side of the steel rims that were bent. For spares I had four wheels and tyres, two were part used M&S quarter studded ice type tyres fitted to the front of the roof in the same way the long-distance rally teams would fit them. The other two standard rim and tyres stayed in the roof box so I finished up with two new ones to the front and the old front ones went on the back making the vehicle legal again. The two rear tyres were well worn, but mainly on the outside almost to the point of a full line of canvas running round the tyre. This was due to two things; one the weight but mainly because of the tracking on the rear was producing too much toe in and made for so much scuffing to the rear tyres. The only other thing I found that needed to be fixed was the nut that holds the small bracket on the end of the spindle into the carburettor was missing. The bracket is where the throttle cable is connected. How long it had been missing and the fact it had stayed in place was beyond me but a new nut would sort the problem.

Having got through my job list and with the weather being good I drove into Fairbanks to shop basically for food and liquids as the forecast was showing a heat wave over the coming week. Now happy to have some fresh milk and fruit I went back to the quarry and my camp deciding I would stay out of Fairbanks for the weekend. I did nothing but sunbath and eat, and the quarry became my own oasis of peace and quiet that would last till Monday morning when I would break camp and head into Fairbanks and a car wash, that I had spotted on my shopping trip. The weekend pasted to quick and Monday would find me arriving at the car wash where I would spend one and a half hours of time on the mini and the much-needed wash to every place to get rid of months of dirt and small stones. Finally finished it looked great and then it surprised me when it started on the first turn of the key. By midday I was on my way opting to bypass the city and keep heading south with some thoughts of how close I could get to Russia.

The weather was perfect and with the road smooth and easy on the mini I made good progress south down the George R Parks Highway for several hours until I came to a turn off to the right and a poster advertising a Bluegrass Festival that was happening the following weekend. This was only Monday and as the festival didn't start till Friday, I was a little disappointed I would miss it. At the junction there was a board showing that the Lions had a RV campsite so I decided to drive the 9km into the small town of Anderson. Following the camp site arrows till I eventually came on a couple of guys putting steel posts into the ground. I stopped and spoke to them telling them I was in the Lions back home. The main guy in charge was Carl and he told me what they were doing, and as I had plenty of time I offered to stay around and help.

Parking the mini out of the way I teamed up with a chap called Jethro putting more steel stakes in for the car parking area. He told me that the festival had been running for 22 years and thousands of people turn up from all over Alaska and the Aleutian Islands. Shortly after Jethro had to leave, so I went and helped Carl for a while before cleaning the rust off the park entry gates before giving them a coat of paint. In the meantime, Carl had organised a meal for us which his wife Karen brought to us. What a meal, spare ribs and macaroni followed by strawberries and cream. We worked till ten that night, then I had a shower in the toilet block as Carl had showed me how to by-pass the dollar slot machine so I could shower as many times as I wanted. That night was a great sleep, having done some proper physical work for the first time in ages. Sleep was good that night along with the thought of helping others.

The previous afternoon I had set up my camping patch in a quiet corner away from the main outdoor stage and the area where the stalls would be. Over the next four days a small team of us worked together till ten each evening, bar one night when we finished at six, when we all went to the pub for a sit down meal and a few drinks and lots of laughter. Friday morning was spent mainly directing traffic and people onto the site to park as the festival would be starting at midday with the music continuing well into the early hours of Saturday morning.

Staying in bed till ten as it was going to be a long day I then walked to the shower block occasionally seeing the odd tent or camper van door open and the first of movement of people that had arrived early. After grabbing a quick shower, I checked in with Carl to see if there was anything that he wanted doing. He asked me to take his quad bike and trailer to go round the site and fit new plastic bin bags into the drums. I enjoyed doing this as I got to stop and chat too many of the people over the next couple of hours who were now on this huge site. That afternoon I got to help for a while behind the bar, occasionally having to climb into the back of the forty feet Budweiser trailer to extract several crates of beer. Later I went for a walk around to have a look at the stalls and the people behind them, as the festival was a mecca for people of all ages with all types of beliefs. The festival was laid back and the music never seemed to start on time even though there was a program of times and musicians. Feeling hungry I went for a burger and a beer that came free with my jobs. I joined the crowd and found a seat close to the stage; the music had started with a group of six guys from Kodiak Island each of them playing different string instruments with my favourite the banjo plucking away in the background, with the occasional solo.

Having enjoyed the music for an hour I thought I would check in with Jethro who was running the bar, but on the way back and threading my way round the many tables of people, I spotted the two cyclists I had met more than a week ago on the haul road at Atigun Pass. I stopped and chatted for a while and lt transpired that not long after I had waved them farewell they had decided to get a lift from one of the big trucks the rest of the way back to Fairbanks then cycle on to Anderson and the Bluegrass Festival. The guys had decided to stay overnight so I joined them for a couple of hours before going to bed with the music still playing strong till about two or three o'clock on Sunday morning.

We had been so lucky with the weather and on Sunday morning there was definitely a slow start for everyone as people sat around talking and slowly packing their vehicles to make ready for the trip back home. This gave me the opportunity to seek out one of the banjo players from Kodiak who had offered to give me an hour's free lesson on my own banjo. Eventually finding the musicians tent that distinctly looked like the site of a prospector's camp, the musicians beckoned me to join them. I stayed a while in their company before returning to the mini with my banjo having been shown a few practice cords to learn.

Being in that part of the world gave me a different aspect on life, one that I could easily get used to, so I was more than happy to stick around and help the gang and start the big clean up that would take us through Sunday and Monday till about 9pm that evening. With what seemed like everything was done the last six of us that sat round a log fire pit roasting large pieces of steak while knocking back a few well-earned beers till about midnight. It was then Carl jumped up and said "Come on let's go and take the Quad bikes, you can take the grey one Dave and follow us." So with that thought I jumped on the quad bike and took off after the others, who had disappeared by now into the bushes? I eventually caught up with them as they had stopped; pulling up next to Carl he asked me if I was ok. I told him I was and I was enjoying this madness along with the smell of the wood around us. That's when he turned and looked at me and laughed "That smell is legal in this state." I got off the bike and walked over to Carl and asked him to slap me, to which he replied if you would like some ask Karen. I smiled and said "No thank you, I am fine just to follow your tails" and with that we sped off for the next two hours driving in and out of the undergrowth and river just having a great time under a brightly lit sky.

Now into my eighth day at Anderson and having had a late night it was ten before I got up to join Carl and Jethro for a couple of hours and the last bit of tidying up. Happy that all the jobs had been done we went back to Carls for something to eat. Karen had cooked a meal and invited fellow Lions along to join us as I had planned to leave at about two in the afternoon. My last hour with those wonderful people was quite emotional, as we all reflected on the past week on how we had raised forty thousand dollars for good causes. Come three o'clock, I picked myself up and hugged each and every one, wishing and hoping that one day I would return and be able to do it all again. Little did I know but the following year would be the last festival year and like many good things in life it would disappear for ever?

As I drove back through the woods in the direction of the main highway, I came to a junction where I turned left and on stopping I looked to the right and in the distance I could see a sign post that read the word Clear. I did not think much about it till I looked straight ahead, that when I could just about make out a substantial high fence, that when I put two and two together and realised that beyond the fence and hidden in the trees was the American top secret tracking station run by the US army.

That afternoon I only drove for three hours, as I felt tired and I had decided to pull in at Cantwell RV camp and set my tent before heading straight to the laundry room as I had a full sack of dirty washing from a dusty festival week. That evening while chatting with the camp owner he told me about the fires that were burning and with the wind they were spreading fast. I told him that I had been at Anderson for the festival and that was when he told me one of the fires was only about two miles from there and it is thought that Anderson/ Clear may have to be evacuated anytime.

Next morning, I was up bright and early to check on the fires as I wanted to arrive in Anchorage today and would need to keep an eye on the fires that were burning. It was about 200km to Anchorage and for the first 100km I could see several fires and lots of smoke. Further on I passed Mount McKinley on the right and by early afternoon I arrived in Anchorage to track down a music shop to get some spare strings and steel picks for my banjo as I was told by the guys back at the Blue Grass Fest. They also gave me the directions to get there, they were spot on and I stayed a little while looking round and talking to the owner before heading to the Visitor Centre. Just as I got to the Visitor Centre a Range Rover pulled alongside and waved, It was a couple I had met at the festival who had been responsible for all the sound electronics and speakers over the weekend. We talked and agreed to meet up later on that evening for a drink. Inside the centre I picked up some information, and one of the young girls told me about a small campsite almost in the middle of the city, at a place called Ship Creek. Before thanking the staff they insisted in taking some photos of me with the mini outside the information centre.

It was still reasonable early as I climbed back into the Mini so I went for a drive round to find the pub where I was to meet up later on with the sound crew. The drive round Anchorage was easy and it would be difficult to get lost due to the block road system the Americans use in their cities. One place I wanted to visit was the rail head of the Alaskan railroad, if only to hear that great sound from those huge horns, especially when heard in the interior of the wilderness. After visiting the rail station, I found the campsite that had to be the smallest one I had stopped at so far. Having said that, it had everything the traveller needed so I booked two nights stay. Washed and dressed I walked the short distance to the pub to meet up with the guys from the Bluegrass bash. We had a great evening of music along with a huge meal of seafood that comes from the glacier waters in this part of the world. God bless them, they paid for my meal and told me they would love to go to Scotland. The music lasted till midnight and shortly after I made my way back to camp, pleased that they had spotted me in the city earlier on in the day. My sleep that evening was only disturbed by the occasional sound of train horns some distance away.

Next morning after breakfast and as the weather was so good I went for a walk round the city centre looking at its many shops and especially the Hudson Bay company stores where I finished up having my lunch, before making tracks for the industrial hub of the city and taking in some of the workings that keeps so many parts of the interior supplied all year round. Next morning, I finished of some laundry and had a couple of hours on the camps internet sending messages back home, I even got to have a short talk with my daughter Louise before I left at three in the afternoon from what was again an oasis on my travels.

Leaving anchorage on Saturday meant I had to join the weekend traffic. My destination was the end of the road at Homer but that was at least three or four days away. The highway runs parallel with an inlet called Turnagain Arm and this area is steeped in Captain Cook stuff so when I got to Cook Inlet, I stopped to read up on him at one of the turn offs that gave information. It seems Cook had arrived here thinking it was the North West Passage but had to turn round as there was no way through. Once again, I was pleased with my adventure as I had learned something I was never taught at school. The drive crosses many rivers which run into the sea and I couldn't help but notice people fishing in the river many of who were women with families enjoying the good weather. That night I stayed at the small ski resort of Girdwood. It was out of season and quiet, so I found a corner in the car park to camp and then took a walk round the huge log lodge that was beautiful and covered in flowers and roses.

The next morning, I was up and away out of the car park early in case I should not have camped there. The morning drive wound left and right as the road made its way inland for a little time, and eventually I came to the turn off for the small historic mining town of Hope and my campsite for the night. People still lived there in the old buildings that looked like they could fall over any time. Driving through the town of no more than a dozen buildings I came to a dead end and found a spot to camp in the corner of a car park. After setting up camp I went for a walk to look at the buildings, the mine entrance, and the old equipment that goes back to the 1900's and has been preserved. I was able to get a real feeling of how it must have been all those years ago. Walking back, I came upon an old timer outside a small wooden building. He was sitting on a bench having a beer so I stopped and we chatted. He nodded his head upwards and I raised my head to read the sign above which said Saloon. He then told me, if you're going in for one, and then observe the notice by the door that read, Leave All Guns behind the Bar. It would have been fool hardy of me to have come this far and not to go in and have one on such a warm evening, so I stayed and had a couple of beers, really getting a sense of the history as the Saloon just looked and felt right, as I ran my eyes round the room.

As I looked across the fields that evening, I settled down to cook some salmon that had been given to me when I stopped to watch some people fishing on one of the rivers. I slept well and just had toast and marmalade for breakfast before packing up and getting back on the road for ten. Having good weather made driving through the Kenai Peninsula a joy and before long I reached the junction for the Stirling Highway that would take me west towards the coast again. Just before four o'clock I reached the town of Soldotna where I stopped to do a shop for food, and while packing the van a guy with two young people came over to talk to me. The older man was an American, his name was Shamus, and his son was called Patrick and he was accompanied by his girlfriend Jemmy. They were on vacation and had rented a cabin there in town on the Kenai River and as they had a spare room, I was invited to join them for the night. They told me to use the shower and laundry facilities, and that evening I joined them outside for dinner and beers on the patio. I even tried to do some fishing later on in the evening all to no avail.

Next morning, I woke to the smell of breakfast with smells I could easily recognise and entering the kitchen I found Shamus had set the table and was ready to dish up. While at the table he told me about a problem he was having with his Cadillac and wondered if I could take a look after breakfast. Fearing the worst, I said yes. The only vehicle I had seen was the 4x4 they had at the shops and when I went out to the front, Patrick got in the 4x4 and reversed it out of the way from the door of the garage at which point Shamus backed out this huge big black Cadillac that gave me the frights, thinking what have I let myself in for, as the engine sounded like a bag of spanners.

"I have a problem with the suspension Dave", said Shamus "as it won't stay up for long on the rear."

After asking a few questions I soon found out that it was not like our standardised suspension, but air cushioned. Trying to show willing I offered to have a look if they would leave me to it for a while. This seemed to work as they went away to do some fishing. I spent the next hour trying to follow and figure out how the system worked and with Shamus having told me the problem was on the rear, which was where I started to look. Mindful that the suspension would not stay raised, I started the monster up and went to the mini to get the two spare wheels from the roof box and place them under the car for safety. Crawling under the back I found that the suspension canisters units had plastic pipes going to both of them. Eventually I found that on the nearside lift unit and where the input air pipe is fitted, if I bent it slightly it leaked so I reckoned what was happening was that air would leak out each time the car went over any bumps as the movement caused the pipe to flex and leak a small amount of air. Happy in my mind this was the problem I went and caught up with Shamus and explained what I had found. He agreed it made sense as it did not happen all the time. I took him outside and got Patrick to go under the car and I pointed out the pipe that I thought could be fixed with just a cut of the pipe and the fitting of a new olive. Shamus offered to pay me but I declined his offer and told him and his family that it was time for me to move on. I collected my few things together and stored them back in the mini before thanking them for their kindness. Shamus and his family asked me where my next stop was.

"The end of the road" at Homer I said "Then Russia if possible." "Well we wish you good luck with that my friend."

Chapter 12
This is the end of the road

A couple of hours driving would find me reaching the top of a big climb, I pulled into a flower covered viewing point to stop and take a look at the panoramic surroundings. To my right far out to sea was the Aleutian Islands and turning to my left I could see the Kenai mountains and glaciers running into Kachemak Bay. Bringing my eyes back across the bay I could see below me the edge of town and a dark piece of land shaped like an explanation mark running into the bay, which could only be the Homer Spit.

I was magnetised seeing the spit and I had to go and seek it out having heard so much about this small piece of land. I climbed back into the mini, passing a sign that read Homer the Halibut Capital of The World. The downhill run was quiet and when I reached the first houses there seemed to be a relaxed feeling about the place that I liked. Before long I found myself on the spit. I drove all the way to the end then turning round I drove a short distance back where I had spotted a fish and chip shop. It had been some time since I'd eaten that very much British meal out of paper, so I purchased a large portion and went for a wander round. My first port of call was the small souvenir shop from the Time Bandit one of the fishing vessels from the TV program the Deadliest Catch and while inside I spoke with the girl who ran the shop. Her name was Lu and I told her my daughter's name was Louise. She told me her dad had named her Lu so it could not be shortened.

While on the spit I called into the Salty Dawg Pub. It was the size of a small garage and is well known in Alaska having the walls and ceiling covered in assorted dollar notes. When I spoke with the owner Jim, he gave me a sticker for the rear of the van.

Digression
Homer Spit is the world's longest drive out into the sea, and at almost five miles long it has lots of things happening there all connected to the sea. The small boats harbour takes up a big part, and equally does the basin for the sea going boats many of them well known for fishing king crab. On land you can find assorted small interesting shops even a London double decker bus that has been turned into a café. Little did I know in the years to come I would return to Homer many times and also to the Spit? ~~

Digression
The following is a short story from a forthcoming return to Homer. It was tinged with sadness that was soon followed with a celebration of the lady's life.

My involvement had come about when myself and a friend had been asked if we would go along to a small birthday party being held for a lady who had cancer and was very, very ill seems she did not have long to live. The idea was that the two of us would drop in unannounced on the all-female party one afternoon and perform the Full Monty all unbeknown to the lady who was ill. The afternoon went well and the lady was very pleased. I remember her husband coming to me while in the Salty Dawg during the celebrations and thanking me for giving his wife such a memorable moment in the last few days of her life. Whenever I hear Donna Summer and "I Need Some Hot Stuff Baby," it takes me right back to that day. The boat harbour on the spit would also become a place to launch a few different adventures in the years ahead and perhaps one day I will recall them. ~~

I could camp on the spit, but as they wanted twenty dollars for the view and no facilities, I went in search for a place out of town in the country. After eight miles I found a spot close to a Russian village that had a great view across the bay to the glaciers. That night I settled for chicken noodles, as dinner had been earlier with the fish and chips. Bed time came at nine after sitting watching the sun set behind the Glacier Mountains.

I woke at 9.30 a.m. to a dull overcast day, but I could still see the glaciers with the tops covered in low cloud across the bay. Breakfast was cornflakes followed by egg on toast and a mug of tea. Decamping I was keen to restock my food stores, so I drove back in to town to the large super market I had seen the previous day and interestingly enough it was called Safeway, a name that used to be familiar back in the Uk once upon a time. The Safeway store became a much-visited place over the coming month as I could buy most of what I needed there. The internet instore was great for catching up on people back home, and most mornings I would appear and order my first coffee of the day called a 16oz drip, the refill was half price, so I would stay a while and watch the world go by.

Happy having updated everybody back home I decided to head back to the mini. When I got to the vehicle a lady was looking at the stickers on the rear door and commented on the one the Salty Dawg Pub had given me. We talked a while and she told me that she owned the local book store and if I follow her to the shop, she would like to give me another sticker to put on the van. I duly followed her back to the shop and to get my sticker and while there I learned her name was Mary. She asked me if she could ring her husband who ran the local newspaper to come along and interview me for an article. Eventually I gave in and said okay. Looking out of the shop window I saw a big Jaguar pull up and an elderly guy get out and look over the mini. He walked into the book shop and introduced himself as Bill De Creeft telling me that he had a 1961 mini cooper and would I come round and see him. We walked outside and I had a look over the Jag. We continued our conversation, and before Bill left, he gave me a piece of paper with his details on, and I promised to call round after seeing the guy from the Homer News.

Two cups of tea later Mary's husband Michael turned up at the shop and we sat down to do a short interview. He asked me a lot of questions, one of them, why Homer as this is the end of the road? I told him I believed there was stuff happening here as there always is at the end of a road to nowhere, and I wanted to find out more. When we had finished the interview, we went outside and Michael took some photos of me with the mini. I went back inside to thank the staff for their kindness and climbed back in the mini I headed by the Safeway store and onto the narrow causeway with the float plane lake on my left. Taking the next turning I arrived at Bill's office on the edge of the lakeside where I met Bill and his wife Barbara.

We sat and drank coffee while Bill gave me a run down on his life and how he had now closed his business called Kachemak Air Service that he started back in 1967. At seventy-seven years of age he was now retired and he told me about the many planes he had had over that period of time, and how he now just kept one small float plane on the lake by the old office. Keen to show me the mini cooper I jumped into Bill's pickup and we drove over to where he lived. Pulling up at the rear of his log house I could see an old wooden open fronted shed that had a mixture of car and plane bits in, mainly covered in dust. We both got out and I followed Bill to a huge shed with two very big doors. Opening one of the doors I walked into a world that was back in time. Looking at the vehicles alone there were two old Jag's, a Mini Cooper and a very old and rare American Peirce car plus a jeep, hanging from the roof where a couple of plane wings. Before leaving Bill told about a problem he was having with the distributor on one of the Jag's and I promised to take a look the following day.

Back at the lakeside Bill told me I could set up my camp and use the office bathroom and shower whenever I wanted, so I set about laying out my camp and while fitting the tent to the rear of the van Bill came over and said "Hurry up the weather is good so we will go for an hours flight over the glaciers across the bay." I was completely stunned by his offer which I gratefully accepted, but I was just a little nervous in flying in such a small plane for the first time. The plane was tied up just on the dock in front of us. Bill completed a few checks then shouted over to tell me he was ready for heading out, so I jumped in through the side door and got into my seat that was positioned behind Bill due to the plane cockpit being so narrow. Slowly we taxied across the lake checking for any incoming planes and on reaching the western end of the lake Bill made a few adjustments to knobs and levers before pushing the throttle forward, and I watched the wave of water coming off the two floats as the nose lifted into the wind. We were soon clear of the water and making a turn for the bay. Looking out of the right-side window I could see water and turning the other way all I could see was sky. Soon after we levelled out and I started to relax, admiring the stunning views. As we got closer to the mountains and the glaciers, Bill pointed to things while talking to me over the head sets. Now we were flying close to the glaciers and he told me that as a pilot you had to be so careful when entering a gully or small valley as the wind could stall the plane and you would find yourself with not enough room to turn. Not long after it became very noticeable how the wind was starting to buffet the plane around like a leaf in the wind, and shortly after Bill decided to abort going any further up the glacier and with a well-timed turn on a gust of wind we exited the gully, and I sat back pretending not to look at the steep side of the mountain. We flew for another half an hour before returning to land safely back on the lake. I had fully enjoyed every moment, even when I was nervous, but I trusted my pilot he had been flying for years and had nothing to prove for a man of his age. Before leaving Homer I would fly again with Bill and several other guys.

As I sat down that evening at my lakeside camp, I reflected on the day's activities thinking how much I had enjoyed the many friendly people that I had met on my first full day in Homer.

I was up early the following day and had eaten by the time Bill came down to the lake. We headed out to a car parts store to get some new points to go in the distributor of the V12 Jag and back at the shed I fitted the new parts. Bill was happy with what I had done and he asked me if I would dog sit for a few days while he and Barbara, along with their granddaughter, went to Anchorage the following day on a shopping trip to buy clothes for the youngster.

The weather had turned to rain, so I walked the short distance to the laundrette as my sleeping bag and clothes needed washing properly. This was another great place to spend a few hours, they had great showers and perfect internet access and it was a place that I would get to use many times then and also in future years. Getting back to the lakeside I found the location I had parked the van, but where I had put the tent up had flooded. There was a couple of inches of water in the tent area with my plastic boxes were floating around inside. Seeing this I decided to sleep in the van and just to leave moving it in the rain, hoping it would stop raining during the night and that the water would go down.

The following morning was dry and my pond had disappeared so I packed my campsite up and headed the short distance to Bill's house, as he and the family would be leaving that morning for Anchorage. I drove the van round to the rear and parked the mini under the shed taking out the plastic boxes as I was happy to sleep in the van where all my needs would be around me, just leaving the use of the bathroom and washing facilities in the house. I had just finished setting up the mini when a guy arrived, his name was Mike. It seemed seems Bill had rung him the previous day so that he could come and meet me. Mike was a pilot and a medic, just to name a few of the talents he possessed. He and I hit it off pretty quickly and soon after, the two of us were under a 1938 Dodge pickup truck belonging to Bill taking the gearbox out. Mike must have seen my capabilities because he soon whisked me away in his truck down to the air field to his hangar and his hide away. Walking in I soon felt at home as it was full of interesting things, with most of them in bits. The biggest bit was a Russian Antonov AN-2 Plane sitting on the right-hand side of the hanger. The plane was minus its wings with a deer head sticking out of the pilot's cockpit window. In the bottom left-hand corner of the hangar was the open office come work bench come canteen come bedsit with couch, well you get the general idea, and it looked great and lived in. That afternoon we messed about outside at the back of the hangar trying to start an old campervan all to no avail, even when we tried to pull start it. Little did I know at that time this was a sign of things to come as I would join Mike McCann on a many more adventures in the years ahead?

Digression
I first met Mike McCann in Homer in 2009 and during my month long stay we met up and did lots of things together. Mike was born in New York and in his youth he enjoyed some interesting times before hitching across the US and making a base in Montana and Alaska. Mike always had many of his own projects on the go, far too many, and he would jump from one to another. Normally you can work round and achieve a finish, but the trouble was that Mike would make himself available to one and all, never turning anybody down if they needed help, so it would look like he was going backwards with his own projects and endeavours. One thing I learned early on was to hang on to his shirt tail as hard as you could. His generosity far outweighed what he may have got in return, but rarely did he ask for anything in return. Mike is a giver, not a taker. Over the years I have spent time in Ireland, Montana and Alaska with Mike and a huge chunk of the time in Alaska flying with him in his Piper Cherokee plane, getting around to places like Homer, Fairbanks and Tanana on the Yukon River. We did things that will stay as memories in my mind forever. Mike is friends with many people round the world and each of them have their own stories and connection with him as he has with them. Mike is a one off in this world and you would have to have spent real time with him to understand why I say that. I often wish we had met twenty or thirty year ago, but then I stop and tell myself how lucky I was the day Mike McCann walked into Bill De Greefts big shed. There aren't many days when I don't look out for Mike's shirt tail, well why wouldn't I as you never know where it will take you or what we may get up to. Mike has written a couple of books that I can guarantee you will enjoy. One is, Give Me the Hudson or the Yukon the other is, Return to The River.

For me Mike is a special guy and I miss our time together. Mike can be seen now and again wearing an old T-shirt or top with Run-a-muck Tours etched into the clothing and if you get close enough you can read his motto, No Plans – Shit Happens. Long may you let me be proud to wear my Engineer/ Co-Pilot top whenever we get together? Thank you Mr President and Bela, Vice President. ~~

Later on, Mike dropped me back at Bill's place and while we were there, he received a phone call from Bill telling us that there was a problem with the Jag and he had put Barbara and his granddaughter on a plane at Kenai airport and he was limping back to Homer. About an hour later Bill arrived explaining there was a shudder problem with the brakes. I told him that I would take a look the following day, so with that, and Barbara not being there, Bill took me for a pizza and a beer before I went to bed.

Next morning Bill was round at eight, as I lay in the van parked under the shed, to tell me breakfast was on the go. Soon after I was working on the front brakes of the Jag and soon established that the problem was a couple of sticking pistons, so I freed them off and cleaned the pads and rebuilt the units before fitting the wheels and road testing. All was good. What I did find was a sticking throttle and eventually sorted that by making a new bush and fitting it to the accelerator shaft. Job done and Bill was more than happy. Just then Mike turned up so all three of us went down to the airfield to have a look at the gearbox we had taken out of the old dodge pick-up. We took the top off the box where the gear stick goes in and found a worn part that we added a little weld to, that would sort the problem. Happy with the outcome we went for a burger down on the spit. These two guys were great fun to be around and I could listen to both of them all day. Mike went his way and Bill and I went back to his house as he was going to collect Barbara from the airport. Bill suggested I took the van down to the lakeside office and bedded down there.

Next morning, I drove to the café just by the laundrette and had scrambled eggs on toast with tea, and while there, Bill arrived out front as he had tracked me down, which was not hard to do in small place like Homer. Bill came in and joined me for coffee and gave me the local newspaper with the article about my travels. The article made for a couple of interesting days for me. I was recognised while dropping in on shops with the mini, even to the point that whenever I went to the gas station the attendant would come out and fill the tank for me. I still had to pay though as I was not that famous yet. I finished breakfast and Bill suggested I left the mini there while we went in the Jag as he wanted to show me a few places where I could get nuts, bolts and the such like, so I climbed in the car and sat back while we drove passed the back of the airport were Mike's hangar was situated, then on passed the boat yard to a huge warehouse called the Gear Shed, a place that was stoked with tools, equipment and all things small, that you can bolt, screw and fix with. While having coffee with Bill that morning we had spoken about the Mini Cooper and that he had been thinking of having it restored. I offered to strip the car back to the bare shell and suggested that if he sent it away to a specialised restorer of mini bodies, which could be found in Canada, then if he was happy I would return and rebuild the parts back in to the restored body as and when, if he wanted me to.

Monday morning found Mike coming round to help Bill and myself get the Mini Cooper out as it was buried in the back of the big shed. We had two Jags' and a couple more cars to move before we could get the mini into a workable position for me to make a start. It would be the afternoon before we finally got all the vehicles back into the shed. I told Bill I would just drain the oil and water off, and make a fresh start tomorrow as it would give me a clear day to focus on removing the engine and all the equipment from under the bonnet. For the next four or five days I got into a routine of getting up and going to the boat yard café for breakfast, then coming back and working on the mini then in the evening going round to the laundrette to shower and doing any washing that was needed. Slowly I began to strip the mini of its mechanical parts, then the bodywork, down to a bare shell. The condition of the shell was not bad for its age. One thing that did mystify me though was the dotted marks on the paint work all over the car's roof and wings. Eventually Bill told me that they were caused by volcanic ash following an eruption many years back. His answer led me to understand why so many signs can be seen on the roads close to the sea that said, Tsunami Evacuation Route.

The weekend found me invited to join Bill and Barbara for a cocktail evening at one of their close friends, who it seemed, wanted to meet me as I was from Scotland and they had seen the article and picture of me with the mini. I headed early to the laundry and showered so I would get to Bill's on time for five as agreed. Once there he asked me if I would follow him to the venue in the minivan and he would go in the V12 Jag. The drive from Bill's took us from sea level up a tight and twisting road known as the Skyline Road to the top of the mountains overlooking Kachemak Bay and I soon realised Bill wanted to prove something with the Jag, but I resisted being drawn into his little scheme as he was well into his seventies and Barbara was sitting alongside him. We arrived at our destination; it was a lovely big log cabin with many out buildings. I stepped out and met Jim and Jean, our hosts, and once inside I was whipped off with Bill to Jim's den to check out the malt whiskeys. Jean had prepared a spread of food for the many people who had come along for the evening. I decided not to eat too much as I had an eight o'clock appointment with a group of young people at the small village hall. This had come about because I had been approached by a teacher when I was getting into the van a few days ago, and she asked me if I would come along and give a talk to a group of youngsters about my adventures. The evening had been another great experience of being treated so kindly almost like royalty among such wonderful people. Returning to the lakeside at ten thirty I bedded down in the office just as the rain started.

Next morning, I was back at the boat yard café for breakfast and by now I was familiar with the locals who came in, and also the staff who looked after me so well with extra large portions and endless tea. Returning to the lake I found Bill was getting ready to take two people out on a paid flight over the glaciers. I watched him take off and I settled down to write up my log. Mike came down to do some work on the Stinson float plane that had almost sunk a short time back when one of the floats had sprung a leak, causing it to submerge on one float. Mike was very lucky to have saved it because the sunken float had hit the bottom close to the shore and had it been any deeper it would have been a lot worse if the engine had been submerged. I remember him telling me how he had jumped in the lake to save the plane by trying to keep the wing from going under water while wishing and hoping for help. The plane float had been repaired and Mike was happy with that, so that side of it was fine, leaving just an oil change and a check on the port side wing fuel tank which needed cleaning out and the t-piece for the fuel line changing. Not having this part, we went for a drive to one of Mike's pilot friends in search of a replacement part.

While out trying to locate the fuel line part we met a man and wife team from Australia who had been driving round the world for four years in a homemade buggy, based on the range rover chassis and engine with their homemade cab adapted to the frame. After a short conversation Mike suggested that if they were still here next Saturday, they might like to come along to the village hall and listen to Diddy Dave's talk about his travels. Once outside I asked Mike what was this talk I was giving as I knew nothing about it. "Well I've asked a few friends to come along and have a get together in the hall on Saturday."
 "So how many people have you asked if we need a hall" I enquired.
 "Don't worry the women have organised the food, it is all sorted."
 "Right, so it's too late to cancel then."
 "Yes."
With my head buried in my hands we headed back to the lake not having found the part we needed.

Next morning Mike turned up with the new fuel part which he fitted. With that job done, he set about some final checks while I poured fresh fuel in the wing fuel tank and with that completed, Mike said he would like to run the engine up and taxi round the lake to make sure everything was working. He hinted to me if I wanted to come along then jump in. I climbed in and took up the seat behind Mike. The wind drifted us backwards away from the jetty enough for the power to be increased allowing us to taxi across the lake. All seemed okay as Mike turned round and gave the thumbs up to which I replied with the same signal. Next thing, he said "Go to the back and get me a life jacket from the store box." Asking him why he said "We will see if it can fly." Doing my best, I scrambled along the plane's floor to the rear, opened the box, and searching inside, I could only find one life jacket. Turning round I scrambled back to the front and passed the jacket to Mike telling him there was only one life jacket and none for me, to which he relied "You won't need one," and with that he pushed the throttle foreword while checking the dials. Slowly we started to lift from the lake, and I said to him "Did you see that?"
"See what?" "That incoming plane that's just gone over the top of us." I don't think he believed me as he didn't reply. It's interesting to note while writing up this story I found a photo that I took at the time of the aforementioned plane just passing over the top off us. Clearing the end of the lake we turned out towards the bay and flew round for half an hour with me trying to figure out which would I favour, a crash landing on a mountain side, or landing on the sea with no life jacket. However, all went well and we returned to the lake and tied the plane up at the jetty for the night. It was good to see that Mike seemed relieved after such a close call of nearly losing his plane to a watery grave.

That evening we had an invite for dinner to Mike and Heidi Neese's house, out of town. Later that evening the four of us sat around the table and talked. I was interested to hear about some of the guys flying experiences, and also about Mike and Heidi's travels to Africa which they did every year. They stayed in Africa for months at a time and travelled round in a land rover they keep stored out there. The talking went on till late as Mike had so many interesting stories to tell. Just before we left Mike Neese said that if I was down at the airfield at tomorrow afternoon, and up for it, he would take me out in his bush plane. Thanking him and Heidi for their hospitality we left and Mike dropped me back at the lake about midnight.

The following day Bill turned up and asked me if I would clean out the fuel tank on the V12Jag, so I suggested we went to the big shed and had a look. When we got there, I asked him why he wanted to take it off and clean it out. The more we talked about it the more I was convinced we did not need to take the tank out and that we could flush it through. In addition, we should fit a commercial type fuel filter that had an easy screw on filter that he could change easily. Happy to go with that Bill and I went round to the large motor factors called Napa, a company that has stores all over Canada and the USA. This wasn't my first visit to the Napa store, and just as before, they were more than helpful once I told them what I wanted to do and within twenty minutes we had the right bits. Rather than go straight back we rode round the back of Homer to the Gear Shed as Bill wanted to get some nuts and bolts. I waited in the vehicle and not long after he returned giving me a bag saying "Take this." Looking inside I pulled out a gun, an orange one. I turned to him and said "But Bill I don't do guns."

"It's a flare gun" he said "and could be useful in a couple of ways, as it may give you time to get away from a bear if your fire it at him and you never know, you could be in distress and could let one of the flares off."

"Thank you, Bill," what a great idea, bush craft at its best.

Back at the shed Bill went off to get some coffee for us both and while he was away Mike turned up with a plan, well a request really, to see if I could help him get a float plane out of the lake and down to the airfield hangar for storage over the coming winter. Just then Bill came back with three cups and we stood round drinking coffee, while Mike explained that he would like to do the job that afternoon as he could borrow a trailer to put it on. I agreed to help him so we set a time for us to meet up at the slipway not far from Bill's office.

Over the next couple of hours, I mounted the new filter system in the boot and made it easy to access. Bill was very pleased when I joined him and Barbara in the cabin for a sandwich, before rushing of to meet up with Mike who had already got the plane round to the slip. As it was my first time of taking a plane out of water, I asked Mike to run through what he wanted me to do. In theory it was like putting a boat onto a trailer, so while I backed the trailer down the slip Mike attempted to guide the two floats onto the flat trailer without getting his feet wet. The job went better than I thought it would, as Mike kept shouting half a dozen different orders such as "Keep going or we will get stuck trying to get out" and "Mind you don't hit any trees with the wings" and finally "Stop before you get to the main highway." Clear of the water I stopped and got out of the pick-up and realised we had to keep going as the truck was only two-wheel drive. Mike thanked me for a great job and I stood and wondering how the wings came off the plane to enable it be transported down the highway. Mike assured me they stayed on and we just picked a quiet moment and took the road to the front of the airport where his security friend Arnie would open a gate and we could slip across the runway to the hangars on the far side. Telling myself that Mike must have done this before I ran out in front of the rig keeping an eye open for traffic while watching the wings didn't hit any trees, all of this while trying to take photos as proof that this moment did actually happen. Thankfully the distance was only about half a mile and we arrived at the gate safely, where once they were opened, we dived across the runway to the hangar and slid the plane off the trailer into safe storage. I often smile to myself about this operation and tell myself yes, we did take this plane down the highway with the wings still on.

Mike Neese was doing pre-flight checks to his bush plane for our evening flight. The three of us chatted for a short while before I climbed into Mike's tiny two seat plane and we took off down the runway and out across the bay. We didn't go to the mountains where Bill had taken me, but we went more towards a flat wooded area, as I think the plan was to locate any bears or moose. We skirted over the top of the trees and after about half an hour of flying Mike descended over the top of some trees and on seeing a short gravel bed he showed me what a bush plane could do with the big floatation tyres, by landing it in such a short distance by dropping the plane out of the air at such a low speed then spinning it around before we ran out of suitable ground to take off again. All the time I kept thinking how lucky I was to be inside this everlasting bubble of my adventures. Back safely in the air, Mike pointed with his hand in the direction of Homer then gave me the signal to take the joy stick and fly the plane, while pointing to the two clocks on the top of the dash, one showing me the direction and the other showing the trim of the plane. I respond with thumbs up, as Mike sat back, and I carried on for the next twenty minutes across the bay. As we got closer, I attempted to offer the controls back to Mike, but he just gave me a few hand signals that brought me in line with the runway. "Go on you can land it." I so clearly remember the approach as Mike signalled me to keep on this course and slowly I descended to about hundred feet of the runway and at that point I asked Mike to take over, and we touched down and taxied to the hanger while Mike God bless him told me that he was happy for me to have landed his plane. Mike McCann was still in his hangar when we got back so I went over and found him tidying up the rear of the hangar. He told me he was flying out to Anchorage at the weekend for a few days and I was more than welcome to bring the minivan down to work on under cover on a level floor. I was really pleased with this suggestion as it gave me space to completely remove everything out of the van, enabling me to make a full check before the twelve days run to Vancouver. Mike dropped me back at the lake and reminded me that tomorrow night was Friday and I was headlining at the village hall with my talk.

The next morning, I woke and decided to have an easy day, if I could keep out of the way. First move was to get dressed and head to the boat yard café for breakfast and start to work out the upcoming work I wanted to do on the van while in Homer. I had thought at one time I would do the work when I got to Vancouver but it made more sense to do it here as I could source anything I needed. After breakfast, as I was driving passed the back of the airport in the direction of the spit, Bill spotted me and stopped me, telling me as it was such a nice day he was going out with his plane and if I wished I could join him. At eleven thirty we took off from the lake, heading once again across Kachemak bay in the directions of the Glacier Mountains. The weather was good so we flew much further and lower than last time. The sky was so clear and with the lack of wind we were able to circle the tops of the glaciers. Some of them pure white, yet others were tinged with black. It seemed the black came from volcanic ash. In my rush to join Bill I had forgotten to bring my camera and I was very disappointed that I was unable to capture the glaciers from those heights. Bill seemed very relaxed and was enjoying his time up in his plane and I was very grateful to him, as these opportunities and occasions never come to most people in their lives. Not having headsets to talk to each other it became difficult to have a conversation, so we used hand signals to communicate, and after for about an hour Bill signalled back down the bay away from the mouth. We flew for about half an hour, and then turned inland for a short distance before coming on a small lake with a cabin at its edge. Bill explained that the cabin was the family's place they used to use a lot at one time, but now not so much. We flew round the lake a few times with Bill looking out of the side window. I too did the same thing, while thinking it's too small to land and take off on but what did I know, I wasn't a real pilot yet. We carried on circling with Bill trying to explain over the noise of the engine that it was possible to land, but there were trees at one end and at the other there were rushes. In the end he aborted the landing telling me it was because of the trees. He reckoned they had grown so much; we would be too high on our approach and that he would be unable to sit the plane on the water soon enough to stop before we ran out of water. We had now been out flying some time so we headed back for the lake touching down just before four o'clock. After tying the plane up, I told Bill I would see him and Barbara later on at the hall as I now wanted to find some clean clothes and have a shower as Mike would be picking me up at seven.

Bang on time Mike picked me up and we headed out on the fifteen-minute drive to the hall. When we got there a few men were putting chairs out and Mike stepped in to give them a hand while I went to the far end of the hall to look at the stage and find some chairs and a table. I thought if the two Australians did turn up and join the audience, I could at any time invite them on stage to recount some of their travel experiences. A microphone was found and placed on the table. I went into the kitchen that was adjacent to the stage to talk with the two ladies who were getting out cups and plates. Just then Mike joined us, making the kitchen full with very little room to move. I stuck my head round the kitchen door and saw the hall had started to fill with a few more people, and amongst them I spotted the Ozzy's. The two ladies collected what they needed and left the kitchen, and I continued to talk to Mike about what he planned and what time we were going to start. Mike said "It's you doing the talk."
"Yes, I know" I replied, "But it would be good if somebody introduced me." Just then I turned round and looked out of the kitchen door to see that Mr Ozzy had climbed on stage. Turning back to Mike I told him he needed to go on stage and get hold of the microphone before the Ozzy got hold of it as he would not get it out of his hand once he started talking. Taken aback Mike was to slow to react but by now both Mr and Mrs Ozzy were on stage and the evening was underway, and for the next one and a half hours the happy couple regaled the audience with their stories. It was too late to stop anything now, and Mike and I were firmly stuck and we couldn't retreat as there was no back door out of this tiny kitchen. Finally, both Mike and I emerged from the side of the stage once the clapping had stopped, and we joined the gathering at the rear of the hall where tea and cakes were being served. The rest of the evening was quite amusing as I went from person to person with my cup of tea, constantly being asked the same question. "What happened to your talk Dave?"
 "Well once your speaker of the night got the mic, my night was over." Well everybody seemed to laugh about it, and that is all that really mattered. The evening ended for me with Bill and Barbara at their log home that is quite small, but very simple and a place I could easily live. Bill and I had a couple of whiskeys and it wasn't long before he got the pipes out to play a few tunes. It must have been close to midnight before I walked the short distance to the lake and the comfort of my sleeping bag.

The following day was Saturday and Mike was heading out at 10.30 a.m. by plane to Anchorage for a few days and he had left me his pick-up should I need it. Close to lunch time I got down to the hangar and set about emptying the minivan of everything, stacking the boxes in a corner as I would need them in the coming days. I started the work by jacking the vehicle up and removing the wheels and tyres. Then I removed the sump guard which would leave me with my last job of the afternoon, unscrewing the sump plug to allow the engine oil to drain overnight. Now that I had made a start on my own vehicle, I was very pleased. Mike had not put any pressure on me so there was no rush, and I finished at four, deciding that as it was Saturday, I would have a shower and walk the four miles down the spit to eat and have a few beers at the Salty Dawg.

With the weather being so good the walk along the spit was pleasant especially with the everlasting view of glaciers in front of me. The first couple of miles were just road and a pavement and not much more until I reached the wider part and the left turn to the small boat harbour. Walking on I reached lots of small assorted wooden buildings that made it look like a shanty town but all of this made it a great and memorable place to spend some time. The buildings were tourist and sea food type business. Having had the fish and chips last time I went for the pizza that evening then it was round the corner to the Dawg to join the evening buzz for a few hours, chatting and mixing with people and enjoying this welcoming land mark. During one of my many chats I was offered a lift back down the spit to the airport turn off, and that would just leave me a ten-minute walk to my lakeside bed.

With Mike leaving me the pick-up to use I made the excuse that I should drive to Mike and Heidi's house and take the chance that they were in. I arrived just before midday to find Mike working on an outboard engine outside his shed. Heidi was gardening and on seeing me she stopped to say hello. Mike came over and suggested it might be a good time to stop and have a coffee break. I stayed around a while giving Mike a hand before heading back into town.

It was a twenty-minute drive back into Homer and while driving I thought I should call at the hangar to collect my camera and drive to the main harbour entrance on the spit. As it was Sunday the spit was quite busy with traffic, and after a couple of miles I reached the left turning that took me round the back of the small boat harbour before reaching the main fishing industrial harbour that held some of the biggest boats I have ever seen. I found a place to park close to one of the walkway entrances that would get me onto the pontoons. At the entrance I looked down the walkway that was sitting at a forty-five-degree angle, obviously due to the tide dropping to its lowest point. Gingerly I walked down the sixty feet walkway to reach the pontoons main walkway. At the bottom I looked to my right and left and figured that the pontoons must run for a hundred feet each way, with lots of large boats tied on each side, many of them familiar from the TV series The Deadliest Catch.

I must have spent a couple of hours looking round and taking lots of photo, one of the things that impressed me was the height of the poles that keep the pontoons in place, these poles allow the pontoons to rise and fall some forty to fifty feet freely due to living almost on top of the world.

I had enjoyed my freedom over the weekend, and I finished it off with fish and chips before bedding down for an early evening as I wanted to spend the following day on the minivan. Next morning, I was up early and at the boat yard café for seven thirty which was when they opened. As I walked in Joe said "Morning Dave, is it the usual?"
 "Yes please" I said picking up my mug of tea. I stood and chatted at the counter until my breakfast of eggs, done easy over, with bacon and very small square cut potato bits that have been fried accompanied with two slices of toast were ready and a second mug of tea. All this for nine dollars.

Back at the hangar I screwed the sump plug back into the oil drain and disposed of the old engine oil into the big waste oil drum. There were two jobs that need serious attention. One was the two inboard drive pod rubber boots that had held together for months across Canada and Alaska with cling film. The other job was to get to the bottom of why the shock absorber bolts were breaking. First job was the drive train, so I unbolted the brake callipers from each hub and I then disconnected the top and bottom ball joints, which let me remove the drive flange and brake disc, complete with driveshaft and pod out of the gearbox leaving the simple operation of knocking the inboard pod off the drive shaft to clean the dirty part up. Having cleaned the pod, I decided to go to Napa car parts with the pod joint and drive shaft to see if I could source new boots. They were a great bunch of guys at Napa and very helpful considering they must have opened every box of boot kits they had. Some of the kits came close but would be let down by the size. They could be wrong at one end or the other or maybe they had too many ridge rings. As a last resort the head man Ron, started looking in the drive train catalogue that gave the sizes and a picture of the full range, so armed with my micrometre we measured up and found a suitable boot that was available and I could have two new kits on the next delivery. I thanked Ron and he told to come back after lunch time on Wednesday, and I left feeling good. I pulled into the Safeway store for coffee and a catch up on any messages from back home and while at the store I got some milk and a large bag of cookies. On the way back to the hangar I called in on Bill to let him know that the guys at Napa had sorted me out and I was going to be busy for the next few days focusing on work that needed doing on my mini. While I was there, I told him it would be sooner rather than later that I would have to cut free and leave Homer to head for Canada and British Columba. Returning to the hangar I set about looking round the underside of the wing mainly to check that the extra cooling fan was okay and the fine mesh had kept small stones away from the radiator. While doing this I cleaned round and removed any excess mud with a wire brush and for some reason I sat back on the small stool and looked at the body mounting for the shock absorber. What I noticed for the first time was the mounting had been fully welded onto the body, why I was not sure, as the standard four bolts is all that is needed to keep it in place. The mounting was at eye level and I was looking directly at the mounting and something looked wrong. Then the penny dropped as I could see the mounting bracket was oblong and that the horizontal mounting position was not in the centre of the bracket, it was offset. They were upside down and fitted to the wrong sides. Pleased to have solved the problem I called it a day and tomorrow I would set about removing the brackets. I was grateful to Mike for the use of the pick-up as it meant I could leave the minivan to work on as I wished. Calling in at the Safeway store on the way back to the lake I used the internet to check for any messages and while there I picked up a microwave meal that could be heated back at Bills lakeside office.

We were into September now, and getting off to sleep was still a problem with the long hours of daylight. I usually got to sleep by taking a deep breath and burying my head inside the sleeping bag, only to find myself waking up in the middle of the night sweating. I did not sleep too well and finished up lying on top of my sleeping bag, and finally giving in at five thirty because of the heat, I went down to the hangar to work on the mini. It was interesting talking to people about the weather in Alaska as most think it to be a cold place. Yes, come winter it can be extremely cold, but the summers are short and very pleasant with the long days and interior Alaska can get very dry and hot at times.

My first job was to work on removing the welded mounting brackets with an angle grinder without damaging the bodywork or the bracket. The job took some patience and time and eventually I removed enough of the weld to use a flat chisel to break the mounting away from the body. That completed it just left a small amount of grinding to the bracket and the body. Now very happy that the mystery had been solved and I had got the welded brackets off it was time for a late breakfast at my favourite café. Now feeling upbeat I returned to the airfield hangar and to the refitting of the brackets on the proper sides of the vehicle by just using the standard four bolts on each mounting. That done I would have to leave fitting the shockers until the following day when hopefully I would have the new boots for the drive train. Work on the rear of the vehicle took the rest of the afternoon and before leaving I removed the roof box as it was cracked and damaged and it need fibreglass from Napa to make the much-needed repairs. Tomorrow would be a busy day and my plan was to clean out the interior of the van in the morning then go to Napa and collect the new boots just after lunch, and while there get some resin and matting for the box repair so I could use the afternoon to make the repair thus giving it plenty of time to harden overnight. After packing up for the day I called at Bill's to update him on my work progress. Barbara asked me to stay for something to eat and this prompted Bill to get the pipes out and play a short tune, giving him a good reason to get his bottle of whiskey out. This was the start of a pleasant evening which was had by all.

Following morning I was back to my routine of breakfast at the boat yard then into the hangar to take on the cleaning of the van interior. This went better and quicker than I thought giving me time to go through all the plastic boxes to clean and throw away unwanted items then repack ready for storage in the van later. When lunch time arrived, I went to Safeway and ate there as Napa was just round the corner. Come two o'clock I drove round to Napa and met up with Ron and collected my two new boot kits. I opened the box to examine them, the quality was great and they so excelled the original ones, and I wished I had ordered two more as spares. I picked up the resin and matting and paid for the parts thanking the guys for their help and the free coffee. Back at the hangar I set about making good the roof box by moulding two strips of wood into the base of the box with resin, then repairing the cracks with matting and resin leaving them to harden before refitting the box in a couple of days. Just as I was finishing off Bill pulled up at the hangar door in one of his Jags and while chatting, he asked me if I had time to fit a module he had been advised to fit on his other Jag, the one with the American V8 engine in. "Sure Bill, I will come round after breakfast and fit it for you." I then knew what Bill's next words would be and I was spot on.
"Be round at the cabin for about eight thirty and Barbara will make pancakes for breakfast."

Next morning, I went round to the cabin and climbed the wooden stairs knocking on the door. Bill shouted "Come in, come in Dave breakfast is ready" so I sat down and started on the warm pancakes adding maple syrup and blueberries, followed by a mug of tea. Time was passing and I was keen to get back to the hangar so I asked Bill if he had the module so I could look at how it fitted, hoping it would just be a simple bolt on the bulkhead job, but no it had to go in the distributor. "Right Bill, I'm of to the big shed to make a start" and at lightning speed I was out of the rear door and under the bonnet. The job took just under the hour to complete before I got out of the shed and back to the hangar. I wanted to get back as I was expecting Mike back round lunch time. Bill was happy so I left and got back to the hangar to fit the new rubber boots with special grease to the pod joints, then before fitting the special clips that hold the boots on, I fitted the pods onto the drive shafts then finished off by fitting the clips. The whole drive train unit was now ready to refit and by the end of the day both sides were back in place just leaving the rims and tyres to be cleaned, then refitted along with new oil and a filter. The jobs were now getting less. Bill popped round to tell me Mike had been delayed and would not be back till tomorrow. That was leaving things a little close, as I had set my mind to leave on Saturday and that was the day after tomorrow. After Bill had gone, I decided to stay on and do some of the following days planned work that evening. I started by refitting the roof box and packing my tent and spare wheels back inside the box. Final job of the evening was to screw a new oil filter onto the engine then add five litres of oil to the engine and oil cooler. Feeling better that I had completed the extra jobs; I threw the four wheels into the back of the pick up as I would wash them down at the car wash, next to the laundrette, in the morning before breakfast. Hopefully Mike would be back tomorrow and I could get a clear day to finish off the last couple of jobs as I wanted to spend some time with Mike as he had been so good to me. Not only that, he had secretly been good for the healing process I was going through. I was up and active finding I could clean the wheels and tyres on the side of the pontoon at the lake thus giving me a head start to the morning and my chance of breakfast just after eight. The boat yard was five minutes away from the back way into the airport so I would find myself in the hangar for nine. The process of fitting the wheels did not take long and I soon had my trusty steed back on the ground not long after Mike walked into the hanger shouting "What's new buddy, let's go and get some coffee." Boy it was good to see him. We jumped in the pickup and headed to the Safeway for a couple of 16 oz drips. While we were there, I told him I was hoping to head for Anchorage sometime tomorrow, and Mike told me that he too would be packing up soon himself and going on vacation south. Dropping me back at the hangar Mike went to his place to unpack and sort a few things out. I had only to tidy round and brush up where I had been working leaving my few plastic boxes in a pile ready to go in the van as the last items.

My last evening was down at the lake with Bill and Barbara for pizza with red wine. During the evening I thanked them both for welcoming me into their lives and helping me so much to enjoy my time in Homer. It must have been quite late before I turned in, as for the first time it felt as though the dark nights had made a start at coming back.

Next morning, I was up at eight and made my way to the laundrette to wash my sleeping bag on a free wash that was given, as a valued customer. After having my wash card stamped each time I used the machines my seventh wash was free so while the wash was on, I showered, also for free. I called round to see Mike before going to hangar and collecting the last of the boxes to go in the van. It was now close to lunch time, so as I would be passing Bill's, I called in to make my farewell. This turned out to be a bad move as no soon as I stepped inside Bill told me he had a problem with the V8 Jag. One of the problems with the Jag was is that dear Bill did play with things. It would seem the module I fitted a few days earlier had not solved whatever problem the car had, in Bills mind it was faulty so he sent it back, and the parts company sent him a new one which I fitted. It made no difference at all to the running of the car. I was secretly frustrated as time was moving on and I wanted to make Anchorage that night. I told Bill I will take the Jag for a run to see if I could find the problem and after a couple of miles, I figured that I might know what was happening. I pulled up and lifted the hood asking Bill if he had a small screwdriver in the car. "Yes, I have one in the glove box" that pleased me and set my alarm bells ringing. While Bill was getting the screwdriver, I spotted a section of flexible fuel line was double bent below the engine on the bulkhead and this made me think it could be causing the problem as the car would tick over okay and then drive a given distance before starting to falter. My thought was fuel was getting though but the restriction in the tube was not allowing enough through for the higher revs and not the air fuel mixture as I first thought could be the problem. I showed Bill the rubber tube and asked him if he had a knife which he duly pulled out of this pocket and I shortened the tube by a couple of inches. We both got back in the car and I drove down the spit at above the recognised speed limit. The Jag took off like a rocket and drove smoothly all the way back to Bill's and as we drove down to the big shed Mike was standing at the open doors looking a little bemused. I stepped out and Mike said "Are you still here" to which I just lifted my eyes and he smiled back at me. Bill got out shouting that the Jag had never gone so well since this engine was fitted three years ago. That made me burst into laughter while Mike grabbed me and put his arms around me whispering "Thanks buddy" in my ear. I turned to Bill and shook his hand telling him I had to go as Canada was beckoning me. I climbed back in the mini and as I headed up the track from Bill's I kept looking back in my wing mirror at two legends that would forever stay close to my heart and always in my mind. Completely unknown to me at the time the impact they had on me would draw me back one day to the place they call Homer, a small drinking village with a fishing problem.

Chapter 13

New friends

I arrived in Anchorage much later than I wanted to; worried as I had not pre booked a place at Ship Creek Campsite where I had stayed a month before. Pulling in the manager recognised the mini straight away and told me that they were full, but he would find me a spot as the vehicle was so small. A spot was found by some trees and I was able to get under the branches with the van and set up a simple camp as I would go out to eat, and not set my tent up but just take out the boxes from the van and place them at the side giving me enough room to bed down when I got back later. I walked the short distance to the pub where I had met up with friends from the Bluegrass Festival last time I was there. The pub served food so I knew I could eat and have a beer before returning at a sensible time for bed.

The following morning, it was back to cornflakes and while I still had the chance, I sent an e-mail to Rick Higgs from the Vancouver mini club letting him know that I was back on the road and that I estimated I should get to the Canadian border the following afternoon. From then on, I would try and keep him posted on my location every couple of days, as I had estimated it would be ten days until I got to his place at Maple Ridge.

With my boxes back in the mini I was soon on my way and driving the Glen Highway. The weather was fantastic, but you could tell that summer was on its way out and autumn was taking over as the country side had been transformed into one mass of colours the likes of which I had never seen before, and as I drove, I tried to count the colours to pass the time away. In the end I gave up counting and decided on green, red, yellow then divided each of them into six shades. Added to the scenery, the bright blue of the sky the black of the mountains and the pure white of the glaziers, and all of that topped off by the lack of vehicles and I was thinking, I have not reached British Columba yet a place world renowned for its autumn colours and beauty. I travelled at a steady pace on the paved roads and by five thirty had covered just short of 300 miles before reaching my forestry camp site at Tok. Setting my tent up for the first time in a while I found myself fancying fried spam and sliced fried potatoes for my evening meal. After washing up I went for a walk round the lake with Bills flare gun in my back pocket for company, should I get an unwanted visitor. Bed time was early as I wanted to get underway before nine the next morning.

My night's sleep was good and with my breakfast of two boiled eggs I had kept my previous night's promise to myself and was on the road for eight thirty, making a quick dash into the gas station at Tok as this was the final place I could get fuel at these cheapest of cheap Alaskan prices. Back on the road I covered the ninety miles to the US border by midday, and as I got close, I got my paperwork ready put a smile on my face, not too big, and took my dark glasses off, as they like to look into yours eyes. As I pulled up at the barrier the dark window to my left opened and the lady officer bid me good afternoon. "Sir where are you going?"
"Vancouver and then Russia"" I answered. They only like single words at a time, but I slipped in a second one for good measure just to sow the seed that I would not be staying.
"Any guns Sir?
"Just a flair gun."
"That's ok. Any beer or tobacco Sir?
"No mam."
"So, what's in the steel box by your side?"
"They're my tools."
"OK sir, have a good day." The barrier raised and off I went noticing I had left my camcorder on, that made for some interesting listening to later that evening.

I had expected to reach the Canadian check point sometime soon, but this did not happen and it would be twenty miles, sorry kilometres, before I got to the check point, all the time thinking who owns the bit in the middle and could I claim it for my own? The road was very quiet and when I pulled up at the check point the officer stamped my passport and cleared me to continue on my journey, confirming that it was labour day in both the US and Canada. I covered many kilometres that day stopping only at Whitehouse to refill my fuel tank then I drove 50 more kilometres before stopping once again at the Five Dollars Forest Camp sites by a lake.

Many times, I had to put the tent up but I didn't mind in the least as I always derived great pleasure from the fact that it was something that I had designed and made, and it had turned out to be so useful in so many ways. That evening food was noodle and chicken soup followed by flat round fried chip butties washed down with tea, all cooked on my Matty stove. Before bed my final duty of the day was to bring my log up to date.

During the night something disturbed me at about four in the morning but I was unsure what it was or why. However, I fell back to sleep until eight when I awoke and packed up camp and drove out of the forest onto highway one in the direction of Watson Lake that was four hundred plus kilometres away. The drive would find me needing to take a right turn onto Highway 37 about fifteen kilometres short of the town. I had passed through Watson Lake some months previously on the road where I had run out of petrol at Ross River, so with this in mind I decided it was wise and worth the time and effort to pass the turning and fill my petrol tank as the 37 was a dirt road and all possible encounters of animals and the lack of gas stations needed to be assumed. I filled up with fuel and bought some more food before back tracking to the 37 turning on through the Yukon once again, where I continued driving for some time well into the evening. I started to worry, as it was getting dark and animals like to start appearing more at dusk, and it was becoming imperative that I found a place to camp for the night and soon.

Digression
As someone who has never been afraid to take up driving, I found it quite interesting on this part of the drive as I started to analyse just how much effort goes into some periods of driving. Take crossing the Prairies of Canada as being simple. The road is paved and mainly runs in a straight line for mile after mile and can be very boring, you can relax just occasionally having to think about traffic. Now take travelling on the dirt road and that is a whole different story. It can be dangerous, as speed, road conditions and animals come into play for longs hours sometimes requiring days of relentless concentration. Your eyes have to observe the road and its condition both in front and ahead of you while constantly looking for animals that can come from the left or right as close as the front line of your vehicle. The fear is always there on these roads that if animals appear in front of you from nowhere it will hit your vehicle. Should you be lucky and it pops out ahead then you roll the dice as to what happens next, can I stop, should I swerve or will I finish up rolling down a bank all of this in the blink of an eye. Meeting bears on the road I didn't mind as they move quickly, but the moose is slow and moves like wobbly jelly. The other animal to be aware of is the porcupine, it is small and covered in spikes that can puncture your tyres. ~~

At eight thirty I reached Deaselake and spotted a sign in the middle of nowhere saying RV site 3 kms on the right, and sure enough a track soon came up that took me to a log cabin and my stop over for the night, where I could shower and get internet access. The site was the only place for more than sixty miles making me think I could enjoy living there. That evening after dinner and showering I managed to get on the internet and read Rick Higgs' reply to an email that I had sent him some days back. Basically, he was informing me that if I could get to Vancouver as soon as possible something was being organised. More than that his message did not really say, which left me a little confused.

Next morning, I was up early and away from the camp by seven, as I wanted to cover a good distance that day and by running the van at 100 to 120 kms I would try and make it to Prince George the same night. My next main junction was Kitwanga at the southern end of the 37 where it met the 16 from Prince Rupert to Prince George. I made a quick stop for fuel at the junction and set off on a great section of dirt road that must have lasted for 50km before getting very narrow and wooded, making it necessity for me to drop my speed. A black bear came out of the undergrowth on my left about twenty meters in front of me and started to walk down the road. I leaned forward and opened the lens cover and pushed the record button on the dash cam. Why does it take forever to start! By then the bear has decided to disappear into the bushes and I had missed a fantastic chance to get some real footage while driving. I made it to Prince George that evening by nine, covering 900kms after driving in the dark, something that is not recommended by the locals or me. However, I had pushed myself too hard as my body was telling me, along with my sore eyes that looked very scary in the mirror. Before bed I filled the petrol tank and bought a sandwich, and finding that I could get wi-fi I sent an e-mail to Rick telling him I thought my eta at his house would be Saturday at the latest. Rick must have been on line as he replied straight back to tell me that would fit nicely as the Vancouver mini club were going to have a get together and a barbeque for me on Sunday.

The last couple of days had been warm and the next morning was no exception, so I went for a shower before breakfast and then repacked the van for another full-on day of driving. Just before leaving I spoke with the campsite owner about my journey to Vancouver and enquired how long the drive would take. He told me it was about one and a half days, and when I got to Cache Creek if I turned right it would take me down through Whistler to the northern end of the city. The other way was to carry on down the 97 passed Hells Gate and in by the US border. I thanked him and he wished me well as I turned out of the gate and onto the 97 and onto what looked like a brand-new paved road. For the first time in ages I felt more relaxed as I was driving on a good solid road, not having to look out for an ever-changing surface. The stunning colours of the forests that had been with me for so long were slowly disappearing giving way to large flat areas with fields of beef cattle and irrigation. Then as quickly, it changed, this time to rivers and narrow gorges and the site of a Canadian Pacific train hauling an endless number of rolling stock containers as it weaved its way round the gorges and rivers. As I drove there was more and more traffic and I started to get that city and fast lane feeling, something that is not on my list of pleasures. The closer I got to Vancouver the more excited I became and with it an urgency to push on and keep driving to meet these new friends from the other side of the world. The trouble was, if I did push on, I would arrive very late and trying to find Rick's house in Pitt Meadows could be difficult so I opted to stop in Mission at Rowley Park for the night about 30kms away from my destination.

I set my camp up and paid the five dollars before getting my Matty stove out and cooking the meat chops I had bought at Prince George gas station. After dinner I messaged Rick to tell him that I had knocked two days off the journey time, and was camping in a place called Mission that night and if it was ok, I would arrive at his house about midday the following day. He offered to come out and meet me but I told him I would be fine and I wanted to make the final run in myself as this meant I would complete the journey under my own guidance. Rick fully understood my reasons for wanting to finish this way telling me that he and his wife Elaine would look forward to seeing me the following day.

Now well into September and with the weather still holding with long hot days, I was looking forward to some time off from driving, and as midday came it was time to re-join the highway and the drive into Pitt Meadows using the instructions Rick had sent me which worked out to the last letter. Finally getting on the last road listed I looked for the street number and drove along for a while before spotting a driveway with a very nice yellow and black mini parked outside, with enough space for me to pull in and park. At one o'clock I walked to the front door and rang the bell. Elaine came to the door and welcomed me calling to Rick telling him of my arrival. Going in I met Rick and thanked him for all the support he had given me since I had first contacted him. Rick had been through a heart valve operation, he had told me some time ago he was waiting for one, but had been lucky and it had been brought forward so my arrival was perfect timing, and if I was up for it while I was still here would I jump into the driver's seat of his jeep and run him around. That was not a problem and over the next ten days I would make myself available to chauffeur him when needed. An hour later Elaine was off to work at the hospital and Rick grabbed at the chance of getting out, so he asked if we could drive over to his younger son Jeremy's house to say hello, and I could take a look at his mini and the work he does. Before leaving Jeremy's, Rick reminded him to be round at Pitt Meadows later for a family barbeque in the back garden. That evening I met Jeremy's wife and son Quinn, and Elaine's son Richard who was wheel chair bound due to a terrible accident some years before. We all ate well and I really enjoyed having a family for company for the first time in ages. During the evening I spent a lot of time kicking a football round the lawn with young Quinn. At ten thirty I asked to be excused as I felt the pull of my own room and a proper bed with white sheets and curtains that blanked out the light and it was all just too much to resist.

I slept well as the family left me to sleep in. I emerged at ten and I could see Elaine outside working in her vegetable plot. Shortly after Rick came up the stairs from his basement den to say good morning, as Elaine appeared asking me what I would like for breakfast. I settled for a light breakfast of cereal and toast and Rick joined me for coffee as we chatted about going out in the jeep. Rick wanted to make a few calls and if possible, I wanted to call in at a travel agent because I had a return ticket to use. I had bought the return ticket to keep the border agencies happy so I didn't get too many awkward questions to answer on entry. I wanted to see what could be done with the ticket out bound from Halifax in ten days.

Now ready to go with me in the driver's seat we drove into town. Pitt Meadows was a really nice clean place, with lots of trees and flowers with the village just a short distance from Rick and Elaine's house. Our first call was the travel agents to see if they could tie in a flight out from Vancouver with the ticket I had. The nice lady took my details and said she would phone back when she had found some options for me. While in town Rick made his couple of shop calls, and I followed him, enjoying my walk about before driving out of town as Rick wanted to show me some of the lowlands or the delta as it is known, then returning back to base along the Frasier River. While driving back Rick told me about a barbeque he had been organised for the following day at Larry and Ann Sutton's house in Maple Ridge, close to the top of the hill overlooking the valley and the Frasier River. I asked if I could take the van and Rick said "Yes please do, we have lots from the Vancouver mini club coming and they are keen to see the minivan. Jeremy has offered to pick mum and dad up, so yes bring the van." Back at the house I unloaded my boxes and stored them in the garage, before giving the mini a wash and polish. As the weather was so good, we ate outside on the large porch talking about my travels and Rick informed me that he had entered me in a rally called the all British Run the following weekend in Whistler, and we would take the Sea to Skye Highway to get there. That really excited me as I had travelled that road a number of years before when it was under construction and Whistler was being developed into the ski resort it is today.

Sunday morning was bright and warm boding well for the afternoon barbeque at Larry and Ann's. After breakfast on the porch, I offered to help Elaine outside with any jobs that needed doing as Rick would be off duty for a while until he got the all clear from the hospital. One thing I really enjoy in life is being able to join in and help other people, especially outside were I can use my strengths and knowledge and work and alongside people on their way in life be it for just a short time.
The following is a short part of a poem that I so like.
"We shall pass this way but once and if there is any good I can do let me do it now. We shall see this day but once and if there is any good let me do it now".

It seemed there was an overdue job right at the rear of the garden where the tool shed stood, so I set about clearing the moss and growth from the shed and the paved floor, and the work kept me going till lunch time. The weather was outstanding and I was getting excited at the thought of meeting likeminded people and their minis who Rick had told me had promised to come along. We arrived at Larry and Ann's early afternoon and I could quickly see an assorted selection of minis including a Mini Moke and various mini saloons and an outstanding almond green and white MK1 Cooper S. Larry and Ann's place was lovely, surrounded by trees to the rear and a front garden of flowers and small shrubs. There was plenty of space for parking so I parked and met up with our hosts Larry and Ann, who asked me what I would like to drink, while Larry took me round and introduced me to the club members before we all started to eat a well laid out selection of food that Ann had prepared. During the afternoon I tried to talk to and thank everybody for turning up and making the effort, as some had travelled a fair distance. Later on, when people started to leave it gave me the opportunity to spend some time with Larry. I had found out the Cooper S belonged to him and he took me over to have a closer look at the pristine vehicle. We talked for a while and I learned that he had been in the film industry for some time, but was now retired and enjoying life with Ann who was originally from Australia. Larry also mentioned that they do house swop holidays and many of their trips took them to the UK.

The last few people were saying their farewells when Rick came over to say that Jeremy was going to take him and Elaine home and asked if I would be ok to find my own way back. I told him I would be fine and would follow them a little later. Most of the tidying up had been done so I joined Larry and Ann in their house for a cup of tea as I wanted to thank them for all the planning and effort, they had put into organising the afternoon. During the conversation Larry asked me what I was going to do with the mini when I go back to the UK.
 "I have to hold my hand up" I said "As I have not even thought about that, and it had completely slipped my mind till that moment." That was my honest answer; I truly had not given it a thought.
 "Come with me" he said, so I followed Larry out of the rear door and across the garden path to a large oblong building that looked like a second house, which turned out to be a wonderful combination of rooms. We entered the building through a single side door, and on the left was a set of stairs that led to an upstairs flat. On the right was a single door that Larry opened. He turned the light on to reveal a mini that his daughter owned and he was keeping there in dry storage. Larry then turned to me saying he would make space and that he was more than happy to store my mini while I was out of the country. I recall not replying straight away, but just standing there silent with tears running down my cheeks before thanking him for his unbelievable offer. There is a saying "Cometh the hour cometh the man." "Just bring it along when you are ready to store it." We came back out through the single door to take a look in Larry's man cave that was next to the stairs, and like all good man caves it was well packed with workshop items. Coming out of the room and turning left we walked a short distance and via a single door we entered into a large double garage that was both clean and tidy. I got the impression there was a place for everything so long as everything was in its place, truly a man after my own heart. We went back inside and I had another cup of tea while asking about next weekends all British Run to Whistler. It seemed it was not a rally, more like a pleasant drive to Whistler. It was now about seven thirty so I made my way back to Rick's who was just about to settle down and watch the hockey match with a beer. Elaine had gone to work so I joined Rick to watch the game telling him what Larry had offered to do for me over the winter months. I went to bed that night having had a really good day making new friends and finding a safe place to store the mini.

I was up next morning at about eight and came down stairs to find Rick sitting in a chair reading the newspaper. Elaine, I guessed was in bed having worked the previous night. I helped myself to breakfast cereals, knowing where to find them as Elaine had given me the kitchen tour a couple of days back. Rick got up and made himself a coffee whilst telling me that a couple of the mini members were also members of the MG and Jag Club and tonight was there monthly meeting. A lot of them will be going on the Whistler run, so if I would like to meet them, we could go in the jeep. That worked for me. I was more than happy to drive Rick around and it gave me a chance to find my way about and to meet new people, so the following days were very laid back with the weather being at its best. Just before lunch time we received a phone call from the travel agent saying they had sorted out some flight plans so if we could call in, they could be finalised. My travel itinerary was flying from Vancouver to Montreal then onwards to Heathrow and Manchester. Not what I really wanted but it was the best that could be done with the return ticket I had. Travel plans sorted, we headed over to Jeremy's to find him in the garage working on a cylinder head for a customer. During the conversation Jeremy mentioned to his dad something about going to the club night on Wednesday, where I popped in the words "No its tonight."

Rick replied with "Hold on Diddy you're right and Jeremy is also right as it's the mini club monthly meet on Wednesday and we were hoping you will come along and give a talk on your travels." My response was a big chuckle and a smile.

Leaving Jeremy, we headed for the town of Mission and to call in at Cedar Garage to see owners Nolan and Deanna Kitchener about booking his mini in for a tune up. I had met these lovely people the previous afternoon at the barbeque and once inside the reception area Rick struck up a conversation with Nolan while Deanna made me a coffee, before I was taken on a tour of the workshop that was well set up for all sorts of vehicles. I spotted lots of mini bits on the shelves and outside could be found the odd mini of one form or another. While there I learned that Nolan ice raced a mini over the winter months, something I would love to do.

Back at Rick's we had an early evening meal before we headed out to drive someway into Vancouver for a couple of hours of well, I will just say MG and Jag talk that I know nothing about.

Over the next couple of days, I spent time in the garden doing a few jobs and painted part of the porch. The work kept me going till late Wednesday afternoon, when close to five o clock, Rick, Elaine and I all went in Elaine's car to the pub, joining others early to have a meal before the main motor club meeting started. It soon came apparent that they had a good membership and were well organised. They were a friendly lot and I could see that by the way the tables were placed in a U shape with nobody seated on the inside, which meant that no one had their back turned to anyone. The main course came and was enjoyed by all, and along with others I ordered a dessert, that would seem to signal the start of the evening's proceedings. The Chairman started the meeting by asking for apologies then welcomed me, announcing that I was to give a talk on my travels after the club business had been dealt with. As with most clubs they pushed on through to any other business quite quickly and to the closure of the agenda. Dessert dishes were cleared and everybody was asked if they wanted tea or coffee while others went to the bar to top up their glasses. When everybody was settled back in their seats, I was asked to give a short version of my travels and I took the opportunity to use the word short. To break the ice and kick start my talk, I started by telling the room that with a fair wind and good weather it would take them about twenty days to do coast to coast, but for me it took 135 days. I tried to cover as much of my journey as I could and after about an hour, I stopped thinking a beer break was a good move before returning to see if anybody had any questions. That move seemed to be welcomed, as it kept us going for another hour before I packed up and was thanked by all in the room. It then went quiet and I was asked to step forward as they had a presentation to make to me in the form of a certificate which read.

The North American Classic Mini Brigade
Honorary Patron Dave Vizard
Certificate of Membership
David Diddy, Dave Thomas, is hereby accorded membership in the North American Classic Mini Brigade dedicated to the preparation, use and enjoyment of the classic mini and the fellowship of mini owners on the continent, given for no stop journeys over 5.000 miles

I was deeply touched by the presentation that night and to be given the certificate by what I believe is one of the best mini clubs in the world, an evening that will stay with me for a long time.

The following day was the All British run to Whistler so I decided to do oil and filter change for the drive, and because of the winter storage, this would mean when I came back the mini would be ready to go. Saturday morning and the weather was ideal for the drive and just after breakfast Jeremy turned up with the family in his up rated BMW Cooper S, Rick was to go with Elaine in her car and I would follow in the minivan, so at about eleven o'clock we headed out of North Vancouver to the start of the Sea To Skye Highway passing through Squamish, Garibaldi and my favourite place name, Function Junction, then into Whistler. The road was now perfect and in places very fast as we wound our way up and down and around the mountain road that was built for the Winter Olympics. Arriving I made my way into Whistler Village and then to the check point where I joined the many British cars that had already parked close to one of the ski gondolas. One of the Marshalls found me a place to park among the MG's Jag's and Triumphs to name but a few. I left the mini and walked around, eventually finding our group before having a bite to eat. Rick asked me if I was going to do the rally which I declined as I did not have a passenger seat, and anyway I was more than happy to stay around and talk to people who wanted to look over the mini. The selection of cars was outstanding and I was surprised being this side of the world, that the following was so big. Most of the vehicles were old; some of them very old and you could see good money had been spent on them to be able to enjoy them on days like today. Come four thirty people started to leave so we to join the exit and the drive back to Pitt Meadows as I would have to prepare the mini for storage tomorrow at Larry's.

On Sunday I went through the van removing things that I would take back on the flight such as gifts and paperwork. I packed it into one of my big plastic boxes which were sealed, and labelled with the help of Rick and his printing machine. I had also decided to ship my banjo out so this was labelled and by afternoon I had delivered the mini and stored it at Larry's. Rick had come along and was now driving himself a little so after thanking Larry and Ann we headed back to Ricks. I appreciated my last evening with Ricks family, Elaine cooked us all a lovely meal which we all enjoyed out on the patio.

Sunday was to be a very early start for Rick and me, as we would have to be up at five and on the road soon after to make sure we did not get stuck in the early morning traffic. We made good time and arrived at the departure car park at six thirty. Rick gave me a hand with my extra items and helped me to the check in. All went well at the check in desk with my paper work, which just left me the banjo and the plastic box of gifts and papers to check in at the plane hold desk. I was informed that as I was passing through Montreal and Heathrow, I would be able to collect the two items on my arrival at Manchester. I said my farewell to Rick and told him I would let him know when I got back home to the Isle of Mull. With that we shook hands and I headed to the baggage clearing. There with no problems, and I took up a place in the departure lounge to sit out the next hour before boarding the first of three planes that would get me to Manchester.

When I touched down at Manchester, I had been travelling for twenty-four hours and with only customs and the baggage carousel to complete I was looking forward to being collected by a friend who had looked after my car while I had been away. The airport baggage area was busy as three planes had arrived at the same time. Patiently I waited for my two items to show up and the longer I waited the more worried I became and I finally ended up being the last person standing at the carousel with nothing to be seen. Soon after a lady can over to me and asked if she could help. I explained about my two items so we walked over to her desk to check what had happened to my baggage. After a few minutes the problem was solved when she told me that the items had not been put on the plane at Vancouver. The lady apologised and said that they would be despatched today and they would be delivered to my door. I explained to the nice helpful lady that I lived on an island off the west coast of Scotland but she assured me that I would get my two items. I thanked her but felt a little unsure that I would ever see my items again that were still sitting on the other side of the world. My friend John was waiting to collect me and we headed back to his house where I stayed for the night before driving back to Mull the following morning, as I was keen to get back to see my family and not miss the last boat. I was away early enough the next day to make the ferry in plenty of time. It felt a little strange, yet welcoming, as I sat on the boat this time crossing water to get home as I had been away for so long. My first port of call was my wee home and as I got out of the vehicle, I could not help but look west across the sea thinking, that's where I've been for a while. I closed the driver's door and picked up my travel bag making my way to the back door and on opening the unlocked door I nearly tripped over my missing items, they had beaten me back from Canada.

Chapter 14

Dead in the water

Seven and a half thousand kilometres separated me and my mini from Russia where I would continue my attempt to go the wrong way round the world. Over the winter months back home the thought of how I could get the mini across the vast Pacific Ocean was a worry especially with limited funds. Initially a very elaborate plan seemed to offer a solution as my friend back in Alaska, Mike McCann, had offered to make a few phone calls to see if one of his aeroplane buddies could put a mini in an Antonov cargo plane and fly it into Russia. I truly believed they would have pulled it off as Mike was a bush pilot who flies food for the thousand-mile Iditarod sled dog race from Anchorage to Nome which is just about the closest you can get on foot to Russia. However, the time of year and the lack of roads on the Russian pacific coast put that idea to bed.

It was while at home that winter I received an e-mail from Rick Higgs asking me if I had made any plans for my return to Canada and if not, then would I like to go to Mini Meet West for the four day get together of everything that is mini. It was the turn of the Canadians to organise the event at a place called Penticton. The Canadians have never failed to impress me with their generosity and friendship and this has made it very difficult for me to cut my ties with this fantastic part of the world, so come April I flew back out to Vancouver with no fixed plans other than having a road trip to Penticton. Rick met me at the airport and after a meal and a good night's sleep he took me to Larry and Ann Sutton's to renew my friendship with my mini. Rick had brought a set of jump leads but I told him that I knew my vehicle and I wouldn't need them. I lifted the bonnet dipped the oil and pulled the coil lead off before cranking the engine three or four times until the oil pressure rose. After refitting the coil lead the engine sparked into life so with a big smile, I couldn't help but turn to rick and say "I told you so." Over the next few days, I did a spanner check and left the oil and filter as I had done those items before storing the van, and I took time to check the contents of the plastic boxes to get to know where everything was for the forth coming road trip. A few weeks later I would be back in the driving seat and reminding myself of the real deep reason I was here and the two people that I had lost forever on that day in February.

Now in convoy with Rick and Elaine we were winding our way through the interior of British Columba, the roads were great and the scenery was stunning, and we arrived in Penticton early afternoon to check in at the hotel that would be the base for the Mini Meet. The meet proved to be great fun and well organised and I found out that there is a Mini Meet every year. One year the event is held in the USA and the next year in Canada then each year it alternates between the east and west coasts. The meeting brings lots of minis and people together who have travelled great distances to get there from both Canada and the USA. I've been to a lot of car shows in my time but of all of them, I have always found no matter where in the world they are held the people that go to mini meetings are the friendliest, as their cars are the people's car and that makes us all equal. The first couple of days were spent looking over the many different versions of the car while mixing and meeting old friends and making new ones. The third day was a navigational rally, timed at what was considered a safe speed. The rally involved getting to different locations such as vineyards, museums and eating establishments so as I did not have a second seat in the van, I jumped in to the passenger seat of Steve Kovac's mini to read the notes. Steve had a really nice orange mini traveller that he had driven to the meet from Washington State. Steve and I got on really well and we had a laugh. The trouble was it was Steve's car and he was the driver.

My problem is, I am very competitive and wanted to win and I would use every trick in the book I could to make up time, with no cheating being involved of course. I remember one check point was at a vineyard and I managed to convince Steve to give the wine tasting a miss and in doing that it got us ahead of the pack while everybody else opted to sample the vines. That evening back at the hotel was the grand dinner and prize giving, and I finished up with an award for the minivan. The whole show had been great fun and I took away so many memories from my experience at the Mini Meet. Thoughts of leaving Canada were furthest from my mind and Russia would be for another time, so after the Mini Meet I spent the following months travelling round British Columba revisiting some of the places I had passed through on my drive across Canada the previous year.

During my return and with no real urgency to leave Canada I joined Rick on a road trip with his jeep into the interior, camping under canvas. It transpired Rick wanted to return after a period of twelve months to the location of his last hunting trip where he had lost his camera, one that was not unlike my own. We arrived late afternoon somewhere in the middle of a huge forest having driven up and down so many different forest roads as Rick was trying to figure out how to get as close to where he thought he and son Jeremy had been hunting. Eventually we stopped in the evening by a lake and set up our tents before making a camp fire and cooking the evening meal accompanied by a couple of beers to finish off the day. Next morning after breakfast we decamped and set off once again to try and find the right forest road, which we eventually did. Seeking out the route they had taken from the road into the bush by foot was the difficult part, and all the time Rick was trying to remember back to when he taken his camera out from his jacket pocket. We eventually got out of the jeep and walked up and down the track a couple of times before Rick made the decision that we would walk and make our way slowly uphill from the track, ever mindful to keep an eye out for his camera that could have fallen out of his coat pocket on the walk to the top of the hill. Rick walked ahead and as I climbed, I had mixed feeling of both hope and there was no chance of finding the camera as time and winter had gone by since he was last there. We pushed on for about half an hour before cresting a small plateau where Rick remembered he and Jeremy had been standing looking out for moose or bear. "This is the spot we stopped at Diddy" he told me, "I remember we had a great all-round view from here but I can't remember taking any photos." Rick must have been twenty feet away from me while talking and trying to recall how it had been on that ill-fated trip. Meanwhile I stopped to take a leak, and that was when I spotted I small shinny thing lying in the grass just to my side, it was the camera. Rather than jump up in excitement, I finished what I was doing and hatched a little joke to play on Rick. Checking that he was not looking I picked up his camera and put it in my coat pocket and wandered over in Ricks direction and chatted about what we would do next to do before heading back to the jeep. Just as we were about to make our way off the hill, I pulled out the camera and with it in the palm of my hand and said "Here you are, this is yours."
"Don't be silly that's yours as I've seen it before."
Rick was not for leaving so with that I reached into my coat pocket and pulled out the other camera and said "Who owns this one then?" It's not often Rick gets stuck for words but he was at that moment. It's interesting to say that when we did get back to Pitt Meadows and the camera was cleaned and with the battery recharged it worked and there were some great photos of the past hunting trip.

Still uncertain about when and how I would make it to Russia Larry and Ann Sutton offered to store the mini once again over winter so I could return to the UK. Back home over the winter I did some research on which route I would like to take once the vehicle had crossed the Pacific Ocean. Having worked in Kazakhstan my first thought was to revisit the country, so I used that part of the world to reverse a route backwards that would find me travelling the silk route through China. This route through China looked good as it gave me not only a starting point, but also a port to ship the mini into, so I set about finding out what I needed to do, paper wise for me, and also the mini to make sure everything was legal. The system was not easy to navigate and I could have made it easier by passing it to an agency but that would be completely out of my budget, so I set about doing it myself, looking at what I would need personally when it came to documents and paperwork. Over the winter I did my research and established what I needed for myself before setting about the requirements for the minivan. That turned out to be a nightmare, as it seemed I would be entering the country with a vehicle and myself therefore the following would apply. I would have to re-sit my driving test, the vehicle would have to be vehicle checked (MOT) and insurance was needed both for me and the vehicle. Ok all pretty standard stuff but then came the crunch, I had to seek permission from the army, police and the government and be accompanied by an official of some sort, to make sure I behaved, and this was all at a cost of seven thousand pounds. I was very disappointed because I so wanted to drive the Silk Road into Kazakhstan but at those costs it was never going to happen. I did at the time think that some of the requirements were a scam, but I closed the door on that idea and searched for another way.

That was when I realised huge ships transport cars across the pacific from Japan to the western seaboard of Canada and the United States so they must have return shipments of cargo. Whilst I was looking into the shipment of the mini, I received an e-mail from Rick asking me if I was interested in another Mini Meet next year, this time down in Arizona at a place called Prescott Valley. I took a couple of days to think about it as it would mean crossing the border into the United States and a country that quite honestly, I was in no rush to visit if I was to be truthful. It's true I have spent time in Alaska and I have since been back many times and there are similarities to the lower 48 but you cannot compare the two as being the same.

Eventually I emailed Rick to say I would go, with one stipulation, that we ran the slow pacific coast route 101 and not the fast interstate route as I was now looking into the possibility of carrying on down the Pan Pacific Highway to South America.

That winter back home I got very busy looking into two possible ways that my future travels might take as I had now promised Rick, I would make the trip to Arizona and possible South America. I would have to head to London and the American Embassy to be relieved of several hundred pounds for my ten-year visa. The interview was very interesting and did test my patience. Fortunately, I have learned to be precise and use as few words as possible. Finally I also learned never laugh or joke as it could cost in some way or other whether in time or money with any Border personnel.

Now well into the New Year and back on Mull from my visit to London, I started investigating the potential shipment of the van across the pacific into Japan purely as an exercise for now, but I would at some time have to make that journey. The research was worthwhile, as I found it was possible to load the mini in Vancouver and ship it to Yokohama. This idea was also further advanced when Chris Harper at Minisport gave me the name of a person to contact who could possibly help me in Japan, so when I flew out of the UK for Vancouver in April, I felt quite pleased with myself and the outcome of my research.

I always get a kick out of landing at Vancouver airport. It's so friendly and I have always been processed quickly, so I soon found myself once again being treated so kindly by Rick and Elaine in Pitt Meadows, two very special Canadians who have always helped and supported me. As my flight had landed in the morning I was determined to stay up and get myself into west coast time, so we talked about the upcoming road trip. Rick reckoned that six or seven days would do us to get down the pacific coast at a steady pace. One thing that could be a problem would be the heat when we started to go inland from San Francisco, so fitting an extra radiator would have to be undertaken. As the mini had been in storage over the winter months, I had maintained contact with Larry and Ann Sutton. Larry knew of my pending trip and that some preparation beforehand would be needed so he kindly offered me the use of his garage, and I could stay in the flat above making it easier for me to work when I wanted. Their help and generosity over the years has far outweighed anything I could ever do for them in return.

Digression
My adventures have given me a chance to meet many kind and helpful people on my journey, it's not until you stop and reflect which I did more than ever in this part of the world. I was truly humbled by the people that live in and around Vancouver, British Columba. ~~

Now based at Larry's I settled down to look over the suspension problem of breaking knuckle joints all the time. While I was back in the UK I had spoken with Daniel Harper about my problem and he reckoned the fitting of coil springs all-round should cure the problem, so while placing a shipment order for new tyres and rubber cones, the coil springs were added to the order for me to try out. With the suspension stripped and awaiting new parts I set about improving the cooling system by fitting an extra frontal radiator, which Rick had given me. Larry and his small workshop were to help out with making fitting that would enable me to fit the radiator whilst I could still keep the Winch in place. Both these items I felt would be important not only for this road trip but also if I was to take on South America after the Mini Meet in Arizona.

I received notice that my shipment of parts had left the UK and that they should be with me by the end of that week. Everything was moving along at a steady pace and we were well ahead of our time to leave for Prescott Valley so Larry and Ann offered to take me out for the day to a place called Hells Gate, if I was up for it. Sounded like my kind of place "Let's go for it" I said. We headed out early morning, driving north out of Maple Ridge through Mission and onto the road I had used when I first arrived from Alaska, so I was finding it quite interesting to see what I would find once we arrived at Hells Gate, knowing I had passed by before and what I could have missed. After a couple of hours, we arrived at a car park and proceeded to walk down a foot path to a narrow link span bridge crossing the canyon suspended a hundred feet across at the narrowest point of the Fraser River. There was quite a lot of history attached to this place. Early in the nineteen hundred, during the construction of the Canadian Pacific Railway, a large rockslide was triggered by the construction works and the banks of the canyon fell into the river, thus reducing the width of the river greatly, causing such a volume of water at this point, it became virtually impossible for pacific salmon to swim upstream to spawn. It was impossible to remove the landslide due to the nature and the location so it was decided to construct huge concrete cells that would baffle the water on one side of the narrows, so allowing the salmon to rest in each of the cells and make their way into calmer water. The walk across the hanging walkway while listening and seeing such a torrent of water was pretty spectacular and this was only April, so to come back in spring with the melting snow and when the logs started to move must be something special.
My stay at the Sutton's was comfortable and very easy going. I remember going out for breakfast one morning into Mission with Larry and Ann. I ordered a breakfast that Larry thought I should try and when it came, I took a deep

breath at the size of the plate. Trying to be positive I thought I would give it a go but, in the end, it defeated me. On the way back I received a message to say my shipment of parts had arrived at Ricks and that he would bring them over after lunch. Just after two o'clock Rick arrived with a boot full of new parts and as there were new tyres to be fitted, he offered to collect me the following day and take me over to his local tyre fitting shop to get the new ones fitted. With that agreed I unpacked the rest of my order to look at the coil springs and what was involved in fitting them. That task turned out to be simple and was completed by the end of the day.

Next morning Rick was at Larry's by ten to collect me and the four new tyres, plus the wheels and tyres that were to be changed. After a quick coffee we headed over to Pitt Meadows and the fitting shop. I thought I would have to leave them and come back later but no; they gave great service and sorted my needs in no time at all. On the way back we called in at Ricks for a bite to eat before the short drive to Larry's where we fitted the new tyres and wheels to the van. Now happy that the mini was ready for the trip to Arizona I took the van for a test drive. It was not long before I decided that I did not like the coil spring suspension set up, that was now fitted to the van. I returned to Larry's and decided to remove the coil springs and refit new rubber cones and the adjustable suspension. With all the preparation done on the mini I finally packed my clothes for the start of our journey in the morning, while Rick was outside making the finishing touches to his mini as Elaine packed their travel needs in the house.

Start time was not going to be too early in the morning as the border crossing at Bellingham was not far away, and Rick reckoned it would take half an hour to get through the border, and I was confident as I'd already been to the US Embassy in London and acquired a ten-year visa. The crossing was not that busy so I followed Rick and stuck on his tail deciding to use the same booth. Rick was sent through but as I went through, I was told to report to the passport office. As I pulled outside, I saw Rick's car, the two of us had been stopped, apparently at random, but I think they thought we had drugs in the minis. We both got out of our cars and walked to the passport office while dogs and border officials walked around the vehicles. Once inside we joined several others and sat down awaiting our turn to be interviewed. During this time nobody spoke and the only time you heard a voice was when a name was called. All we could do was sit and watch as a collection of both male and female officers, of various sizes from sixteen stone to twenty odd stone pranced about armed with every offensive weapon I could think of, strapped to their waists while walking up and down. Trying to lose weight, I kept telling myself. That was when I remembered this was one of the many reasons I had never been in a rush to visit this side of the border, but it was too late now to turn back. Half an hour passed before Rick was processed and, on his way out of the building, but for me it would be another hour and a half before I was summoned to a desk to be grilled on my details, which they already had. Finally, they hit on me with the words "What is your itinerary I want to know your itinerary?" The word itinerary is not a word that I use every day so it took me a little time to translate the words into real English. The delay in responding as I tried to figure out a short reply did not do me any good because I told him that I did not have an itinerary as I was driving round the world. The questions went on for a while and I could feel myself getting nowhere. I had been stuck in there for ages and at one point I remember going back to the van and collecting my folder that was full of al the paperwork on me and the mini. Back in the office the border official took a look through my paperwork, but it made no difference, that is when I realised, he was just using his authority to play with me, and I had to keep my cool, until he finally stamped my entry and I walked out of the door. Any border crossing has to be taken seriously and I always remember not to joke until after the paperwork has been stamped, but even then, it pays be careful. Of all the border crossings during all my travels this had to be the worst. It was scary. You guys need to sort your own country out as I am convinced it will implode one day. Rant over.

Back outside Rick must have done a runner with the alleged contraband as I could not see him, Elaine or the mini and it was at this point I did consider doing a U-turn at the next junction and head back to a sensible part of the world but as luck would have it I caught up with Rick who had stopped at the first possible place to wait for me. Once on the road I started to enjoy the drive before arriving in Seattle to meet up with a guy who Rick had arranged to collect some mini parts from. Eventually we left the big city and made it to the coast where we picked up the 101 highway which would take us south. We continued running down the pacific coast and on through Oregon where there were red cedar trees. Their size has to be seen to be believed and at one point I got to drive the mini through the centre of one that had been cut out as an arched tunnel. The weather was really good and with the road hugging the coast it made for pleasant driving with us stopping each night to camp at some great locations. About three days into the trip we reached Gold Beach and camped for a couple of days as it was Ricks birthday and he was keen to take one of those fast jet boat rides on the river. I joined Rick and Elaine along with a few others on a slim lined boat that darted and weaved its way round the bends of the canyon while avoiding the many rocks and shale banks. The trip covered about a hundred miles and was great fun with most of us finishing up with wet cloths.

After a good night's sleep and a hearty breakfast, we returned to our drive and the heat of the day that was ever increasing as we travelled south. The only thing that made it bearable was the breeze that could be felt coming from the coast. Eventually we arrived in San Francisco, where we stopped to take some photos of the Golden Gate Bridge then it was onward through the city to re-join the coast road as far the town of San Luis Obispo where we would turn in land and onto interstate 40 which was made famous by the film Convoy.

Just before the town of Bakersfield I broke another knuckle joint and again I do not know why, but decided I would continue till the evening and change it at our campsite in the desert. Trying to sleep in the evening did not come easy as the heat made it very difficult to get any proper rest. I kept remembering when we had pulled up at gas stations and the attendant asking if we had air con. We'd say no and they'd just laugh at us telling us we would find the hot air hard to breath in the middle of the day.

Next morning, we were up at a sensibly time and pushed on through Kingman still on the 40 that had by now formed part of the famous route 66 taking us through the Mojave Desert. The outside temperature was about 120 degrees and the heat was akin to having hairdryers blowing in my face. It was unbelievable that the steering wheel was so hot I found it difficult to hold. Any water I had could not be kept cold and would become warm to drink. Try as I could to deflect cool air into the mini it was a waste of time as the ambient temperature made it impossible to cool down. I had been keeping an eye on the vans water temperature gauge as it would raise quite high even on some of the small hill climbs we had to make. Equally the temp would drop back on the downward side if I held it in a lower gear. The desert drive had become a worry as the heat was endless. If there was any comfort it had to be the fact, we did not have any steep climbs, they were shallower and long and in keeping with the terrain. I remember looking in the mirror and having to stop to go and collect one of the two chevron marker boards I had on the rear of the van, as it had fallen off due to the heat and the glue had said, "I give in." Progress to the meet was good and we were on course to arrive at the meeting that same evening. We decided to stop for a big mac and a cold drink at lunch time and as Rick pulled in I parked alongside him. Once inside and feeling the benefits of the air conditioning we sat down for a welcome break and some shade.

We probably stopped for about forty-five minutes before returning to our vehicles with Rick getting away before me as he had backed in to his parking spot. I had driven in to my parking spot so I had to reverse out. Starting the engine up I instantly recognised it did not sound right and it began to falter as though it had a plug lead off. Looking under the bonnet all the plug leads were in place, so I got back in the mini telling myself that it would clear its self once I got back on the interstate. After a short distance it did seem to run ok but then I noticed the temperature had started to rise to over one hundred degrees with the engine starting to falter again losing power. All the while I tried to keep moving as I wanted to make it to the meet where I could take a proper look at the problem. I was now really starting to worry about the possibilities of what could happen and I knew it was now only a matter of time. The heat was bad and trying to process things in my head was difficult, and drinking hot water did not help. Rick was running ahead of me; he knew I had a problem so I did my best to keep up with him. My thought was to stop and see if there was anything that could done but the trouble was there was no shade, so I shelved that idea. Then I realised we would be turning of the interstate shortly so with a bit of luck it should have an underpass where I could find some shade. My speed now had been reduced so much I was dragging the mini along at thirty miles an hour due to the lack of power from the engine. With a quick glance at the temp gauge which had now registered one hundred and forty degrees on the clock, it was at that moment it all went wrong, with a bang and a windscreen full of brown water. If I was to have any luck it was the availability of a hard shoulder to run onto and cruise as far down the freeway as I could to the turn off that could be seen in the distance, but unfortunately, I came to a halt short of the exit. Rick by now had stopped and was starting to reverse up the hard shoulder. In the meantime, I had lifted the bonnet and I decided that I would remove the cylinder head and look at the gasket. Rick offered to give me a hand but I insisted that he and Elaine should carry on to the meet and check in as it was far too hot to sit around. I would then follow when I had sorted out the problem.

Now on my own I set about removing the cylinder head as quickly as I could. After a short while the road became unbearable to stand on, and I could see the tar joints in the concrete melting so I had to improvise by taking turns to stand on a piece of wood then the inside of my tool box. After about half an hour a Mini Moke stopped and backed up the freeway the same way Rick had and out got Nolan and Deanna from Mission offering to help. I spoke with Nolan who was a mechanic and I told him what I was planning to do. I assured him I would be fine and I would see them tonight. I returned to stripping the top end of the engine and eventually I lifted the head off and placed it on the floor. While working I was conscious of getting dehydrated even with the hot water, I was forced to drink. With the head off I inspected the head gasket, the like of which I had never seen before. A large part of the gasket had blown away from the water gallery next to number three cylinder and the other place was between number three and four cylinders. My thought was to clean everything up and fit a new head gasket. I found some emery tape and a rag and as I started to clean the oil and water from round the cylinder block face with a rag, which was when I spotted a large crack in the face of the block between number three and four cylinders. I remember standing back on that day and taking a deep breath telling myself that I was now dead in the water and I could do nothing about it. I was concerned what my next move would be as I was now stranded in Mojave Desert. What made me take my next move has puzzled me to this day, maybe I did it because that is the way you would normally continue with the work. I picked up the emery cloth and started to clean round the crack and in desperation my thought was I could fill the crack with metal mender from my first aid kit for vehicles. With a bit more rubbing and cleaning, I spotted a ring round the combustion chamber. The engine had been built with new cylinder liners so on closer inspection the crack was only in the block face. The liners had prevented the crack from entering the combustion chamber, so I might be able to limp out of the desert and get to Prescott Valley. I finished cleaning all the parts and fitted a new head gasket.

I had now been standing the sun for some considerable time and I could tell that it was starting to affect me. I was beginning to have trouble remembering things and that was not helped by the fact any water I had would be needed for the radiator. I could feel myself slowing up and focusing my thoughts became difficult. Trying to finish the work seemed to drag on. The operation for resetting the inlet and exhaust valves which was normally a simple operation became a challenge and, in the end, I had to write the details on how I should do it on the underside of the bonnet in white to help me complete the work correctly. My next job was to check the oil and test it for water, a process that can be simply done by using the flame from a lighter or a match. All you have to do is hold the flame under the end of the dip stick and if it splatters then you have water mixed with oil. Right now, my luck was on the up, as the oil test showed the oil was good. The last job was to fill the cooling system with water and I was fortunate to have enough, by using my drinking water. With fingers crossed I climbed back into the mini and burned my backside on the seat and almost left steering wheel burn impressions on my fingers. Turning the key brought new life back into my trusty steed, and the engine and oil pressure was good. After checking I had left nothing at the side of this famous road, I gingerly crept away down the ramp praising my mini and my luck while watching the temp gauge register normal and thinking we can make it the two hundred miles this evening. The further I drove south the more the scenery changed for the better. The day was now turning into evening giving a cooler temperature and with that came the confidence that I could complete the journey. Now feeling more relaxed I started to reflect on the nightmare that had tested me to the limit. Sure, it was the heat of the day that had brought the vehicle to a standstill but that alone I felt was not the only reason for it to happen. I had done everything that could be done back in Vancouver by fitting an extra radiator and new coolant in the system. It had been exceptionally hot outside on the journey and as long as we kept moving, the hot air would blow into the engine bay, and the cooling system could cope, so why did it all start to go wrong after we had stopped. That kept me puzzled for some time before the penny eventually dropped. The damage was done in the car pack while we sat and ate inside. I had unknowingly caused the start of the failure because I had parked the mini turned the engine off and literally walked straight into the restaurant. That was a cardinal sin in those extreme temperatures. I should not have stopped the engine, but left it running for a while as this would allow the temperature to come down. I should have known better from my rally days, if you stop your car instantly the temperature will rise and continue to rise for a short time after you stop. Late that evening I arrived at the hotel where we were all staying. I pulled up outside the front door to be greeted with a beer by a few mini friends who stood clapping and drinking beer. It soon became obvious that word had got round about my troubles and the odd bet had been placed on my chances of making it. Over the next few days, I would relax and enjoy my time at the meeting with lots of offers of support it I needed any parts for my engine.

On the third day of the meeting Elaine, Rick and myself decided to take the day off and drive in the direction of Flagstaff to the Grand Canyon and take a look at this great wonder. On the way back we stopped at Williams a small town that is just off interstate 40 on the old route 66 so we could have something to eat, and as luck would have it the town was re-enacting the Wild West on the main street with gun fights and stage coaches which we all had to get involved in.

The final day of the meet was at a race track with lots of the minis taking to the track before we had our last evening together for a meal and prize giving. I was truly touched to win the People's Choice Award but all the time at the back of my mind I was wondering if my repair would last. Sadly, this would ultimately lead to a change of plan. I still wanted to head to South America as I'd already done a good third of the leg that would get me down to the tip, but I had to re-evaluate my position. I needed to focus on getting the engine sorted and that would be a lot easier back at Ricks place in Vancouver if we could make it. That evening while enjoying the awards, Rick and I came up with a plan that would see both our minis leaving the next morning at 2 a.m. to set off out of the desert to use the coldest part of the day to our advantage, when we would be heading for the coast to where the ambient temperatures were cooler. It was dark when we left heading west and by 4 a.m. I could see the light starting to appear with a hint that the sun was about to follow and it was not to long before I could feel it on my back. The worry of us making it safely returned to haunt me for the rest of the day. We both pushed on back along the interstate 40 and were reluctant to stop till we got close to Bakersfield where we would join interstate 5 to head north into California. On leaving the Meet we had been instructed to stop in Sacramento by one of our mini friends. She told us that the keys were under the front door mat and she would meet us in a few days. It was so heart warning to meet such wonderful kind people. We had been travelling for 36 hours non-stop and the mini had held together. We would take a two day stop over at our friend's home and in that time I would e-mail back to Minisport in the UK and ask what the possibility was of a new block, the same specification, being sent to Vancouver. Before the end of the day a reply came back telling me they were on it and would process it straight away. Now feeling a weight had been lifted of my shoulders we turned our backs on Sacramento and an oasis that had set us up to be able to push on for Portland and Seattle and those nice people at the Canadian border crossing who even gave me a smile and told me to enjoy my time in Canada. We had covered nearly 3000 miles and in the next half hour we would be back in Pitt Meadows.

The next few days would see me remove the engine from the mini and strip it down. The new block arrived on Saturday morning; the service was better than I had ever seen before, two and a half days from the UK to the west coast of Canada. It would not take me long to rebuild the stripped parts back into the new block and late afternoon on Sunday I only had to refit the head. On cleaning the head up, I found the old head was cracked beneath one of the valve seats. (We found out later it had two more cracks), so the work came to a stop that day. Fortunately, Rick had a spare head sitting on a shelf, it's not the same as the UK where you can just ring up and buy one. Rick said he'd had it a couple of years but it hadn't been used. I feared that it may have been a leaded head, the valve stem oil seals might have gone brittle so I just changed them and put the head on and it worked. It wasn't till I got back to the UK that I found out it was indeed a leaded head. With a fresh start on Monday I refitted the engine back in to the mini, and by early afternoon she was up and running. While having our dinner that night Rick said that he would ring Nolan Kitchener to see if we could run the mini down to his garage for him to check the timing and a make a few adjustments.

I spent a couple of days cleaning and tidying the van before taking myself off on a short tour, with a determination to revisit my favourite Diner just past Function Junction at a place they call First Tracks. The van ran perfectly so I returned to Vancouver and with the blessing from Larry and Ann I could once again leave the mini in storage. So, to my mind the car was running fine again. That would stand me in good stead, but I definitely needed to make plans to get to Russia, in fact I actually asked my Canadian friends to kick me out! I just love that place and its people.

Chapter 15

Yanking my chain

I have always thought how lucky I am to have made the transition from mainland England to an island off the west coast of Scotland many years ago. The move gave me control over my life without the pressures of life's mainstream do's and don'ts. There was a time in the early days when friends would ask me, how do you pass you time? Since them most of them have visited and no longer ask that question. Don't get me wrong life is not perfect but it is me who makes the decision to stay in or to go out when it rains. This particular winter was no different when it came to rain in fact I am sure we got to see close on three months of rain virtually every day so apart from going out to fetch logs for the wood burner I knuckled down to putting serious plans in place to ship the mini into japan.

Having been given the contact details of Shinobu Kitani from Garage Grace near Yokohama by Chris Harper I e-mailed Shinobu and asked for some guidance on shipping the mini into japan. Over the winter months we both kept in contact and through his knowledge and understanding my work became very easy, leaving just the vehicle shipment to organise. Little did I know at the time that Shinobu had been shipping a team of rally prepared minis for a number of years from Japan to the Isle of Man to compete in the historic class on the Manx Rally? Each year the cars were put on a container ship for the two months journey, and the team would fly out to enjoy the rally and have a holiday, before the consignment was all shipped back to japan. Before I could book the vehicle passage, I had to make the decision on what day I wanted to land in Vladivostok, I would then apply for a visa to start on that day to cover me, thus maximising the 30 days the visa would give me to cross Russia.

The visa for Russia was easy and was helped considerably by the staff in the Edinburgh office. They translated my passport, driving licence and vehicle details into Russian, they even gave me a covering letter telling any authorities that stopped me what I was doing while in Russia. I now had a fixed date the third of June so I now had a timeline to consolidate my plans. The next step was to find and book our passage by boat from Japan into Russia that would arrive on the visa starting date and not before. I eventually found a ship that sailed from Japan to Vladivostok via a port close to the north south border of Korea. North Korea looked like it was going to war and I would be calling into Korea, too late I had my visa and it was convinced they wouldn't shoot at one of their own ships, would they? This was my only choice and the ship would arrive in Russia two days after my visa started therefore it did not eat into my visa days to much. Mind you I was very aware that any delays in customs or on the road such as possible breakdowns could eat heavily into my 30 days. With the visa and my passage sorted I turned to booking the pacific crossing for the mini. This was easier as I could book some flexible time for the arrival of the vehicle into Japan and give me over a month to stay there while meeting the people that Shinobu had mentioned in one of his e-mails.

Now happy that I had linked together the passage of the mini from Canada to Russia all that was now left to do would to book my flight out of Vancouver to Tokyo. I knew what day the mini would arrive in Japan so I made some enquires and with it a startling revelation, that once I had put the UK origin of my payment card into the system, the price became stupid. In the end Rick Higgs booked and paid for the flight back in Canada and when I arrived in the spring I paid him back all at half the price I had been quoted. Big lesson learned there. When eventually I leave the UK for my final leg, I will be into my fourth year of this adventure. I was still ever mindful of why I had taken on my journey of searching, and mending the loss of close ones and that it was a private matter that I had to deal with on my own. When I first started thinking about taking on the challenge, I can remember being approached to film and document my days on the road then send in a report two or three times a week. At the time I was glad I had turned the offer down; however, it did motivate me to keep a log that I am very grateful for.

With many years having passed I decided to set up the Wrong Way Round site on Face Book. The decision did not come easily but I felt a need to give something back to the many people who had not only helped me but were keen to follow my adventures and this seemed the best way to go about it. For almost a month I worked on what to put on the site. An easy way was with photos, I had hundreds, and so with that in mind I began with the vehicle build and the preparation, which soon became popular with the mini fans. Then I followed with posts of the start in Halifax and continued on through my travels in Canada and Alaska I eventually caught up with adventure before leaving for

Japan. The outcome of the Face Book site was startling as people from all over the world either liked the site or joined in by sending me messages with some of them very touching. The site for me was at its best once I had arrived in Russia. Word had got round and the feedback was great, but my problem was getting internet access or the lack of it which could go for days on end.

Spring time would see me back on a plane heading for Vancouver with Rick once again collecting me from the airport. I am forever telling myself and others that I don't do any planning well maybe a little but you will be glad to hear that I had now convinced myself I must be able to string together two plans otherwise the next couple of months could lead to disaster with me having to get the cavalry to come and find me. Feeling relaxed as payments and plans had been made, my journey would soon take on totally new challenges. I had set my route of counties to travel three years before, knowing the good and easy stuff would come first, leaving me to take on the greatest challenge of all committing the mini for shipment across the pacific and the point of no return. I was starting to get those uneasy nerves again the type that tests you to perform at your best.

I would stay in Canada for a good few weeks as I had to prep the mini for shipment and Rick had entered us in the classic car Rally they call the Spring Thaw. We would use his mini over three or four days along with a whole host of ancient and classic cars again run similar to the one we had at Mini Meet West in Penticton two years before. This was the second year I had been invited to join like-minded people and friends. Many of the competitors are from the Vancouver mini club. Larry and Ann Sutton were out in there standard 1964 Cooper S, one of the finest standard forms I have come across for a long time. They could be seen enjoying the freedom of the road like many others. Sadly, we would come across the other type of driver the one who thought he had something to prove to the rest of the entrants. The weather was good for the time of year with snow only found on the very highest mounts of the interior. I really enjoyed the get together both during the day then later on in the evenings. The route and the views were stunning and the event was something I would put my hand up and return for anytime.

My final couple of days in Canada now seemed a little sombre as I would be leaving for good, and it was starting to sink in no more so than when I went to collect my much-reduced flight ticket to Tokyo. I would be leaving good times and many good people that had treated me like family. Unknown to me Rick and Elaine had organised a barbeque in their back garden on my last night in Canada, inviting family and members from the Mini club that included Nolan and Deanna, Larry and Ann, Ken Martin and john Goolevitch and his wife to name but a few. The weather was good and the conversations and eating went on for some time, probably close to midnight. Finally, I stood up and thanked everyone for treating me so kindly over the years, and I was genuinely leaving tomorrow, but I would be back some time in the future to pick up where we had left of.

I did not sleep too well, as I found myself buzzing all night reflecting on what I had achieved so far, yet tinged with anticipation of what lay ahead of me. Rick ran me to the airport that morning and I can remember shedding a tear. Rick had been the instigator of many good and great things that had happened to me in this part of the world. We finally shook hands and I turned and headed in to the crowd looking for gate 13 and a plane that would cross the International Date Line somewhere in the mid Pacific Ocean and onward to the land of the rising sun.

Before the trip to compete alongside Rick on the Spring Thaw Rally I spent a few days prepping the mini for shipment on the container ship. There were two ways I could send the mini. One was a twenty feet container which was the safest way of shipping, but the costliest by the time all the expenditure been added up, so I reverted to the same system I used when I shipped the vehicle across the Atlantic and booked a Ro-Ro Crossing as it is known. It is much cheaper as the vehicle is simply driven on and off, the biggest problem being possible damage and the safety of any contents in the vehicle. The Atlantic crossing had been fine with the vehicle arriving in Halifax with no problems and when I did collect it from the docks a note had been left on the key ring by someone telling me to enjoy my travels. I knew the pacific crossing would take about twenty days after leaving the port in Vancouver and the ship would also call into Seattle and other ports down the west coast of America before heading off in the direction of Japan, so with the vehicle being at sea for so long I decided to remove all the contents from the rear of the van and make a timber head board behind the driver's seat and then repack the van. By doing this, I thought it would give me the security of protecting the contents. With the day of delivery now here, Rick guided me down to the port and we eventually found the office of All Cargo Express, where I was to leave the mini as they would deliver it to the ship. Most of the paper work had been done so both Rick and I assumed we would get away reasonably quickly. The fact was it took longer than expected due to me being asked questions I had already answered when filling in the paperwork some time before. I was starting to get a little restless with the repeated questions considering payment had been made some time before. I recall walking round outside waiting for someone to come out and at least look over the vehicle.

Rick kept trying to calm me, with me telling him I was in control. A chap came out with a clip board to check the van over for bumps and scrapes which is standard practice, and. he seemed happy with the roof box and tyres bolted down the top of the roof, all of which I had made known on their shipping form. Finally, I thought we were getting somewhere, but then he opened my door to look inside and noticed the partition board behind the driver seat asking me what was behind the board, to which I replied my clothes and spares that I listed on the contents shipping form, "sorry but you can't leave them in there, they will have to come out repacked and sent separately." There is a saying that is used this side of the pond. "You're yanking my chain," the British way of saying it is "You're extracting the water," or words to that effect! I was not best pleased, and turned on the man using words as mentioned, telling him that if what he was telling me I now had to do, after having completed all the paperwork months ago, then this vehicle would not be going on the ship and I would cancel my order. I remember thinking no, I have done my part correctly you are in the wrong and if I separate my things then there was a good chance of not seeing them again. Not only that but I felt that a request for another payment would follow. Sorry but you have had your money and that was not going to happen. With his tail between his legs and me feeling I had shot myself in the foot, the guy set of in the direction of the office. I could tell Rick was a little nervous at the thought of what could happen. Shortly after the guy and his clip board came back and told me that they were more than happy with my paperwork and the vehicle could now be put into the bond area. Smiles all around, and Rick and I headed back to Pitt Meadows in his little yellow mini to prepare the car for our trip into the interior in a few days' time.

Chapter 16

Run in with the law

Once again I was now in the air and I would find myself passing the mini while it was on the high seas. I eventually touched down at Narita airport on fifth of May some 40 kms from central Tokyo and its neon lights very late in the evening. My plan was to get a bus in the hope that I could find a hotel near the Japanese automobile federation as they would have to authenticate the mini to give me clearance with customs. I eventually sourced a reasonably priced hotel in Tokyo. The next day I found the Japanese Automobile Club building and in no time, they signed off my paperwork and gave me clearance to proceed to the customs office in Yokohama Port. I was there for what seemed like a lifetime and it wasn't until four in the afternoon that they had cleared all the paperwork which allowed me to go to their subsidiary customs office at the docks and collect the mini, but just as I was leaving, I was suddenly stopped and asked to return everything. After some confusion it transpired the ship carrying the mini was still at sea.

Now unsure when the ship would arrive, I spent another couple of nights trawling around Yokohama looking for cheap hotels and in doing so discovered the seedier areas of the city. Having walked round the Chinatown area I eventually found a small hotel, The Hotel Happy. Not able to speak Japanese was a disadvantage, but I was fortunate as once inside the prices were displayed on a large board fixed to the wall, showing six different tariffs. I decided on the cheapest which included a double bed and settled for that. Looking round for the reception area a small hatch suddenly slid open and a little old lady's face was peering at me, saying something I could not understand. I gave her the correct money, as indicated on the pricing board, and she banged down a key and shut the hatch. Pleased at last to have found a place to put my head down, I made my way upstairs to the room and took a long shower before climbing into bed. At midnight I got a strange phone call that somehow, I eventually understood. I was being told my time was up and I had to leave the room. Still not fully awake or understanding why I had to leave I got up in a pretty bad mood and put some clothes on to go downstairs and ask the woman what was going on. I left the room and walked along the corridor to the lift and waited for the door to open. I walked inside and turned, just as the door was closing, and on lifting my head, I could see a glass cabinet in the corridor displaying an assortment of sexual items. As the lift door closed the penny dropped and my pulse rate went off the scale, thinking that men with axes and swords would come and get me if I stepped out of line. Now down stairs and fully understanding what had happened I stood at the hatch trying to negotiate the rest of my night's sleep, finally paying a few more yen for the ok to stay? It sure was one scary moment brought on by my own naivety.

After a few days of exploring I decided to contact Shinobu, and we came up with a simple plan for me to catch the train and travel to the station nearest his garage where he would meet me. This relatively simple task turned out to be a small nightmare, but one I am glad I experienced. The Japanese railway is so efficient and I remember standing in the main station looking at hundreds and hundreds of people going about their day in an orderly manner, no pushing or shoving, just respect for each other and it was a pleasure to just stand and watch and it felt good to be a part of it. As I only had the name of the destination station it took a little time for me to convince myself which train, I needed to catch. Eventually I arrived at the correct station and was met by Shinobu in his Morris Minor van. We put my travel bag in the back and I climbed into the front seat to enjoy a steady and peaceful drive back to Garage Grace. Shinobu made some calls to the customs office and we were told the ship was sitting at the quayside. Armed with all the paperwork we finally collected the vehicle, but I was instructed to drive it to their inspection area where they would do checks on the vehicle. This was all a little strange to me as I had to take the mini and drive it across town to the customs check area, so I just followed Shinobu who was in his BMC 1800 land crab. While on my way the temperature gauge on the mini shot off the scale, so we stopped and topped up the radiator with some water that Shinobu had in the boot of his car. We eventually arrived at a very clean and tidy customs facility and I was instructed to drive through a huge building which was suitable for trucks where they were scanned for drugs and people. I then went into a building and was asked to remove the contents. This was when I discovered the van had been broken into while at sea. I had put a board up behind the driver's seat to protect my stuff but someone had managed to get an arm behind it and pulled out anything that was loose. All of my bedding had been taken plus some clothing. Fortunately, that was it for any further setbacks. The customs people were really friendly and courteous as all they were interested in was looking for drugs, and my layout of parts and personal items was fine with them.

Because of the water loss problem with the mini, Shinobu towed me back to his house as by this time it was quite late. As the day had been so busy, I had not even thought about where I would be staying that night, but that was all settled when Shinobu told me to bring my case as I was welcome to stay there. I went in and met his wife Hiroko and their daughter Aoi. Their house was lovely, not very big but most Japanese don't go in for large properties. The first thing I had was a cup of tea, made with proper English tea and in mug that had a picture of Big Ben on it. Everywhere I looked I could see many things that would not be out of place back home which I found very comforting and made me feel at ease. There is a saying, "When in Rome do as the Romans do," so that night I went to sleep in my room on the floor with a rolled-up pillow under my head and slept well, so much so, it was late when got up for breakfast. Hiroko was in the kitchen and she asked me what I would like for breakfast which turned out to be Kellogg's cornflakes, toast and marmalade with that mug of tea again. Thinking it was a work day I asked Hiroko if Shinobu had gone to work, but she told me not and that he was outside. Finishing my breakfast, I went outside and found Shinobu with the bonnet up on the mini. While he was searching for the water leak, he had found the bottom hose had burst and he was now replacing the part for me topping up the radiator with water coolant. Closer inspection of the damaged hose made me think, rightly or wrongly, the hose had been sabotaged while the vehicle was at sea, as the hose was slit on the bend into the water pump. The vehicle had been fine on leaving Canada and had not done any mileage.

Happy with the work done to my mini I followed Shinobu to his garage and as it was Saturday, there were a number of his friends at his work place. Once inside I realised, I had stepped into a treasure box of minis and man stuff. I was taken upstairs where we removed our shoes before going into a room that had been adapted to a meeting place, with about eight chairs round a table that was now full of Shinobu's friends and customers. I was introduced to everybody and spent the rest of the day talking to people and looking round the garage. I recall looking over Shinobu's Mini Cooper S and also Tsuchiya's Mini Cooper Rally Cars, the ones that have been shipped to the Isle of Man for many years to compete in the highly praised Rally yearly Rally. These two cars were spotless and maintained to the highest of standards you will ever see. The workmanship impressed me that much I just had to tell the man who was responsible for the presentation of these cars. Shinobu's response to me and something I will never forget was to say, no David, you should look at my customers cars. I was quickly learning about the people in this part of the world. They have a totally different outlook and understanding of life and the people that live in it, these people were a pleasure to be with at any time.

Before leaving to go back to Shinobu's house that evening, it was decided that I should leave the van at the garage, and join the group of friends the following day in their convoy of British vehicles, that would consist of Morris Minors, Minis, MGB's and 1800's the idea being they would show me around. Next day we met up at the garage and I took up a seat in one of the minis and over the next few days we did the same thing, each time visiting different places. One of the most notable places I was shown was the location were Honda first started. The site turned out to be no bigger than thirty feet by twenty feet with nothing now standing on the site other than some stone covering the area. Over the next few days, I would visit many places such as parks covered in flowers and trees of petals. The Buddhist temples were very interesting and I can recall visiting one of the biggest Buddhas' to be found in Japan, it was so big I was able to go inside and walk around. I was very grateful to have been taken around and looked after for a few days by such a wonderful group of people, but unbeknown to me the van had been in the garage for the fitting of a completely new suspension system that Shinobu and his son wanted me to have. On arriving back at the garage in the afternoon all the work had been completed on the Minivan, Shinobu informed that he customs officers at head office would like me to call by and show them the Mini. I didn't have to go, but felt that I should, perhaps I had been to friendly with them on my first visit to get my paperwork cleared before they released the van while it was still at sea.

The following day, with the van ready, I went out of courtesy back to Yokohama and the customs office. Shinobu gave me two different routes and the one I favoured was through the country. I impressed myself by finding the main office once more. I parked and took the lift to the third floor to meet up with several people who had tried to help me a week before. As soon as I walked in, they remembered me, and I offered them my paperwork, but they just wanted to look at the mini so we stepped over to the window and by their gestures everyone seemed to be happy.

Back in the van I made my way out from the customs and onto the road, and shortly after I found myself on the toll road system where I was lost, very lost, so much so, it would last for eight hours and a box full of receipts I've never dared to add up, it was an absolute nightmare!

I had so many great days while staying in Japan with Shinobu and Hiriko. One of those days was when they asked me if I would like to go with them to their daughter Aoi sports day which was being held at her school. It was a Saturday, and we joined many others in the playground. We sat on the seats that made up the perimeter round the games area. It was very colourful and once underway it was very well organised and based on team work rather than individuals. At the lunchtime break Hiroko produced a picnic basket she had prepared and we all sat on the ground for an enjoyable lunch. After the lunch break the games continued before the finale which was very colourful and involved the four teams bursting huge hanging baskets of fire crackers. For me the whole day was truly special, I was the other side of the world joining a family for a day in their lives, and I could not have felt more at ease.

A few days later I decided to adventure out and camp with the van to explore the coast road south of Yokohama, calling in on the small fishing ports and camping there overnight. This part of the world is all about fish and fishing each and every day. I would spend the next few days sticking to the coast before turning in land and making my way for Mount Fuji and the race circuit. On the drive inland I climbed a very twisting pass and once over the pass the road was flatter but still has lots of bends. It was on this part of the drive I found myself diving through a built-up town and by luck the name on a building jumped out at me. Kent Garage stood out in green and white, so I slowed up to take a look and it was then I discovered they had rows of classic minis, so I pulled in and stopped. The whole site was full of everything classic mini, and I met the owner Mr Kiyoshi Katsumata who showed me around. We ended up in the show room and an office full of photos of past visitors; Jensen Button from his days at Honda plus a photo of Paddy Hopkirk, who had dropped in at some time. I spent some time in the workshop looking at two of the cars they were working on, one of which was a very nice 1300GT before I made my way back on the road.

My routine was falling back into place, with evening meals, bed, sleep, then breakfast, and on the road again when I was ready. The drive for me was most enjoyable as it made me focus as I took in the twist and bends on my way up and down the very tight country roads which just seem to flow on and on, occasionally passing by small hamlets. It was in one of these small towns I was passed by a police motor cyclist who stopped and I was quizzed in sign language and abrupt Japanese, with me throwing replies back in English. Basically I could feel I was being threatened and was being told to leave the country, he made out I was in big trouble. I just kept my patience and nodded my head in agreement. I figured out afterwards he was looking for a bribe. Now with nervous thoughts, I took off and made a dash to find somewhere to camp for the night. That was when I spotted a sign that said viewing point for Mount Fuji. As I arrived at the entry point, I turned the steering wheel, but the van only wanted to turn a little, with a lot of steering wheel movement. I stopped and turned the steering wheel and felt the wheels only slightly move, my steering had failed. Gingerly I managed to get the van into the car park, which was empty, where I could look into what had happened. It did not take too long to figure out what had happened. The steering column would make endless turns while the front wheels stayed motionless and it was obvious the problem lay in the foot wheel and I would have to take the pinch bolt out from the bottom of the steering column to inspect the threads on the column and the steering rack. I was now starting to worry a little as I did not have a spare column, or steering rack and the thought of changing a rack, if I had one, did not bode well. I have done them with engine and sub frame in place, but it's a struggle. With the column now off, I took a look at the steering rack spline that sticks through the floor. That seemed to be ok, much to my relieve, and on extracting myself out of the foot well, it would appear I had gathered a small audience interested in what I was up to. Now I turned my attention to the column. I placed it upside down and sat it on the steering wheel boss taking a look at the inner end that fits into the rack. Straight away a could see small sliver signs of metal. Yes, the column had failed, luckily in some ways for me at this point as the softest metal had succumbed to my travels. My audience had now increased to about twelve people and I could see they were very interest in the whole event. They occasionally asked me questions, and one or two started to move away, leaving a few to stay and wonder what I was going to do next. Diving into my tool box I got my needle file set out and picked out the small triangle file, then set about trying to remake some sharp edges to the worn-out grooves. The process took a little time before I inserted two blades into my hacksaw to widen the pinch bolt gap. This done I refitted the column to the rack then I found a new bolt to refit in the pinch spline. Using two new nuts with the bolt, I ran the two nuts down the bolt to pull it all together. Happy with the temporary repair I decided to stop and camp at the viewing point for the night, and while cooking the evening meal of pork chops with fried potatoes, I managed to access the internet and e-mail Kent Garage with my problem and told them I would try and make it back to the workshop.

Next morning, I made my way back to Kent Garage where I met up with Mr Kiyoshi Katsumata and his son again, who presented me with two steering columns. I fitted one of them and cable tied the other as a spare to the roll cage. Job done I was now happy knowing the steering was once again safe. I went and washed my hands before going to the office to pay for the parts, but I was told that payment was not needed and if I was happy, they would like me to join them for dinner the Japanese way. I accepted, and the three of us got into a very nice 4x4 Jaguar Estate and set off for a restaurant where I enjoyed the traditional way of sitting and eating real Japanese food. Following the meal, I went back to the garage and spent a little time looking round the many interesting vehicles and parts they had collected, before saying my farewell.

That afternoon I decided to start heading back to the coast and return to Garage Grace the following day. Late in the evening I got to the top of Hakone Pass where there was a pull off for trucks where they could stop and park. I joined the few already there and set up my camp on the tarmac not bothering with food as I had eaten earlier on. Next morning would see me with my Matty stove and a box of eggs making a large omelette, much to the amazement of the truck drivers. By ten o'clock I had packed my things away and was on the road enjoying a steady run back to Shinobu's workshop arriving early on Friday evening.

The weekend would see me first at the garage as Saturday was a get together day, with people appearing with British cars that Shinobu and his team looked after. I walked round outside stunned by the number of cars with several Morris Minor saloon and estate cars, BMC 1100/1300, 1800, Austin A 40's and MG Midgets along with MGB's, and of course no end of Minis and Mini Clubman's. I took time to look at them all and talk where I could with the owners. I soon formed the opinion they loved driving and enjoyed these very old but British cars and it all felt a little like the nineteen sixties and seventies. Sunday, I spent most of the day at Shinobu and Hiroko's house just relaxing as it was decided I would go down to garage the following morning and reload all my many boxes back into the van.

Monday morning would see me having breakfast with Shinobu, Hiroko and Aoi for the last time before travelling to the garage where I loaded the van and filled up with petrol. There was quite a gathering of people with Shinobu giving me the address of Mr Takashi Furuhashi from Dinky Classics. The idea was for me to call in and see him if I had time. Hiroko had bought a map and had marked a route that would take me past Dinky Classics. We all made our farewells, hoping we could catch up at the Isle of Man Rally sometime in the future.

It had been almost three weeks since I had first set foot in Japan and it was time for me to start heading south and west across this fantastic country, heading for the port of Sakaiminato and my departure for Russia. I set off and took the same route, over the pass where I had camped at a few days before, the weather was not good and for the next few hours it continued to rain by the bucket full, fortunately a little after dinner time the weather started to improve, and I arrived at Dinky Classics just after two o'clock. Finding the place was easier than I thought. The double gates had a huge wooden painted poster I recognised from the sixties, of the BMC Mini that won the European Rally Championship. The gates were closed, and I got out of the van. The first thing that stood out for me was the driveway, all very neat and tidy, something you would expect in Japan, but what was unusual were the thousands of bricks that stretched the full length of the drive right up to a building that would look more at home back in Briton. To all intent and purpose, it was a bungalow and a driveway made of British bricks, and it all felt a little strange until Mr Furuhashi came out to greet and welcome me before taking me inside to what felt like a small museum, full of all things mini and memorabilia from the sixties and seventies. We went into his office and drank tea where he told me that Shinobu had sent him an e-mail pre warning him that I may arrive at some time. I was keen to know about the driveway and bungalow and how it had come about, and I asked him how they became to be there. I quickly learned that Mr Furuhashi travelled most years to the UK and attended the big classic auto jumble at Beulieu to purchase items that he would ship back to Japan by container. If he was unable to fill the container, then he would buy products such as doors and building items from B&Q or Home Base to fill the container. Later that afternoon I found myself extremely embarrassed as I had been booked into a very nice four-star hotel by Mr Furuhashi, and he would not hear a no from me, so I checked in and made my way to my room. Once I had settled in, I took a shower and found some clean clothes, as I was going to be collected later and taken to an obscure restaurant that had whole MIG Jet's as part of the decor. The evening was very pleasant, as we were joined by some friends of Mr Furuhashi and the evening went on until late. I had been booked in to the hotel for two nights and after breakfast next morning I was collected by Mr Dinky and taken to meet some of his friends and customers and view their business premises. I have to say how privileged I felt to be driven round and shown the inside of buildings that were full of British made cars. There were two such places I remember well. The first venue housed a mixed assortment of Jags, Martins, Lotus and Jensen's MG, and other assorted vehicles, none of them modern, and most of them as far as I could see, would be capable of being driven from the building. While there I spotted an Aston Martin that sure looked like the original car that a certain Mr Bond used to drive, if the number plate was anything to go by. The second place we visited looked like an old farm barn made of corrugated steel. We entered the building by a small side door and once the lights had been turned on, I was left speechless. I was confronted by rows of pallet racking full of minis that were stacked three high from the floor to the roof. Most were complete cars with the odd body shell sitting on pallets. Having seen all of those cars, the next thing that took my eye was the endless lines of engines and gear boxes all very neat and tidy. This building was a time warp and that was confirmed when I started to look at the collection of front sub frames that still had their engines in. One I spotted still had the hydro elastic units and its Cooper S engine in. The one next to it had its 1071 tag still on the back of the unit, covered in dust, and a rocker box that read Downton. I would have gladly been left all day to look around but I did not want to show discourtesy to my guide. No wonder they're in short supply they're all hidden away in Japan. This country never ceased to amaze me in every way, and people's kindness and generosity came as an everyday way of life. I felt truly honoured to have found myself in this part of the world with a nation of likeminded people. We could learn a great deal from them.

Next morning would see me thanking Mr Furuhashi for the welcome he gave to me. I was now leaving on the last leg across Japan to arrive at the port of Sakaiminato for my departure to Russia in three days' time. As I drove away it started to rain and as I climbed away from the pacific side of Japan into the mountains the rain turned into a monsoon and my pace slowed to almost a stop. Once out of the hilly area the rain eased and buildings started to appear. I was now on the road of a thousand traffic lights and would keep to the 45 kms speed limit. It was well past lunch time and I was thinking of stopping for something to eat. I pulled up at some traffic lights and spotted a police car in my mirror. The lights changed and I moved off, but not long after the police car pulled past me and indicated for me to stop. I stepped out of the mini armed with my big black file of paperwork that even impresses me. The police officer walked back to the van as I laid my folder on the van bonnet and flicked the pages over in the hope that would impress the officer enough to allow me to continue. And why not, it had worked before. After a few minutes I thought that I had succeeded, only to be taken round to the rear of the mini where the British number plate was pointed out to me. Conversation between us was nil and I pointed to the paperwork. He pointed to the registration plate and then made some calls, finally indicating for me to follow him back to the police headquarters in the mini. Once inside the compound I entered the building and went into very large office where there were police detectives. All the time I was shown courtesy and respect, but having said that I was still worried about the outcome despite all the paperwork I had in place. I continued to follow two officers, one I soon formed the opinion was superior, and it would be to his room I was taken to for questioning. I sat down on the chair and placed my file on the table while the officer pulled up his chair and sat down. I then proceeded to open my file, as I did not totally understand why I had been stopped, so I went through my pages pointing out firstly that I had my international driving licence, vehicle insurance for Japan and paperwork for the vehicle that had all been cleared by the Japanese automobile club and the customs in Yokohama. All of a sudden, the police officer asked me in broken English why you have number plates that should not be in Japan. I tried to explain about the Carnet De Passage paperwork that clears the vehicle for use in Japan. Having listened to me he stood up and asked me if would I like some tea and he returned soon after with both tea and biscuits before departing and leaving me again for some time. I had now been in the station for more than five hours with the officer occasionally coming back with a smile on his face and tray of tea and biscuits. He came back and asked me if he could have the Carnet De Passage from the folder, so I pulled out a photo copy from behind the official and presented it to him, which he accepted with a smile.

Digression
Every piece of paperwork in my folder of 84 pages I had photocopied at least four times and each copy had been placed behind the original copy. This was something I had done back home with great pride and even to the extreme of copying my wiring loom plus every box and containers contents, the whole tool kit was itemised also. By doing this it could save me a lot of time at a border with a cocky officer who wanted to know every item in the vehicle. ~~

Finally, just after six thirty the officer came into the room again offered me tea while informing me, I was clear to leave. Sitting down he set about telling me what investigations he had conducted to reach his final conclusion of clearing me to continue using the vehicle. He told me that his police force had never seen a British number plate and I told him I fully understood that. They had also never seen a Carnet De Passage before, let alone what it was intended for, and his investigations took him finally to a government office that eventually confirmed my paperwork was legal and in order. He and his officers had learnt something new. As I walked out of the small office to retrace my tracks to the outside yard, I was joined by six or more police officers and as I walked across the yard, they applauded me all the way to the mini and out through the gate. I had the biggest smile my face that I had had for some time, brought on by a group of well-meaning police. I now drove with confidence knowing that I would not to be locked up and my bed for the night would be in my steel box and not behind steel bars. By midnight I had reached the port and took a quick drive round to find the departure location of my ship before venturing about six miles out of town where I found an empty car park on a headland viewing point where I set up camp for the night. Next morning, I cooked breakfast of eggs and toast before emptying the van and setting everything in place for my arrival in Russia and the port of Vladivostok.

I didn't have to be at the port office till after lunch time where I was to meet with my agent. A little after three a young lady came in to the seating area and joined me introducing herself at Tatiana. She spoke good English and told me everything was in place and we just needed to go and see the customs at four, as the ship would be leaving at seven. The customs were good with me and they talked more than checking or looking at my items. My paperwork was stamped and I was told to drive the mini onto the ship so they could set about tying the vehicle down. I then walked off the ship and back to the ferry building to make use of the internet with Tatiana talking to me and helping out. The time passed pleasantly as we talked about each other's countries and come six forty-five it was time for me to say good bye and board the ship. Tatiana warned me to be careful when I got to her county, and explained that one of her customers was murdered ten days previously. He was a biker and had gone into the forest and hooked up with some guys who'd been drinking, they had a disagreement, which resulted in his death. All this was very sobering as I walked up the gang plank and my thoughts also turned to the fact that tensions between North and South Korea were just about to escalate and we would be calling into the port of Donghae in a day or two.

Chapter 17

Into the danger zone

I was now at sea and the thoughts of what my agent had told me about the possible dangers that lay ahead were very much in the back of my mind. Whilst on the ship something happened which didn't come close to her warning but the similarities were there. During the first night I joined a young Russian guy for a drink, his name was Yuri and he spoke good English and we struck up a relationship over the course of the journey. We would sit and talk, and I soon learned that he makes the trip about six times a year to buy goods in Japan and then ship them by container back to Russia.

Later than I usually like to eat, I decided to head to the bar and have my evening meal. Steak looked the best option and it was at a price that was half the cost back home. On leaving the lounge bar, which was situated at the stern of the ship, I bought a bottle of beer and went for a walk, passing through the central deck area, and I arrived at an open deck that was covered by a roof. The deck area had a couple of large wooden tables and seats the type you would find in a picnic area. One of the tables had a group of people sitting down enjoying themselves and the other was empty. I thought about stopping to sit down but as quicky as the thought came, I changed my mind and carried on to investigate the ship further. Just as I walked on a voice shouted "Dave." I turned round to see who had called me and Yuri the young Russian guy was standing up at the table beckoning me over to join the group. Normally I would be cautious and I would quickly come up with a reason to keep moving, but because we had met, I walked over to the end of the table to say hello whereupon I was introduced to the other five people at the table. All of this was conducted in part English and part Russian. I remained standing and putting my James Bond brain into gear, and assessed as much information on the gathered party, while viewing the assorted items displayed on the table. There were many beer bottles, several vodka bottles and Jack Daniels bottles. With a big smile on my face and a head full of caution I sat down clutching my beer bottle. At this point their hospitality started, as they offered me both the vodka and the Jack Daniel bottle. It was now time to be hypervigilant and remain on my guard. I felt my survival now depended on the half full bottle of beer I had bought in the lounge, which was grasped in my right, hot and sticky hand, and using the internationally recognised hand signs and gestures I led them to believe I was ok with what I had in my hand. While sitting at the table I was well aware of what lay ahead in the future weeks and months. I was entering a part of the world that played by a totally different set of rules and I was not fazed by it, in fact I was looking forward to the challenge as it would I felt, test my character. Over the next couple of hours, I stayed at the table only getting up on occasions and gesturing that was going to the bar to get another bottle of beer, when in fact all I was doing was going to the gents and topping it up with water. While we were all at the table, we were joined by another guy who had seen me early on, and had taken an interest in the mini when it was on the quayside. He too could speak English and before long he asked me if he could take a look at the mini. "Sure," I said "You can look when we come of the boat in Vladivostok."
"No, now" he said.
It's below decks so we are not able to I told him.
"Yes, its ok," he said "Follow me" and with that the whole table got up and walked off, leaving me sitting on my own. Hell, I thought the van could be in for unseen mishaps, so I got up and followed the tail Enders round the ship and below decks, through several water tight closed doors. As I followed, I kept thinking this is not in the script. Just before the last door we were met by a chap in white overalls and I feared the worst, but it seemed I did not have to worry as our leader put his hand inside his pocket and handed him a remuneration, which allowed us to enter the car deck hold. The main party made their way in and I too causally stepped inside, still fearing armed guards could appear any time. The car deck was well lit and right opposite the door stood the mini. It was soon surrounded by half a dozen wobble bodies, each of them wanting their photo taken with me alongside the van. I acted quickly to try and get some discipline in place thinking we could all leave as soon as possible. Thankfully all went well and we returned from the bowels of the ship to the mayhem of the table full of drink. Not long after I made my excuses to leave for my bunk room, telling them I would see them the following day, as the rest of the table had decided to venture along to the forward bar where there was a disco was underway.

I got to the room and turned the light on. My case was still on the lower bunk and the three other beds had bags on but were unoccupied. I undressed and climbed into the bunk and pulled the curtains across soon finding myself asleep. I must have been in bed for some time before I was suddenly awakened by thumps and bangs. Unsure of what was going on I peeped out between the curtains into the darkness of the room lit only by the light of the open door.

Fearing to open the curtains any further, I could see there was a full-on fight happening, with three of the guys that had been sitting at the table with us with early on. All three where kicking the shit out of each other using any loose items, such as the bunk ladders and the two chairs, to hit one another with. This was serious and I could see blood everywhere. The fighting must have been going on for five minutes and in that time, I wondered if they knew I was there and if they did, how long would it be before I got dragged into what was a full-on fight, that felt like it could go on for some time. On the odd occasion the shadow of a body would fall past my curtains followed by a thump. By now the door was closed and the room was in total darkness with the fight still in full action. I kept thinking, how they can see each other, but they were just lashing out at anything that moved. Suddenly the door opened and I looked through the curtain and could see the young Russian guy that I had first met enter the room to try and stop the fight. The trouble was they all turned on him. I now started thinking when will they stop, as it had now been going on for some fifteen minutes or more. Still in my bunk and untouched I started to think why I had not been touched as they had plenty of chances. I began to realise that this was a group of so-called mates full of drink and their frustration and anger was aimed purely at each other. Suddenly things went quiet, so I looked through the slit in the curtains, where I could make out a single tall but thin man standing at the door with a baton in his hand. I remember thinking where the hell have you been till now. He was obviously security, so I slide the curtain a little further open and he looked across at me. I just nodded my head the once and pulled the curtain closed, at which point he marched the whole group off to the lock up cell for the night and peace returned to the cabin. I climbed out of my bunk to take a look at the room. It had been destroyed and anything that could be broken had been, but the scary bit was the blood that was splattered on all four walls. I turned the light off and climbed back into bed. It took some time for me to drop off to sleep. I was thinking about what I had just seen, and how close I had come to running into something that was completely out of my control.

Next morning, I went for breakfast and was surprised to see the young Russian guy, Yuri. He told me that the rest of the group had been locked up and had their passports taken off them, and each had been fined 500 dollars for the damage to the room. He had been cleared of any involvement, other than intervening to try and stop the fight. While we were at the table, we were joined by another chap called Rafi, who obviously new Yuri. He too spoke English and asked me if I would like to join them when we berthed in Korea as he had some business to do and a collection to make. Keen to join them but still cautious I agreed to tag on. When we finally berthed, I just had to sign a couple of papers and I was then allowed to leave the ship, but I had to be back at a given time.

The three of us left the ship and we walked into a town that I thought would have been much bigger. While we were eating lunch, Rafi was making lots of phone calls. Yuri and I talked; he told me that the border was very close and I replied by telling him that my friends back home had told me I was stupid to leave home and that I should not travel to this part of the world at this particular time because of the unease and uncertainty for the future of North and South Korea. I smiled and told him I had to go as my visa for Russia starts tomorrow.

The town had a few shops and while we were walking Rafi disappeared for a while, and then reappeared this time pushing a bicycle. We made our way back to the ship and as we got closer Rafi asked me if I would take the bike and push it on the boat. This was definitely a big no, as the first rule of travel is you never carry another person's items through a border check. You could get a lot of drugs inside the frame of a bike I thought. I had to come up with a plan to avoid his request and as we got to the ship there was a small queue and as luck would have it a toilet off to the side, so I made my excuse and headed to the toilet to employ some delaying tactics. Giving it about ten minutes I stuck my head round the corner and saw the two guys just going up the gangplank. I made my way and re-joined the ship. Once on board I caught up with Yuri and Rafi who were sitting at one of the deck tables. I don't think Rafi was too pleased with me but having said that he presented me with a miniature handmade bike which I still have to this day. Soon after my room mates turned up at the table and they looked as if they had come from a war zone. The first thing I noticed was they all had baseball hats on, and for youths I was surprised to see them being worn the conventional way, covering their eyes, which by now were of differing hues.

After three days we were about to arrive in Vladivostok and as we approached the dock side I could see a couple of huge sailing ships and row upon row of war ships, a stark reminder I thought of the cold war. By early afternoon I had disembarked and had cleared customs with my visa, so I started to walk towards the dock gate and to try and find a place to stay. Once at the gate all I could see were taxis, and I was hesitant, unsure which was the best to choose; all of a sudden Yuri turned up and spoke with a taxi driver. Before I climbed in the taxi Yuri told me that the driver would take care of me and not overcharge me, and that he would take me to a safe place where I could stay. As we drove, I sat quietly and tried to memorise the route from the docks to my destination. The drive was very sombre, and the buildings looked very cold and grey. Finally, we reached my destination and thanking the driver I turned to walk up the six or eight stairs to a heavy steel door that reminded me of my time working in Kazakhstan, where it seemed all the doors were made from steel.

Once inside I was allocated a room that was already occupied by two guys from the UK. They introduced themselves as Bruce and Mike and I learnt that they both had motorbikes and had been waiting almost a week for their bikes to be released from customs. This made me aware that if I was subject to such a delay it would have a knock-on effect, due to my allocated time in Russia. That evening the three of us went out to eat and I arranged to meet Mike the next day while Bruce went to try and sort out the release of their bikes. I instantly got the feeling that Mike was more than happy to let Bruce get on with that side of things. It was while we were walking around that Mike spoke about some of their adventures and how Bruce had come close on several occasions to making trouble for them. It seemed that Bruce had adopted a gung-ho attitude with the authorities on a few occasions. Mike and I had an interesting conversation and I listened to him for some time. It was then I told him, that after the first twenty minutes, when we met in the room, and in that short time how I had decided which one of them wanted to be the leader and who wanted to enjoy the true experience of their travels. By the end of our conversation it only confirmed my reasons for travelling alone on this adventure. Back at our steel box hostel I checked my e-mails and found a message from my agent in Vladivostok, Yuri Melnikov, saying he would meet me down at docks tomorrow as he was hopeful that the mini would be released. Not long after Bruce came into the room a little unhappy that he had not been able to get the bikes, and it could be tomorrow. I turned and winked at Mike as I told Bruce I too had just received the same message from my agent.

As it was still early in the day I decided to go for a walk on my own. This time I turned right out of the building and came upon a statue that I seemed to recognise. The statue had a bald head and then I remembered who it was. It was Yul Brynner, who it seemed was born in the building next to where I was staying. I continued to walk and the more I walked the more interesting it became. There were a lot of statues depicting history from way back, and also from the cold war period. At one point I came across a submarine that had been placed on the edge of a small park close to the sea, and seeing it made the hair on my arms stand up. Eventually I reached the shore line and a very tall steel fence that was sign-posted in English, telling people to keep away. I had come upon the navel yard, and it all looked very scary, but something inside me wanted to see more, so I gingerly walked on towards the main gates. It was there I saw guards marching up and down with very big guns and at that point I chickened out and turned in land hastily walking away. I headed back into the city centre and did one of my favourite things, people watching. I positioned myself at a large T junction with traffic lights and for the next hour I took in the city and its traffic, while getting to look at and watch the people as they went about their daily lives, concluding that I would more than welcome a return to this city to take in more of its history and the people. That evening the three of us went out to eat together again and we planned that we would all go down to the customs together the following morning in the hope of getting our vehicles.

Next day I met up with my agent Yuri and his assistant Anna. After a short conversation Yuri went off to the customs office to see if the mini had been released, while Anna and I watched Bruce getting more frustrated at seeing the two bikes that had been shipped in crates were still sitting on the floor and as yet had not been released. Yuri returned and told me the mini would definitely be released tomorrow, and if I would like to join him and Anna, they would take me for a drive round into the country side. During the time I spent with Yuri and Anna that afternoon I learned a little regarding how Russians feel about where they lived. One of the things Yuri told me was something I had already thought about and was aware of having been told that most people in Vladivostok like the location of the city, and as Yuri said they are 12000 kms from Moscow and most of the time they leave the people alone. As we drove out of the city, the roads were poor and we had to avoid manholes because the covers had either fallen in or had just disappeared. This left me thinking if this was my introduction to what lay ahead. After a short distance we turned onto a well paved highway with fresh tarmac, before making our way onto what looked like a brand-new bridge, which took me by surprise, so much so, I asked Yuri was this the start of something big, to which his answer was short and simple. "G8 made this happen."
"Could you explain more" I asked?
Yuri continued telling me that it was Russia's turn to host the G8 Summit and that it was generally thought that Moscow would be the venue, but sometime latter it was suggested that Vladivostok would be a more favourable location. Moscow in the end agreed to this, and the government had to throw millions and millions in finance and resources into the building of a huge bridge and an all new road system, plus a new complex, to hold just one meeting. It was then that I remarked about the lack of traffic and was told that it does not go anywhere but to a dead end and a building. As we drew close to the building, we turned off onto a dirt road before eventually stopping and getting out of the vehicle to walk the short distance over a dry hill and host of large dug outs and evidence that once

housed a range of large guns with Yuri and Anna explaining that they were still here until a short time ago. On the drive back Yuri gave me instructions that Anna would collect me at lunch time the following day and take me down to the customs to collect the mini. Getting back to the hostel I found Bruce and Mike lying on their beds frustrated that they still did not have their motor bikes. I told them I was being collected tomorrow and it genuinely looked like I was getting the mini. Bruce by now was sounding off as they had been waiting twice as long as me. The evening was further compromised when I told Bruce about my guided trip round Vladivostok. As they looked a bit down, I told then I would treat them to a pizza, as it could be our last evening.

The following morning, I went for a walk and finished up people watching till lunch time when Anna collected me and we headed for the dockside customs house. Within the hour the mini was cleared and ownership was once again mine. Soon after Bruce and Mike arrived and they were both very excited as they too had got clearance for the release of their motor bikes. The customs guy was a really nice chap and through Anna we made conversation while watching Bruce and Mike try to extract their bikes from the wooden boxes without any tools, until I supplied them with a large tyre lever from the driver's door pocket of the mini. Before leaving, Anna asked me when I was hoping to start my trip. I told her it would be tomorrow and she said that Yuri would like to take us out for a meal that evening and they would be round at seven to pick me up. For the rest of the afternoon I checked over the van firstly removing the false bulk head behind the driver's seat, then I bolted the winch to the front and did a quick spanner check.

Spot on seven, Yuri and Anna picked me up from my hostel before driving to the other side of the city and a nice restaurant where I asked Yuri to choose a meal for me to eat and for Anna to choose the wine. The evening was very pleasant and my meal was some sort of meat, I was not sure what it was, but was still enjoyable. We passed a couple of hours together talking about one another's countries, and at ten o'clock I returned to the door steps of my hostel making my farewells to Yuri and Anna. Before going back into the hostel, I went over to the mini and sat in it for a while, reflecting that tomorrow would be my seventh day the city. That was when a voice in the back of my head said you need to start making a move on your visa time. I got out of the van, walked up to my room and started to pack my case. Prompting Bruce to ask me what I was doing. "I'm off,"
"What now? "
"Yes".
"Why?" to get a head start as the city is asleep and that way it minimises my distractions as I leave the city behind and head out into the total unknown of Russia and it's roads.
I then wished my fellow countrymen all the best and off I went.

I remember looking at the time, it was eleven in the evening, and I chose what I thought would be the right direction to get out of the city and find the one road that would take me north. There was little or no traffic about and sign posts were even less. It all felt a bit eerie as there was a low mist that circled any street lamps that were lit. The road condition was quite good and my confidence improved as midnight got closer and trucks started to appear. They must be coming from the north I thought. Then, all of a sudden, the good road ended and I got a taste of the roads that would be with me for the next two weeks and nine time zones. The next twelve hours were a nightmare as I was out of my comfort zone that first night. I felt I was driving into a black hole. It wasn't just dark it was pitch black and there was no lighting of any sort other than the odd glare that came on me from a distance or if I was really lucky a red tail light might appear only to disappear. I kept asking myself had I done the right thing by leaving in the dark; as the road conditions were so unpredictable, as they would just disappear leaving you guessing if you were still on a road. In the end I tagged onto the rear of a truck for a couple of hours to get my confidence back. Fortunately, I had filled up with petrol in Vlad but as yet had not seen a gas station. I was now starting to think I needed to fill up sooner rather than later, and as luck would have it the truck, I was following turned off to right. At the time I was not sure why as I could not see any bright petrol station signs, but as we got closer, I could see lights and other trucks so I followed and to my surprise it was a gas station. I pulled up to observe, firstly to see if it was safe and while doing so learned that I had to go to a steel cabin with a post box size slot and give the hidden person money to fill my tank. That evening I learned to give the right money as change isn't given.

My drive north on the edge of China would take me over two days and nights during which time I learned all about suicidal Russian drivers who would drive at you fast then try and cut you up from behind. I had been well warned about people wanting to commit suicide also by jumping in front of cars and on two occasions it would happen to me before leaving Russia and on both occasions I would have to take evasive action.

I eventually reached Khabarovsk where I would turn west for Europe and continue to run along the border with China. As I did not have satellite navigation I would rely on the sun once again, keeping me pointed homeward by the end of the day. The town of Khabarovsk was skirted by a dirt road with craters the size of bomb holes. I remember being about 10km out of town and being passed by a car with a guy hanging out of the window waving me down. A quick count told me that the vehicle had three occupants making it a bit one sided if I was to stop, so I decided to continue while making gestures that I wished to carry on. Eventually I passed them only to be overtaken again, this time with the same gent waving money at me again wanting me to pull up. I then made my move and once again got in front of their car, and this time they stayed behind me for some time before again speeding passed me and on into the distance with me thinking that was the last I would see of them but no, soon after as I rounded a sharp bend there at the side of the road was their stationary car with the passenger this time out of the car waving me down. What I also noted was, the rear door was also open with the third member lying on the rear seat, with what I figured was a bottle of vodka. On seeing this my thought process became serious and I stepped up my get away into rally mode, as I did not want to be caught by these three. This mini adventure had been going on for about eight kms and over the next three kms I kept them at bay. As we descended a long hill, I looked in the mirror and could not see the vehicle it had gone. Then for some reason I looked to my far left and could just about make out horses and men who looked like they were racing while standing bare back on horses. That's when I saw the car that had been chasing me driving across the dusty field. Our little run in had finished, and the money they had been so keen to give away may be going on a bet as to who would be the winner of the next race.

The next largest town was Irkutsk but that was five days and nights away but before that I would reach the turn off at a place called Never. This Road if you could call it a road would be the road to take me to Magadan and along The Road of Bones. I had been tempted to give it a try but thought long and hard and decided not to.

It was well into June and the weather was hot. I had noticed that the temperature gauge in the van started to read a little high and the next day it became so bad I had to stop and take a look, as something was wrong. Just after midday I decided to stop and pulled off onto a small track that led into a field. My location was very private or I believed it was, as I had not seen any people or buildings for many hours. All that could be seen was endless fields of sun flowers and a road side full of dandelions. On lifting the bonnet and checking I found that the radiator fins were fully choked up with what looked like papier mâché. I decided that I should fit my spare radiator, so I set about emptying the rear of the van of all my plastic boxes to get the new radiator from the floor locker, and in doing this it would give the engine some time to cool down. It's interesting that at times like these I never felt any urgency or rush to get the work done and in that way the work seemed easier to complete. Now back under the bonnet I set about removing the radiator. I was completely on my own as I thought, when suddenly a body walked swiftly past me from the back of the van and as I looked up, I saw my driver's door open. I couldn't remember if I had left it open and instantly, I rushed to look in the van and there on the seat was my makeshift wallet that I keep in the door pocket. The mysteries man was now well on his way as I shouted at him but he just ignored me and soon disappeared into a field of sun flowers. Checking the wallet, the small amount of money that was in it had gone, but nothing else had been touched. I didn't feel too bad about it as the wallet was a dummy and decoy, a trick that I had learned about some time ago when making my travel preparations. What did unnerve me was the fact that he came from nowhere, I never heard him and he disappeared as quickly. Returning to fit the new radiator I completed the work and took a closer look at what it was that was covering the fins. On closer inspection I could see husks and seeds embedded all over the inboard face of the radiator. I then realised that the things that had been blowing in the wind the last couple of day had slowly been drawn in by the engine fan. With another lesson learned I reloaded the van and set off once again. The rest of the afternoon I felt annoyed with myself about how that man had just appeared in the middle of nowhere, without my knowledge. It was while I was driving and still reflecting on the thought that there are good and bad in all countries, I reminded myself that I have to be a bit more aware of potential unforeseen possibilities and no more so than when I wish to stop and sleep on such a journey as this. Having said that I was now finding myself driving for some silly lengths of time as much as sixteen hours a day so finding a safe place to stop and sleep was very important. I remember one evening looking for a spot to stop and camp when I spotted a large cherry tree orchard. The trees weren't very tall but they had been planted in rows so I drove off the dirt road and along one of the rows to take a look. Finally thinking that this might be a good place I noticed that any fruit that was on the trees had been picked, which made me feel more comfortable as nobody, in my mind, would be returning in the near future. I slept well that night out of sight and in safety.

My days where long hot and very dusty, and I would find myself driving in my underpants and sandals for days on end. My sleeping bag was in need of a wash not to mention the condition I was getting into so with that in mind I made myself a promise that when I arrive in Irkutsk the following day, I would book into the first hotel I saw no matter what the cost. I was now about six days into my journey and the landscape was changing from green fields with small lakes and lots of mosquitoes to wide open prairies of cornfields as far as the eye could see. These fields would last for days, it was so vast and useful for me as the night before I arrived in Irkutsk I drove till well after midnight and with being so tied I just turned into a cornfield that was still growing and hid the van for the rest of the night. I remember not bothering to eat I just opened the driver's door and swung my legs out, only to look at my feet and see the collection of dust that was trapped between my toes. Many days had passed since I had been able to wash properly let alone have a shower, Irkutsk and a hotel could not come too soon. I decided the best course of action was to take my sandals off and leave them outside for the night, before sliding into my sleeping bag and crash out.

Digression
This part of my journey would find me discomforted in lots of ways and the more the days went on the more I could feel the strain on my body and mind. I remember posting on my site a picture on The Wrong Way Round of myself behind the wheel then getting a message from my daughter Louise a day or two later asking me if I was alright as I didn't look good. That was when I took a look at the photo I had posted, and sure enough I could have done with a shave and shower but my eyes told another story, one of emptiness. Going by my past experiences I had been able to deal and keep on top of everything that I had been faced with before. This time it was different and of my own making. Firstly my determination to drive across Russia the biggest country in the world as quickly as possible and this would be done I had thought by putting in endless days of continuous driving to the extreme of eighteen hours on some days, heat and dust too was with me most of the time. The lack of being able to clean myself was the biggest contributor to me starting to drift into a bubble that was not positive for me mentally. ~~

Next morning, I woke early from my hiding place in the cornfield having had four hours sleep. While lying there I knew I had to eat something even though I was keen to get moving, so I settled for one of my pot noodles that I had bought in Japan. Should you ever make it to Japan then I insist you have to try one, they are great and my grandson Sam also thinks the same telling me I should have brought more back. Breakfast finished I swung my legs outside of the van to put on my sandals that I had left outside overnight. Slipping on the first one I then struggled to find the other so I got out of the van to take a look as I thought it may have slipped under the vehicle. I bent down but could not see the missing sandal, so I did a walk about as best I could in a cornfield to track down the offending item that was nowhere to be found. Still to this day it is a mystery where that one sandal went and who or what took it away. I have kept the other as a reminder of that day and that part of the world.

My drive that day would find me skirting the southern end of the biggest and deepest fresh water lake in the world, Lake Baikal. I would also run alongside the Trans-Siberian Railroad for a while and for the first time in five days or more I would start to see movement of people and vehicles in bigger volumes. By the afternoon I had reached the south west point of the lake and the road turned north for my late afternoon drive into Irkutsk and the promise I made to myself a number of days ago to book into the first hotel I could find. By five o clock I was entering the city and the experience of driving with and alongside Russian drivers that care nothing about courtesy was a big wakeup call once again. Spotting a shell garage, I dived in and filled up with petrol that cost me under fifty pence a litre and purchased a five litre can of shell oil that cost £6.50. As I was about to pull out of the garage I spotted a sign that was lit up some way in the distance that said Marriott. I sat for a while pondering that of all the hotels I had come across, can this be right in this part of the world. Well there was only one way to find out. I must drive my little vehicle to the front door so I did. I remember pulling up outside and thinking if I can't afford to stay here then I'm going to take a picture of it at least. Dressed in an old holey and dusty T-shirt with dirty shorts I marched into the marbled reception area looking as if I had just walked in from being lost in the desert. The very well-dressed young lady behind the desk greeted and welcomed me in good English asking if I would like a room. Enquiring about the cost of a room she informed me I could have a room with dinner bed and breakfast, with a lunch box for the next day including secure parking for the mini, all at a cost of forty-five pounds per night. The cost totally blew me away in disbelief, so I booked two nights of luxury living.

The hotel was beautiful inside everywhere was covered in marble and was so clean, considering once I stepped outside everywhere was so grey and dusty. Now checked in I drove the mini round to the compound that had a security guard on duty 24/7. Once in my room and armed with my travel case and dirty washing I headed to the bathroom and the best-looking shower I had ever seen. I remember standing in the shower for what felt like an hour captivated by the hot water and my thoughts reflecting on what I had completed since I left Vladivostok some six days earlier. I recall smiling to myself then looking down into the shower tray and the dirt that lay in all four corners making me think I had better go through the wash process once again before stepping out of the shower. After showering and finding some dust free cloths I went down to reception and asked about my dirty washing. I was told that it would be collected from my room, washed, dried and ironed before being returned to my room all at no extra cost. The young lady was really nice and was keen to learn more about my travels in the little mini. While talking she booked a table for me to dine at seven in the restaurant. This then would give me a good hour to catch up with free wi-fi available back in my room. After dinner I went for a walk along the river embankment before turning inward to the city and its many mixed building, most of them very colourful with the rest of them a dark grey and very box like, that would make me think authority of some form. Two extreme types of buildings.

Next morning I took my time over breakfast and maximised both on the food and the service that was being given at such a plush hotel. While at breakfast the waitress told me of a car wash place that would completely valet my car for fifty pence. Yes, fifty pence. Again, my thinking head kicked into action, reflecting on the price of a few basics that I had to buy since leaving Vladivostok, how could this be right, and how could people survive at these low costs. By the end of the day I had concluded that it was cheaper for me to be out of my country than it was to be in it, a thought that is well established in my mind, still to this day.

After being treated so well at the car wash, I headed back to the safety of the hotel compound to check over the mini, as I would be breaking free from Irkutsk in the morning and back into the danger zone with another big push to clock up the many daunting miles that lay ahead. I again dined at the hotel then later on I took a walk into the city before darkness fell. This time I wanted to go a little further and for this I decided I needed to dress differently for my own safety, as I recalled my time working with the hovercraft on the Caspian sea in Kazakhstan, when a couple of my work colleges where attacked and at the time it was believed it was because they stood out due to the way they were dressed in their European clothes. That evening I dressed in darker clothes and my Russian looking hat that had been with me since my time in the Caspian. Suitably dressed I headed out of the hotel about seven thirty giving me a good two hours to look round and take in the buildings and movement of people as they went about their business. The walk went well and I felt safe. I would spot a building in the distance that looked interesting then make a beeline for it before repeating it several times over; in the end I concluded that they were all churches of some sort. With darkness starting to fall I made my way back to the hotel bar, and a couple of night cap beers before bed.

One of the many things I have learned is that you can't get egg, bacon sausage and beans everywhere in the world and certainly none of the food in Russia looked like anything from back home, so it was a nice surprise to find under the many silver serving bowls at breakfast were the items that made a full English breakfast. I made up a take away bag of food and collected my travel bag before thanking the hotel staff for their help and courtesy.

With the lack of readable sign posts I made a calculated exit out of the city in a westerly direction onto the dirt road and as the time ticked by my confidence grew once again. The company of big trucks around me was always a good sign. It was time once again to settle down and start dodging the pot holes and the crazy car drivers and road conditions that would change, mostly without much warning. This once totally dirt road that crosses Russia east to west are now a work in progress for much of the way with the odd hour of driving on tarmac. What hadn't come yet were a motorway network and all the other things that come with it such as modern filling stations, café's and toilets. There was the odd good petrol station mainly in a city, but once on the road they were basically a twenty-foot container with a slot cut in the side to pass your money through and as for the petrol station services and a toilet don't ask. Having said that it did come to my attention while driving that the blue or green port-a-loo's occasionally seen at the side of the newly paved road were not there for the work force, that had left and gone to work elsewhere, but were intended for road users. Doctor Who's blue box has never looked the same since that day and I will never shake from my mind the site of a blue box standing in the wilderness, all alone at the side of a brand-new road. I only visited the one, deciding that I would now use my own travel port-a-loo from then on. The boredom of that day's drive was only occasionally interrupted by trucks that had either crashed or turned over and could be seen lying abandoned at the side of the road. That evening I stopped for the night at what I would loosely call a truck stop where I managed to back the mini into a corner by two skips and set up enough room in the van to sleep without attaching my rear tent. That evening I set my Matty stove up behind the skip and was back to cooking and eating boiled up stew from the hot pan followed by tea and biscuits. Sleep that night was peaceful only broken on occasion by the sound of air brakes as trucks came and went.

Next morning, I decided to go into the café and try some breakfast, what that was to be, I, was very unsure. Walking inside I found myself standing behind a great big guy and the guy in front of him was being served, so I did my best to look over the guys shoulder to see what was in the small glass show case. A quick look revealed nothing I recognised and what little writing there was I couldn't understand so now I was starting to sweat and panic a bit, as the guy in front of me was now being served. Fear came over me, should I be brave and walk out and resort back to pot noodle. Suddenly I was at the counter facing this very large Russian female cook, still thinking what I am going to do. Then for whatever reason I swung my head round and looked at the nearest table to see a guy with two eggs on his plate. I quickly pointed to the table and gave the thumbs up, she just stood and looked at me bewildered where upon inspiration came to me. I stepped back nearly standing on the toes of the guy behind me and did several chicken impressions, by flapping my arms and bending my knees, much to the amusement of the room full of truckers. Back at the mini, after my breakfast, I tidied my few bits up and made haste to get going as there were still a few more of the eleven time zones to cross before I would exit Russia and with memories of the morning's entertainment still in my mind it would help the day go a lot quicker.

Boredom and concentration were now a big problem for me. Every day was just relentless driving for suicidal hours as I found myself on the run to get out of Russia. To keep my moral up I started to sow the seed of taking time out for a week when I got to Volgograd, and divert from my route to the Sochi area on the black sea, as I had heard it was a great place to relax and lie on some proper sand with sun. Over the next few days, I really pushed myself and the mini, while not forgetting to pat my steering wheel at the end of each day in thanks for taking care of me. The feeling of getting closer to Europe and the west started to creep in to my days as the colour of green would appear on the trees and bushes, with the odd hill to climb.

The formalities of the evening never changed as there was always a search for a safe place to spend the night. One particular night I came across a host of trucks parked in a line, four lanes wide, so I slowed up to take a look as I could not see a café. On closer examination, when I reached the far end of the line, I came to a metal sheeted compound and a chained gate where a man was standing. As I walked towards him, he made gestures of steering wheel movements with both his hands, so I replied with the internationally recognised thumbs up, and with that he opened the gate and I drove in to the empty, partly grassed, area to pick my spot to set up camp. The chap walked to meet me, we shook hands and I parted with a few roubles. He then showed me a small wooden building that had a toilet and a washroom complete with shower. The conditions were acceptable and the surprise was that the water was hot, so long as you didn't linger. That evening I sat and entered the last couple of days into my log while in the safety of the high sided steel compound with a guard to keep out the bad guys.

Next morning, I was up early and settled for marmalade on toast with a large mug of tea made on my Matty stove. A quick wash and clean of the teeth and I was ready to open the steel gates and head out once again into a very warm and clear day. As the day went on, I was starting to feel better, I was making progress and Ukraine was in touching distance albeit on the other side of the biggest mountain range to divide Europe and Asia, yes, the Ural Mountains would be my challenge in the coming days.

It had to have been over a week since I was last stopped by the police, but this particular day it happened twice. I was starting to get used to it, but never the less it was always worrying. Procedure was they would jump out in front of me wave what looked like a badminton racket and signal me to stop. I would stop and grab my thick black multi page folder and step out of the vehicle holding it above my head showing them I had come prepared, whereupon I would get a shake of the head and a point to the bonnet for an inspection of my engine. They would then take an interested look round the engine and try to smile or shake my hand and walk away.

Digression
Japan and the police way back was the only place I had needed to open my black folder and never once since then had I been asked to delve inside so my paperwork could be viewed and I accept that as a blessing. Having said that I was a little disappointed having made such an effort into the preparation of all eighty-four pages, now I can hold my hand up as more than 50% of the folder was for show and it looked good visually. The important things like licences, insurances or visas at the forefront followed by wiring looms or how to fix my Matty stove if it breaks and so on Well to me my folder was impressive and was part of the team that would get me through. ~~

By about six p.m. I was starting to climb into mountainous places, with rock faces and trees. Sure enough the scenery was changing but the road surfaces had now turned to broken tarmac as I struggled to weave my way safely round the large holes, with the ever-present sun bringing my vision to zero on occasions. In the end I settled down to follow a large truck carrying a container that would act as my sun vizier for the next couple of hours, before I found a deserted spot to set up camp, this time at the top of a mountain where I hid the van in some bushes. The spot I picked was great as a slight wind kept the bugs down and the view was quite breath taking. The only worry was that several types of wild animals could be found roaming the area, so my evening walk would not see me straying too far, before I prepared the evening meal of sliced fried potatoes and fried spam quickly followed by bed and tomorrows plan that if I made it to Volgograd, what would I decide to do, would I detour for the Black Sea or not?

Next morning, I skipped breakfast but did do my oil check on the engine as I had noticed it seemed to be using a little too much oil over the past few days. A closer look would reveal that oil was slowly seeping from the rear of the rocker cover, so I replaced the gasket and that seemed to cure it. By six fifteen I was out of my hide away and back heading westward. The day's entertainment whilst driving through the mountains would consist of keeping out of danger with all the other vehicles that took to the road which would on occasion shoot out from nowhere in the guise of a suicide vehicle and driver .

Digression
So picture if you can a dirt road that caters for two way traffic and is full of bomb like craters and it has now become thirty meters wider due to ground conditions and neglect. The rules in Russia in the terms of driving standards don't exist. Getting past vehicle is pretty standard in most countries, well almost, so in this part of the world you could come on a line of two cars or twenty-two cars and you would like to overtake the slower vehicles. Normally you would set about choosing the safest moment to make the manoeuvre. But no, it does not work like that here and the rules would seem to be that the vehicle at the rear has it in his head he has the right to pass all of the vehicles without warning, so that's a complete reversal to most countries in the world. Hence that's how I figured out their dirt roads are so wide, also it is not unusual to see two or even three cars side by side overtaking a slower vehicle or vehicles. In fact it wasn't unusual to see a car and truck side by side overtaking a slower vehicle. The trick it would seem was for these suicide drivers to focus on what is coming at them and ignore those you are overtaking.~~

Later on that day while approaching the outskirts of Volgograd the reality of what can happen when it all goes wrong for both driver and passengers was something I was about to experience. As I recall it must have been about five p.m. Cresting a slight hill, I saw a large plume of white smoke rising into the air getting closer to the smoke which had now started to settle a little I could see a large articulated truck that was stationary and just to my left. I was now only about a hundred feet away from what was obviously a very bad accident. I could now see what looked like a car trapped under the trucks large trailer. I could see one person pulling a body out from the mangled car while a second person was pulling a second body by its arms and there feet and shoes dragging on the road directly in front of me. That was when I spotted the motionless body lying off to the right at the side of the road. To my right people were gathering so I resisted making a stop and continued to drive slowly by. The next few miles would find me deciding to get out of both Volgograd and Russia as soon as possible.

The decision had now been made for me; I would not be making that detour south to Sochi. I pushed on and by nine I had found a nice bed and breakfast place in a beautiful location that set me back with the cost of the loose change in my trouser pocket. As a reasonably well travelled traveller there is no better feeling than hot shower and clean clothes followed by a nice steak and several bottles of beer. That evening I did all of those things while reflecting on the sight of the people being pulled out of a crushed vehicle. What did help me to divert my thoughts that night was that in two days' time I should make it to the Ukraine border.

The next two days past quite quickly and I would only be stopped once by police. Having the mini for my travels turned out to be the best choice for me in many ways, and certainly when confronted by the police it has worked in my favour. I have heard many stories of why people get stopped and what happened to them.

Digression
I remember when working in Kazakhstan where we were driven round by a local and it was not unusual to get stopped by the police. The driver would show the policeman his paperwork then pass a cigarette or two over, then climb back in the vehicle and we would carry on. I was interested to know why our team of workers, who were sitting in the back, had not been asked to produce any paperwork. It seemed that all the policeman was interested in was free cigarettes from the local driver. Should any of our team have been at the wheel, then the police would be more awkward and difficult and seek something more substantial than a few cigarettes, before allowing us to carry on. ~~

Late in the evening on the second day I arrived in Rostov-on-Don. The border crossing for Ukraine is about ten miles further on down a narrow corridor of land with the Sea of Azov on my left. As I drove through the city it was very quiet, and poorly lit, so I kept driving eventually coming to a small tarmac area when suddenly out of the Dim Street lighting several police walked from the side walk and gestured for me to pull over and stop. Rather startled I pulled in and reached for my black folder before climbing out and standing by the door, offering the folder to the closest policeman, only to have it pushed away by his baton while the other policeman walked off. My instant thought was to keep calm and see what would happen. Bending his head, the lone policeman looked in to the mini and spotted my silver toolbox that was sitting on the large aluminium tray that forms part of my bed where the original driver seat had been located. Gesturing for me to take it out, I went round the other side of the van and extracted the silver box and placed it on the floor and opened it, while he stood over me and watched. With the box open he could see it was just tools, but then he wanted me to take them out and look inside the socket set. Throughout the whole operation not a single word was spoken between us both, he just used his baton to point and would bang it down on what he wanted taken out of the vehicle. His next move was to point to another box then another box that was when I figured out what he was up to. Now with two boxes on the floor the policeman then pointed towards a second box that is when I decided to stand my ground, I stood up and shook both my hands and pointed back to the open silver toolbox and the socket set. I then bent down and picked up the socket set to show him the contents that is when he turned round and walked off, he'd had his bit of fun and I was not for it going any further.

It was now getting close to midnight by the time I put the boxes back into the van, but just before I got back in the mini, I took a look round. The location felt like something out of a Hitchcock thriller, nothing was moving, any street light had a halo of mist circling around it and I just had the feeling I was being watched. I decided to move on and as I drove round the next corner, I spotted rows and rows of car wash areas. That was when I remembered I must have a clean vehicle at the border crossing or I could be refused entry and turned back. The mini was covered in mud and would need a power wash, but the trouble was all of the vehicle washes were closed and that also told me the border up the road must also be closed, so I decided to get out of town to find a spot to camp before the check point that I figured was ten miles down the road. Driving for about twenty minutes I came across a small concrete bridge then spotted a small track off to my right that doubled back on itself. Deciding to take it was the right decision as the track ran down to a small river where I could hide for the night then wash the mini in the morning. It must have been about one a.m. before I settled down to an uneasy sleep. There were a number of things buzzing round in my head, one of them about being able to get insurance for the mini while driving in Ukraine. I was told I could buy it at the border crossing once out of Russia but if I didn't have any, I could find myself in trouble a few miles up the road as they lay in wait for you to drive by.

Next morning, I was up at first light and attacking the mini with buckets of water from the river. It must have taken me about two hours to be happy with the outcome and one that would also keep the border staff of my back. After a quick cup of tea and an energy bar I was on my way by seven thirty and would find myself at the Russian exit crossing just as it was opening at eight. I joined the small queue and waited my turn. The wait was not long and I would soon find myself pulling up to the window at passport control. I passed my passport in under the glass where the lady checked my visa date, then stamped the page passing it back to me and pointing to the exit, proving it is a lot easier to get of a country than it is to get in, something my own country might consider learning. I then drove out through one gate and continued for about a mile along a dead straight road that was heavily fenced on both sides before eventually the road opened out into a large holding area for waiting cars. Again, it was very quiet and one of the Ukrainian officials waved me and my vehicle to come forward and pull up. The gentleman walked round to my door and I handed over my passport. He took a look inside and walked away returning with a second person shortly after. Now fearing the worst as there were two of them, I smiled and the second officer wished me good morning in pretty good English. "What type of vehicle is this and can we have a look under the front while pointing to the bonnet? The whole procedure was very relaxed and before I had opened the bonnet at least six more people had joined in the process. All the time the English-speaking officer was asking me questions about the engine and the mini in general, then translating my responses to his gathered colleagues who kept turning up from the main office. I could tell their interest was genuine and I remember getting to a point where two of the younger guys where keen to purchase the mini, they even made me an offer. However, I had to gently reply that this was the only way I could get home. The whole episode must have taken an hour and never once did I feel uncomfortable, in fact it was very heart-warming having just spent the last two weeks crossing the land of their nearest neighbour. Finally, we all bid one another farewell and I drove the short distance to the start of the main road to seek out insurance that could be bought at one of the many port-a-cabins on both sides of the road. The only trouble was they were all closed and locked up, with the only cabin that was open being a café so I took myself off to get some breakfast and enquire about closed cabins. I soon learned that they don't open till ten so I sat back and drank extra tea until one opened. Sure enough just after ten, a couple of them opened up and I bought some insurance, well I had a piece of paper and was hopeful it was legal. Soon after I climbed back in to the mini and headed in the direction of Odessa wondering if I would come across the threatened possibility of a police car in waiting to check my vehicle insurance. Well after ten miles I relaxed as no police had tested me and there was little traffic bar the odd truck kept me company.

While crossing Russia I had picked up information that things where kicking off in Ukraine with Russia. The old enemy was none too happy with the Ukrainian government and was putting on the pressure with tanks on the streets. My thought was to keep moving and give Kiev a detour and head for L'viv and my shortest route into Poland. I pushed on through Marupol and Odessa again putting in ridiculous hours making the crossing of Ukraine in two days and nights reaching the Ukraine exit border crossing just west of L'viv late in the afternoon.

Leaving the Ukraine check point was simple but when I got to the Polish entry crossing, the biggest blue euro sign I had ever seen lay in front of me. All I now had to do was get past that and I would feel safe. The whole car holding area was full of vehicles trying to get into Europe and talk was of a minimum waiting time of five to six hours, with the possibility of the border being closed, which left me thinking that things had really taken a turn for the worse in Ukraine and if so, would the euro border crossing be shut down. Back in the mini I just sat and pondered for hours on end what might happen. Nothing was moving other than the odd person climbing in and out of their vehicles. Being parked right at the back of the queue there was not a lot I could see as I was so far from the crossing boxes and border officials. What I could see in my driver's mirror was two officials walking up behind my vehicle and I was not sure which side of the border they were from. Just before they reached me, they stopped and closed two rather big metal gates then threw a padlock round them. It was now dark and I had been driving for two days to get to this point and I was still in the danger zone now going nowhere, soon after I fell into a deep sleep.

Chapter 18

Not telling the truth

After a very uncomfortable night sleeping in the driving seat, I eventually cleared the Polish entry crossing and the back log of vehicles by nine thirty the next morning. Tired and weary I soon picked up the e40 route that would take me in the direction of Cracow. Vehicle insurance now was not a problem as I was in the EU. Poland was an instant hit for me and I could not find fault with anything, the roads were so clean, litter free and well maintained.

Whilst crossing Russia I had not been able to make much contact with family and friends and posting pictures and posts on my travel site had been sketchy. Now in Poland and with a proper phone signal my Nokia 6310 spat out a dozen text messages. I decided to cut short my day and find a hotel early, especially after such a long delay at the border. I stopped at a place before Cracow in a town called Tarnow. Once booked in to the hotel, I decided to head to bed for the afternoon and rise before the evening meal. Four hours saw me catching up with some of my sleep before taking a shower. The evening meals started at six thirty so I got in a good hour replying to the back log of texts.

I had hoped to catch up with some of the people and mini clubs that had been following me while passing through Europe, but this did not really happen due to lack of communication or because people would only be available at weekends and I made the decision I would return one day, and take a full navigation of Europe sometime in the future. In amongst my texts was a message a friend had sent giving me inside information that my daughter would be travelling from the Isle of Mull in ten days' time to collect her classic rally mini, south of the border, from Jim Brindle at R.A.C.E. Motorsport in Chorley Lancashire then return back north to Scotland. Now armed with that information I set about working out a plan to arrive back in the UK and surprise Louise and my youngest grandson before they returned to Scotland. The surprise would only work by not telling the truth about my true location, and that was being followed by so many on my travel site. Over the next couple of days, I started to mislead both the followers on my travel site and Louise by posting information and photos that in fact were two to three days old. This way I felt sure my daughter would assume that we would not meet up till I got back to the UK and had travelled north back home to the Isle of Mull. The UK was now feeling as if it was a stone's throw away, and with those thoughts came the anticipation and excitement of meeting up with my family. I had been away so long. While at dinner that evening I asked the hotel owner if she had a map of Europe I could borrow. A quick look would confirm that the e40 route I was now on would seem to be the quickest route taking me out of Poland and across Germany, Belgium and into France and the port at Calais. Feeling like a new person I headed to bed deciding tonight was to be my last night of clean sheets and comfortable beds before getting back to the UK.

Next morning with a determination to attack the countries ahead of me full on I was first up, taking a full breakfast and a hand full of fruit for the journey that the owner had made up for me. A last check of the engine oil and with a tank full of petrol, I would drive till the fuel tank needed refilling. This I did twice which got me out of Poland and close to Dresden in Germany at some ridiculous time in the morning. Now on the autobahn the traffic was very light so I could just push on and watch the kilometres pass by, stopping when needed at the services where I would fill up with close to fifty litres of fuel each time. Having filled up I took a couple of hours sleep in the car park settling for the driver's seat as my bed. I made great progress across Germany during the night and through the next day. Cologne was how in touching distance and I was keen to get round the city and its traffic the following night. By achieving that I would have almost ticked off Germany and inched into Belgium and the city of Liege.

I was now starting to smell the salt air from the Channel, well that's what I kept telling myself to try and keep focused, and so once I was round Brussels, I decided to stop close to Gent, refill the van and take a break to calculate my arrival time in Chorley. While at the motorway services I went and had a proper meal as since leaving Poland I had been eating just fruit and energy bars washed down with bottles of water. Trying to decided what was the best thing to do next, I sent a text message to my informer asking if they could confirm that Louise would be still collecting the rally car on the coming Saturday which was five days away. Back came the reply yes, it was still on.

I had done so well with the driving I was at least two days ahead of myself, so I thought the best thing to do was to hide up at my sister place between Dover and Ashford for a couple of days. Doing this would give me ample time to drive the short distance from Kent to Lancashire on the intended surprise day.

Messaging my sister my plans she replied telling me she was away in the Greek islands but I was more than welcome to stay and that she would message her son to let him know I would be arriving in the next couple of days. With those plans in place I thought I would spoil myself when I got to Calais and take the euro star train back to the UK getting off at Folkestone terminal, leaving just one junction on the M20 which would find me at my sisters. Now happy with my plans I returned to the mini and made enough room in van to have a proper lie down that evening, leaving me a couple of hours in the morning to make the port at Calais.

Waking about six the next morning I lifted my head and peeped out of the van window to see that the good weather seemed to be continuing. I grabbed my wash bag and towel and headed to the wash room for a shower before taking a much-needed breakfast. The night's sleep had done me good and I was now set up for the short journey down past Dunkerque and into Calais. As I started to file in to the port, I was hopeful of getting the train back and as it was Wednesday, I thought the possibilities could be favourable. Checking at the ticket office I found that there was a six-hour delay so I came back by sea.

Digression
As I was now re-entering the UK with the mini that had been out of the country for four years I was aware the recognition cameras would light up when they spotted my number plate. To get round this problem I had informed the vehicle taxation office of my plans four years back, so all they did was put a note on the system telling of my plans. On getting home I would re MOT and tax the vehicle. Coming out of Dover would prove if the system worked or not and I was sure that between the south and north of the country it would get tested several times. ~~

My sister's home is only half an hour from the port of Dover and on arrival at her house I was greeted by my nephew Christopher. Over the next two days I relaxed, ate well and had plenty of showers. I hadn't updated my travel site for a while so I set about putting more posts and pictures on to reinforce that I was still travelling through Poland and enjoying my time there, thus hopefully keeping my true location hidden from my daughter and grandson. On Saturday I made my move to leave Kent and head north to Chorley. The drive would take me up the M20, to the biggest car park in the world the M25 and the crossing at Dartford, then onward up the M11 to Cambridge where I would cross a huge part of the country on the A14 to join the M6 that would take me north passed Manchester and my destination on the outskirts of Chorley.

Arriving close to R.A.C.E. Motorsport I went into hiding with the minivan, keeping a safe distance until the unsuspecting party arrived. I did not have long to wait as soon after my daughter arrived with a trailer to collect her rally car. I gave the group a little time to start loading the car before slowly arriving myself and pulling up to take the gathered party by surprise. After the warmest of welcomes from family and friends I made my way to Minisport in Padiham as I wanted to call in and thank them for their support and also for taking care of shipping the mini across the pacific into Japan. I can remember being asked many times while travelling if I was carrying any spares, my answer was always the same, saying I have everything but an engine block, and if you can remember those few words would come to bite me back in Arizona, but with a short e-mail that was soon taken care of back in the UK. A spares package had been put together and kindly lent to me at the start. Four years on I would return the spares package minus a few knuckle and ball joints, with so little used, in the end this would be great testimony to the strength and build of this small box on four small wheels. Amazingly Larry and Anne Sutton were also there to meet me. Larry and Anne had been the wonderful people that had stored the mini for me back in Vancouver. They'd been staying in Yorkshire on a house exchange and they'd driven to Minisport to surprise me. Seems, people were scheming up things while I was scheming to surprise them, so it was truly emotional to see them Larry and Anne.

The final part of my adventure was the drive back to Scotland and a ferry that would finally take me back home to the Isle of Mull. It was while I was sitting in the ferry queue in Oban that I remembered my last ferry and the stranger that had taken a liking to the mini while I was in the ferry queue in Calais. We had struck up a conversation during which he asked me where I was going.
I told him back home to the Isle of Mull. "Crikey that's a long way" he said, I just smiled as I didn't have the heart to tell him where I had come from and as yet I hadn't realised what I had achieved in the last 60.000 miles

With mixed emotions I drove my Little companion onto the Mull boat while thinking how close I was to completing this journey but more than that I think I had now come to terms with the past and through my endeavours I have managed to climb my way out of that black hole, the one that had consumed me on that dark and emotional evening back in February some five years earlier. Could I now perhaps take a short holiday just down the road on the white sandy beach at Calgary where I can reflect on how this journey has given me such a different outlook on all things in this life?